7.95

P9-DUK-584

THE DECLINE AND FALL OF
LLOYD GEORGE

*The following books by Lord Beaverbrook
deal with the Lloyd George Ministry*

*Politicians and the War
Men and Power
The Decline and Fall of Lloyd George*

Lloyd George by Low
"With a hey, and a ho, and a hey nonny no"

LORD BEAVERBROOK

THE DECLINE AND
FALL OF
LLOYD GEORGE

AND GREAT WAS THE
FALL THEREOF

COLLINS

ST JAMES'S PLACE, LONDON

First Impression 1963
Reprinted (twice) 1963
This Edition 1966

Printed in Great Britain
Collins Clear-Type Press
London and Glasgow

CONTENTS

ILLUSTRATIONS

INTRODUCTION

On the first day of January 1921 few people stopped to think on the amazing and unprecedented position of Lloyd George. Certainly his own colleagues, Bonar Law, Chamberlain, Birkenhead, even Churchill, showed no sign of consciousness of the extraordinary political situation.

Lloyd George was a Prime Minister without a Party.

Of his own group of followers, made up mostly of Office-holders, many were ashamed of their association with the Tories, and longing to return to their old tried and trusted leader, H. H. Asquith, who was still in the running for Downing Street.

The back-bench Members of the Coalition Liberal Party were "uncertain, coy and hard to please". They could not be counted. They would not stand up. It is right to say that some waited eagerly and impatiently for honours and places from Lloyd George's bountiful hand. They were loyal. The rest, almost without exception, hoped for reunion with Asquith.[1]

---

[1] It was in 1920 that Lloyd George, supported by Churchill and Charles McCurdy, put forward to his colleagues serving in the Government a scheme for merging the Coalition Liberal and Conservative Parties. He was at that time at the height of his popularity and power. He informed his colleagues that he would be the leader of the combined Party. Bonar Law and Sir George Younger had agreed to the plan, Bonar Law having taken this decision after consulting many of his colleagues. Younger made the condition that Lloyd George's Fund, amounting to several million pounds, should be handed over to the joint Party chest. "Gate money" he called it.

In late June Lloyd George met his colleagues and put the plan before them for the second and last time. Ministers, Under-Ministers and colleagues, under the leadership of T. J. Macnamara, Ian Macpherson and Alfred Mond, were in opposition to the plan. They would not sacrifice their Liberal affiliations. The plan was defeated.

From the meeting Lloyd George came to Cherkley, my Surrey home. He regretted the decision. Dame Margaret Lloyd George, who came with him, rejoiced. She never liked the Tories and never failed to say just so.

But the weakness of Lloyd George's following was counterbalanced in the minds of men by the Prime Minister himself. His name made up the balance of his strength.

Then again many Tory Members had been persuaded to believe that their own seats depended upon the Liberal votes in their constituencies which had been delivered to them at the last election by the almighty hand of the Prime Minister.

He was in the eyes of men supreme and indispensable.

Then 1921 ushered in two cruel years which were to rip away all the gold brocade and the tinsel too. The illusions were being shattered and a great tragedy was being enacted for all to see.

The Greeks told us of a man in high position, self-confident, so successful as to be overpowering to all others. Then his virtues turned to failings. He committed the crime of arrogance. His structure of self-confidence and success came tumbling down. He struggled against fate, but he was doomed. So it was with Lloyd George in the year 1921 and into 1922. Then all was over. His plans good and bad came to nothing. He fell and never rose again.

The brilliant schemes and stratagems which he resorted to in war, outwitting Generals and Politicians, Peers, Prelates and the King, and all to save Britain, he now applied with daring and skill to save himself from defeat by the Members of the House of Commons. He was confident that what he had done once, he could do again. To keep the seat of power, the place of patronage, he was prepared to stand out as the leader of Empire-minded men—or appear as the Liberal Apostle of Free Trade: as the Man of Peace in Europe—or the Man of War against Turkey and France: as the hammer of the Russian Bolsheviks—or their noble conciliator: as the

"The soothing voice"
Miss Stevenson—she married Lloyd George in 1943

Tribune of the British working classes—or the Champion of the Tory Landlords against Labour: stern enemy of the Irish—or their tender friend spreading his covering wings about another Celtic race ground under the heel of the oppressor. He took up each position in turn during those tragic years of 1921 and 1922.

Sometimes and simultaneously he took up contradictory standings. His daring was wonderful to look upon. But to those who never forgot his greatness in his great days, the spectacle wore thin and ere long became pathetic. ". . . God hath made man upright; but they have sought out many inventions."

What a world of power and dignity and authority he might have lived in had he taken a different turn. Spurning all paths of pleasantness, he might have walked out into the desert of Opposition. There he could have reunited his disparate Liberals, attracting to himself the youth of Britain. His return to power would have been a certainty.

Yet he could not. The driver's seat was as he believed his rightful place. He clung to the wheel guiding the vehicle of state until he was rudely flung forth—the fate of every politician who stays too long.

Here I endeavour to record the reasons for the fall of David Lloyd George, war leader, whose friends had believed he might be Prime Minister for life if he wished. It is not a history of the period 1921-22. Many incidents and events of immense importance have been passed over in brief mention. It is, however, an attempt to tell of the shifting of political power as I saw and heard it at the time.

Many conversations, records of meetings and accounts of personal conflicts are told at length, while the Imperial Conference and the Washington Naval Agreement are relegated to the task of the historian. My efforts to gather

and preserve vast collections of papers and correspondence may be of more use to that same historian than all of
my writings.

It is my intention to publish two more volumes; first
the "Age of Baldwin", then "Churchill's Victory".
I have gathered the necessary material.

For Lloyd George's triumphs in war, see Appendix 63.

I

DEPRESSION

1921 was a year of sunshine and warmth, while drought prevailed. The nation benefited by the fine weather, though suffering a miserable, severe and disastrous industrial and financial depression with widespread unemployment on a scale unprecedented. Civil war devastated Ireland, with nearly all of the population of the South arrayed against British rule there.

Civil war also reigned in the Cabinet at Westminster, where Ministers quarrelled over personal problems, domestic issues and foreign policies. Many of them discussed their differences and disputes in the Lobbies and Smoking Room of the House.

Fleet Street was as critical of the Coalition Leader as some of his own colleagues. Newspapers had much to say in condemnation and very little in praise of the Prime Minister. An attempt to unseat Lloyd George, the Prime Minister, was launched by several contenders, brought together only by hostility to their leader. Lloyd George, like a beast of the jungle, was hunted here and there by many marksmen who trained their weapons upon him. He described the hunt as a "Plot", and, in an hour of optimism, made a premature declaration that he had scattered his enemies. He was wrong.

For the purposes of clarity, I am obliged at the outset to describe the composition of the Coalition Government and the attitude of the Parties in the opening years of the decade following the war. My readers will, I hope, put up with this recital of Parliamentary dispositions and public issues.

At the General Election of December 1918, when Lloyd George went to the country as Prime Minister with Bonar Law, Leader of the Tory Party[1], as his coadjutor, the Coalition had won an overwhelming victory. As a result, the Tories under Bonar Law had a majority in the House over all Parties serving in Parliament. But most of the Tory Members believed themselves to have gathered at the election a measure of votes which, in fact, they owed to Lloyd George. Some even considered themselves dependent on Coalition Liberal support for their majority.

In 1921, this Coalition Government was sustained by 333 Tories and 128 Lloyd George Coalition Liberals, 12 Coalition Labour and 43 Independent Unionists. In opposition were the Labour Members of the House, who numbered 67, and a group of 31 Asquithian Liberals, known as the "Wee Frees". 73 Members of the Sinn Fein Party refused to take their seats.

At this time, the Protection issue was a stick of political dynamite. Imperial Preference was the traditional policy of the Tory Party. Joseph Chamberlain, after some preliminary skirmishes, had introduced the plan in September 1903. It involved the setting up of tariff barriers against imports from foreign countries entering the British market, while imports from Empire countries would be admitted free of duty or given preferential treatment. The Empire would be invited to maintain tariff barriers against foreign countries and to admit British manufactures free of duty or with a preference.

There could not be an Empire tariff policy without a tax on foreign food, for at that time the principal

[1] Tory Party, Unionists, Conservatives—synonymous terms in this narrative.

export from the Dominions consisted of foodstuffs. It would be useless to seek a preference for British manufactured goods in Empire markets unless a corresponding advantage could be given by providing for the free entry into Britain of Empire and Dominion food products.

But at the election of 1918 a pledge had been given by the Government promising in effect to maintain Free Trade and positively excluding a tax on the import of food from foreign and Empire countries alike. Bonar Law, a strong supporter of Empire Tariffs including Food Taxes, and the long-time Leader of the Tory Party, joined in the election pledge of "No Food Tax", as a necessary sop to Liberal supporters of the Coalition, who were fanatical Free Traders. Their "Free Food" cry had always won elections and they believed the Free Trade cause was invincible. Many Conservative back-benchers held that the pledge did not preclude the imposition of protective duties on foreign manufactures imported to Great Britain. The agitation against iron and steel from Continental sources reached a high pitch as unemployment mounted and industry languished.

The Government gave quarter to the Tory Members demanding Protection by introducing a measure known as the Key Industries Bill, providing for the exclusion of unfair and abnormal industrial competition due to depressed currencies. Much was made of the need for safeguarding British industrial employment, with demands for anti-dumping legislation. The Act, as finally passed, was a poor substitute for the protective measures against foreigners so ardently desired by most of the Tory supporters of the Coalition. It did not satisfy any section of the House.[1]

Lloyd George, throughout the debate in the House, conspired with the newspapers to defeat the Bill and to

[1] See Appendix 1, E. S. Montagu to Lord Reading, May 12th, 1921.

destroy it by amendments. He was firmly convinced that if he tampered with the existing duties by introducing Protectionist tariffs his Liberal following, who were an important section of his total support in Parliament, would run away. They would turn their backs on the Prime Minister and join the "Wee Frees" on the other side of the House—in opposition. He also believed that their constituents felt the same way.

Food Taxes and Protection were bitterly opposed by all Liberals and also by a section of the Tory Party which included Lords Salisbury and Derby, the two Cecils, Lord Robert and Lord Hugh, and Northcliffe in his newspapers. "No Stomach Tax" was the slogan of these Tories. "Tariff Reform Means Work For All" was the answering cry of the Protectionist group.

Lloyd George's fear was that he would find himself the prisoner of the Tories, with his Liberal support evaporated and all prospects of Liberal Party reunion utterly destroyed. He himself had no intention of being tied down to Protection or Free Trade. Sometimes he favoured Free Trade; at other times he toyed with Imperial Preference.

My own position in this controversy was not in doubt. On the platform of Imperial Preference and Food Taxes I had gained a seat in the House of Commons in 1910. Empire Fiscal Union was, in fact, my only reason for entering politics in Britain and for continuing to take an interest in public life. My devotion to Bonar Law, my belief in his Leadership, my faith in his ability to give to the Empire some day, perhaps some day soon, the Union I so ardently desired, had kept me in close and intimate touch with him and his political problems. My newspaper interests were designed to give him support. Indeed, I had undertaken the arduous duty and dangerous financial obligation of rescuing the

The Vineyard—Once upon a time a refuge for Palmerston

The tiny drawing room at the Vineyard—Lloyd George sat near the window. Bonar Law in the same type of chair with his back to the fireplace. Birkenhead and Beaverbrook on the sofa

bankrupt *Daily Express* for the sole and only purpose
of promoting Empire solidarity and the political fortunes
of Bonar Law. For, as I firmly believed, he was destined
to give us of the Empire movement the prize we sought
—Empire Free Trade.

The distressing and most painful economic conditions,
and widespread and growing unemployment, increased
the pressure of the Tory group for rejection of the "No
Food Tax" pledge, too. Lloyd George stood in the way.
Then remove him from the "path to prosperity"! "Tariff
Reform Means Work For All". A powerful group of
enemies of the Prime Minister aimed at his destruction.

Bonar Law, who was looked upon as the main prop
and indeed the necessary support of the Prime Minister
in and out of Parliament, would not depart from the
election pledges of 1918. He was embarrassed by the
masterful and arrogant conduct of Lloyd George, not
only in the distribution of offices, but also in his insistence
on building up a personal Political Fund by the sale of
honours and other methods that he believed reflected
upon the good name of the Tory Central Office. Bonar
Law was worried by the frequent protests of Sir George
Younger, the Conservative Party Chairman. His Tory
followers in the House of Commons and in newspapers
were constantly reminding him of their dissatisfaction
and disillusionment because of the Government's failure
to deal with the problems of unemployment and a deepening depression which was overwhelming the nation.

Meanwhile Bonar Law's health was suffering under
the strain of trying to curb Lloyd George's ambition to
undertake foreign projects and expeditions which might
endanger the alliance with France and even the peace of
Europe. In this unhappy atmosphere, Bonar Law was
attacked by a bout of influenza. His temperature was high.
His spirits were low. He resigned on March 17th, 1921.

Lloyd George, though regretting the departure of his colleague, did not make any sustained effort to retain his second-in-command.   Possibly the Prime Minister was somewhat wearied by the frequently repeated newspaper comment that the Government's fortunes depended upon the support of Bonar Law.   The Prime Minister's friends said that he was confident he would reign successfully without the need for any helper to hold his arms on high.   His hands would be steady "until the going down of the sun".

Saturday, the 19th of March, was cold with bursts of cheerless sunshine.   A blustering wind raced down the Strand.   From Charing Cross railway station, Bonar Law was about to set out for Cannes and retirement.   The little knot of friends surrounding the traveller at the railway station was undistinguished.   Three secretaries about to transfer their allegiance to other Ministers, several members of the family, and I—that was the company.   There were no photographers exploding their flashbulbs and there were no reporters. No Ministers attended on the traveller.   The Prime Minister did not take time off to speed his departing colleague.

Bonar Law stayed the night at the hotel in Dover. He wrote to Lloyd George.   I knew nothing of this letter.   But researching the Lloyd George papers, I came upon it written in Bonar Law's own hand.

Lord Warden Hotel,
Dover,
19 Mar. 1921[1]

My dear P.M.

I hope you will not feel inclined to tell me to mind my own business but I am still very much interested in yours.

[1] Envelope addressed to Lloyd George at Chequers and postmarked Dover 8 p.m. March 20th, 1921.

You will have noticed from *The Times* that Northcliffe has evidently given orders to make a set against Chamberlain.

I think it would be worth your while, if you can do it, to send for Max just to have a talk with him for I think that he could now be easily influenced by you to support you.

He must be doing something but I really believe he has more sympathy with you than with any one else & the feeling he has had that I prevented him having a free hand (of which I admit there was no sign in his action) perhaps made him more difficult than if I had been out of it altogether.

He is certain to take a strong line one way or the other.

Excuse my bothering you about it but I think it worth while making the suggestion.

I hope your family do not bear me a grudge. Isabel says that if you had needed to go instead of me she would have found it hard to forgive you.

Yours sincerely,
A. Bonar Law

It is true that I was asked in late March to meet Lloyd George at Sir Philip Sassoon's house. But as I was committed to taking part in an organized attack on the Prime Minister, the invitation was side-tracked.

The succession to Bonar Law as Leader of the Tory Party was the immediate issue in politics. All the signs indicated that Austen Chamberlain would be selected. He was a traditional Protectionist. Could he be induced, before taking office, to pledge himself to rid the Party of the "No Food Tax" commitment in preparation for another election? It swiftly became clear that the task would not be easy. Chamberlain explained to his Tory followers that there were difficulties in the way. A leader who pledged himself to tariffs as a means of dealing with unemployment after an election would be asked why there should be any delay in applying the remedy. Why not an immediate election?

Parliament had only run half its course. Chamberlain believed and declared that the House was not willing or ready for a dissolution and election. He would give no pledge for the future. Was it possible to subject him to pressure and perhaps win some advantage through opposing his selection as heir to the Tory Leadership?

There were other candidates. A letter to Lord Stamfordham disclosed the opinion of His Majesty, a powerful influence in the ranks of the Tory Party.

His [Lloyd George's] difficulty will be finding a successor to Bonar Law. Could he get the same advice and support from Chamberlain? Personally I expect he would find Horne[1] easier to get on with, but the Unionists will of course elect Chamberlain as their leader.[2]

Lord Birkenhead was favoured by many of the Members of the House of Commons, and he had the advantage of important newspaper support (*Daily Mail* and *The Times*). Lord Curzon was mentioned and also Lords Derby and Salisbury.[3] The prospect of putting forward one of these competitors was of course thoroughly considered and hopefully canvassed by the Empire group as a means of stampeding Chamberlain into giving tariff pledges. He would not respond. His rejection of the overtures was firm, though courteous. The position was summed up by Captain Frederick Guest, Chief Liberal Whip, in a letter to Lloyd George written on the eve of the Tory Party meeting:

[1] Sir Robert Horne, the President of the Board of Trade.
[2] Windsor Archives K.1681.9.
[3] There was no objection at that time to a Prime Minister in the House of Lords.

House of Commons,
Saturday evening,
March 19 [1921]

Dear Prime Minister,

You will probably wish to hear what news there is anent the Unionist Party Meeting arranged for Monday.

Firstly Talbot[1] tells me to convey to you that he expects all will go well for Austen and that small differences of opinion as to proceedings, title, & period are being smoothed away.

There are a handful who would like to push the Lord Chancellor[2] forward but they are finding no encouragement. Hicks[3] is the chief mover; but his motives have an ulterior object, namely the splitting of the Coalition. You will remember that he has been on this line for some months. . . .

Yours sincerely,
Frederick Guest

At the Party meeting on March 21st, 1921, Chamberlain, though not acceptable to some Members, was elected Leader of the Tory Party without a dissenting voice. This unanimity is the common practice of the Party. He was at once appointed as Lloyd George's Leader of the House of Commons.

Although Austen had always been an ardent supporter of Joe Chamberlain's policy, he appeared to be wavering in his enthusiasm. His mind was turning to Irish affairs. Always, however, he was a most attractive member of the Tory High Command.

Mrs. Ivy Chamberlain was the ideal wife for Austen. They were frequent week-end visitors at Polesden Lacey,

[1] Lord Edmund Talbot, afterwards Viscount Fitzalan, Chief Whip of the Tory Party. He was a most popular Chief Whip. He was appointed Viceroy of Ireland and as he was a Roman Catholic it was expected that the choice would be popular with the nation. But the Irish leaders said that a Catholic Viceroy was no more welcome than a Catholic hangman.

[2] Lord Birkenhead.

[3] Sir William Joynson-Hicks.

the beautiful home of Mrs. Ronnie Greville, on a hillside in Surrey. Mrs. Greville was particular in selecting her guests. There it was in the house on the hill that political parties were held. The guests, drawn from the Front Bench, spent happy hours talking of Lloyd George and Ireland, with occasional discussions on fiscal reform, commonly called Tariff Reform. The food was good and the wine well chosen. Mrs. Greville was rich, generous, outspoken and sometimes rude.

Occasionally important members of the outer circle found themselves included in the list of dignitaries. Sir John Simon, a strange bird quite different from the glittering peacocks that always strutted on the well-kept lawns, was admitted to Mrs. Greville's favour after making a Tory speech in Parliament.

It was Sunday night. The dining table was laden with sparkling glass and shining silver. Pyramids of fruit and sweets scattered here and there in reach of everybody. Gay and happy conversation was exchanged from one neighbour to another and also across the wide table.

Only one detail was going wrong. The butler was obviously tight.

Surely Austen was the most important and impressive guest. An effort to invite a discourse on the Empire policy failed. Instead in a pause in general conversation he casually mentioned that the Empire must not be wrecked on an Irish issue. He carried on with an interesting and informed monologue on Ireland and the difficulties confronting his Party. He had reached the story of the momentous decision of the Unionist group in 1886.

Mrs. Greville's attention wavered. On a scribbling pad she was busily writing. Summoning her butler, well known for his intemperate habits, she handed him

the written message—which was indeed amply justified.
It read: "You are drunk—leave the room at once."

The butler placed the note on a big and beautiful
salver and, walking unsteadily to Austen Chamberlain,
with a deep bow presented the message.

Austen paused in his admirable exposition of the
intransigence of the Irish race. He slowly fixed his
monocle and read the startling message, "You are drunk
—leave the room at once." Of course he was astonished.
Why had Mrs. Greville sent him such an incredible
message? Written in her own hand and delivered to
him by the butler who had spent many years in the
service of Polesden Lacey.

Austen Chamberlain was well balanced and fortunately not easily offended. He could not be described
as a touchy man. So he knew just how to deal with such
an emergency. As explanations were resolving the crisis
and brushing away the misunderstanding, the butler fled
from the room midst shouts of hilarious laughter.

Good and friendly relations were restored and Austen
returned to telling the long story of Ireland's grievances
and Britain's patience and toleration.

And like all good dinner-time stories, the dinner
ended and so did the story.

But there it was for all to hear, that Austen, the new
leader of the Tory Party, and the heir apparent to the
Prime Minister's place, was not meditating on the why
and wherefor of Tariff Reform and Imperial Preference.

What now? The Protectionist section of the Party
and those who favoured abandoning the "No Food Tax"
pledge were themselves driven to abandoning hope.
Chamberlain, they said, had rejected the faith of his father
(Joe Chamberlain). He would not be acceptable as an
alternative Prime Minister. Harnessed to Lloyd George
by ties of common policy and by bonds of loyalty, he

would not be available as Lloyd George's successor.

But how could Lloyd George be defeated? That was the question anxiously debated by dissident Ministers, dissatisfied Protectionists, and the ancient houses of Hatfield and Knowsley (Salisbury and Derby), traditional Tory strongholds. There were many factors which favoured the Prime Minister against his antagonists.

(1) His right to ask and obtain a dissolution of Parliament. This right, if exercised, would send many Members of the House unwillingly to their constituencies. Some would object because they would sustain defeat. Others would dodge because they would be obliged to pay election expenses. Lazy fellows would want to be left in occupation of their seats. Only the ardent and faithful seekers after the defeat and destruction of Lloyd George could be relied upon to accept willingly the upheaval of a General Election.

(2) His patronage of office and honours which counted with all those who were striving after promotion.

(3) His strength in the constituencies, though dwindling, his reputation abroad and his war record.

He would be a hard nut to crack.

But, on the other hand, the tally of worries and troubles besetting the Coalition and its Prime Minister was long and formidable. These liabilities, his enemies had a right to hope, would help to bring down the old bad system of Coalition Government by Lloyd George, his captive Chamberlain, and all of the Coalition Liberals. A Tory Government would come in, without the Coalition Liberal allies and without Lloyd George. This was most ardently desired by many Tories of right and left, by nearly every Tory newspaper, and by the aristocratic Tory landed and titled families, then of real importance in political circles.

(1) By the summer of 1921 trade conditions were the worst in a hundred years. Unemployment was mounting —by June there were over two millions out of work. Wages were reduced in every industry. Agriculture languished under the devastating flow of foreign imports. Bankrupt farmers and poverty-stricken farm workers distressed and dismayed the shopkeepers, seed and feed merchants and implement dealers throughout the country districts. Wages fell; in Yorkshire the pay of women employed on the land was cut down from 10d. to 7d. an hour. The prices of commodities tumbled: food and raw materials by one third; wheat, pig iron and steel by one half. The cost of living fell 24 points between January 1st and mid-March. The Stock Exchange was in the shadows. With stock markets plunging down, unemployment figures mounting up, and the shipping industry almost at a standstill, foreign exchanges were in chaos.

(2) Serious friction had broken out between the two wings of the Administration, Tory and Liberal. In Parliament, Lloyd George's group of supporters, the Coalition Liberals, were relatively few in number, but held an unreasonable share of offices in the Government. The distribution of honours was also a continual and exasperating cause of dispute. Tory claimants were neglected and a disproportionate share in the list of honours was allotted to the other Coalition Party.[1] Another cause of bitter complaint among the Tory

---

[1] Lloyd George did not take part in the distribution of honours. But he did take full advantage of the benefits to himself and his Coalition Liberal supporters. Recommendations were finally dealt with by J. T. Davies, principal secretary, who reported to his Chief in Welsh, and to the Palace in English. When Lord Stamfordham criticised the Knighthood for William Watson because he had written *The Woman with the Serpent's Tongue*, Lloyd George insisted upon keeping the name on the list because he said Watson had written *The Man Who Saw*.

hierarchy was the activities of Captain Guest, Chief Whip of the Lloyd George Party. He was gathering corn in Tory fields. "Spoiling the Egyptians" did not entirely summarize the case against the Coalition Liberals. A more serious complaint against the Coalition Liberals was the charge by Tories that they were debasing the coinage. A gentleman (whom I will not name) had become a Baronet in the New Year Honours List. Sir George Younger complained violently. He directed the Conservative Central Office with unchallenged authority and was the guardian of the Party's financial interests. He wrote to Bonar Law[1] at the outset of the year 1921, when the New Year's Honours were announced, strongly criticising the apportionment of awards and the unsuitable character of . . . .[2]

(3) It was known to the Tories that Lloyd George was discussing reunion with the "Wee Frees"—the Opposition Liberals. Many Conservative Members of Parliament believed that a Lloyd George plan existed to ditch the Tories by means of a Liberal reunion and a "No Stomach Tax" appeal to the electors, under Lloyd George's leadership. Miss Stevenson,[3] the Prime Minister's secretary, who was familiar with every move

[1] Bonar Law's own attitude to honours is summed up in a short letter written to Sir George Younger—"My dear Younger, Many thanks for your letter of the 23rd. I am very pleased to hear what you say about Walter Neilson. I think we should almost give him the Order of Merit for not wanting a title! . . ." (B.L.P.101/3/53). (The reference is possibly to Lieutenant-Colonel Walter Gordon Neilson.)

[2] See Appendix 2, George Younger to Bonar Law, January 2nd, 1921.

[3] Miss Stevenson joined Lloyd George's staff as a secretary in 1911. Her diary with frequent entries between September 1914 and the end of 1922 has not been published. It is a startling political document. In 1943 she married Lloyd George. He became Earl Lloyd-George in 1945. Her autobiography, written after Lloyd George's death, contains much valuable material. It has not been published.

of her master, recorded in her diary meetings between Lloyd George and the "Wee Frees":

Meanwhile the Wee Frees are making frantic advances to D. [David Lloyd George]—lunches,—dinners etc. A meeting was held on Wednesday when they discussed their position, and *all but four* voted for taking D. as their leader (with certain conditions of course). The four opponents were Asquith,[1] Maclean,[2] Wedgwood Benn[3] and Thorne.[4] Hogge[5] has given an interview to the *Evening Standard* saying they are willing to join D.—with certain conditions. It appears that Hogge's great grievance at the moment is that he has never met D. socially! What a change of front from six weeks ago, when they were howling down D.'s portrait from the walls of the Nat. Liberal Club. But they find Asquith is no leader and they have no hope or trust in him.[6]

(4) Ireland aroused growing political interest throughout the year 1921. The issue always tended to sever the two wings of the Coalition—the Tories and the Coalition Liberals.

(5) A violent and cunning campaign for economy, carried on by the Northcliffe newspapers, found many supporters among the Tory Members of the House of Commons. Three independent candidates, dubbed "Anti-Waste", won Conservative constituencies at by-

---

[1] Herbert Henry Asquith, Leader of the Liberal Party, former Prime Minister, driven out by Lloyd George.

[2] Rt. Hon. Sir Donald Maclean, fifty-seven years of age; he was well-liked on both sides of the House. He was interim Leader of the Liberal Party while Asquith was out of the House following his defeat at East Fife in 1918 until his return for Paisley in 1920.

[3] Capt. William Wedgwood Benn, M.P. for Leith. Small of stature, vigorous in debate and swift in repartee. He joined the Socialists in 1927.

[4] George Rennie Thorne, M.P. for East Wolverhampton, Chief Independent Liberal Whip since 1919.

[5] James Myles Hogge, M.P. for East Edinburgh, 1912-24. Joint Chief Whip Wee Free Liberals, 1918-22.

[6] Miss Stevenson's diary, June 24th, 1921.

elections against Conservative nominees. This movement agitated many Members with narrow majorities,
who feared that the "Anti-Waste" opposition might
destroy their chance of election to the next Parliament.
The criticism of these anxious supporters alarmed the
Prime Minister and excited his Ministerial colleagues,
thus weakening the Government and strengthening the
forces hostile to Lloyd George.

(6) Stanley Baldwin, stalwart Tory and fervent
advocate of Protection for the steel industry against
German competition, was considering resignation. Although he did not at that time rank as a leader of opinion
in the Party, his discontent was of importance. It
reflected back-bench sentiment. He wrote to Bonar Law
to say—"I nearly took advantage of the shuffle to go back
to private life and to business."[1]

(7) But most important of all useful instruments for
removing the Prime Minister were the discontented
Ministers serving in Lloyd George's own Administra-
tion: Churchill, Coalition Liberal and Free Trader;
Birkenhead, Tory and Protectionist; Curzon, Tory and
often a Protectionist, sometimes a Free Trader; and
Montagu, Liberal and Free Trader. Two Tories and
two Coalition Liberals—two Protectionists and two Free
Traders. Then there was Lord Derby, leader of the
Tories in Lancashire and hostile to Lloyd George, and
Lord Salisbury, irreconcilable, the hereditary leader of
those Tories who gave their allegiance to "Hatfield
House".

It was a goodly list of discontents. But what was to
be done with them?

Should the Protectionist and Imperial Preference
movement undertake the task of raising throughout the
country the old Joseph Chamberlain cry of "Tariff

[1] See Appendix 3, Baldwin to Bonar Law, April 2nd, 1921.

Reform Means Work For All"?   Certainly the vast
numbers of unemployed might be expected to listen
with attention and possibly with approval too.   The
farming community would respond with enthusiasm.
Most Tory Members of the House could be relied upon
to rally to this cause.   Lord Salisbury had said, on the
subject of Protection, that the Conservative Party was
like dry wood; that any man with a match would set it
ablaze.

No.   Although there was much to be said for a
propaganda campaign in favour of tariffs and Imperial
Preference, with emphasis on this cure for unemployment, it would be necessary at the outset of a revolu-
tionary movement against Lloyd George and his Free
Trade Liberals in the Cabinet to make use of the
grievances of Ministers who were convinced Free
Traders.   If Lloyd George could be defeated—then it
would be soon enough to manœuvre for a new Government, pledged to go to the country on a programme of
Imperial Preference and Food Taxes.

Churchill, a confirmed Free Trader, and Lord Salisbury were both bitter opponents of Lloyd George and
also of Protection.   They could be mobilised for the defeat
of Lloyd George, but not for the victory of Tariff
Reform.   Derby was also a Free Trader.   And Northcliffe,
who was the foe of Lloyd George in *The Times*, the *Daily
Mail* and other newspapers, might waver if the
"Stomach Tax" became an immediate issue.

There should be no compunction about making use
of the Free Trade elements to promote the prospects of
the tariff cause.   They knew the faith we held.   They
would not hesitate to make full use of the Empire group
in furthering their own designs.

II

FOUR DISCONTENTED
MINISTERS

As for the four Ministers who opposed Lloyd George, they did so each for a different set of reasons.

Churchill disagreed and rebelled over several public issues. The Prime Minister, for his part, believed he was being harassed for personal reasons, and his attitude to Churchill was harsh and overbearing, at times almost insulting. Relations between Lloyd George and Churchill were never entirely comfortable. Lloyd George was explaining a point when Churchill interrupted him, saying: "I don't see . . ." Lloyd George broke in sharply: "You will see the point, when you begin to understand that conversation is not a monologue."

Churchill advocated peace with Turkey. On February 22nd, 1921, he wrote to Lloyd George a letter which showed prescience. He foretold accurately the course of events in the war between Turkey and Greece.[1] By inference, but very clearly, he charged Lloyd George

[1] After being defeated in the war, Turkey was subjected in 1920 to the Treaty of Sèvres, by which Greece gained possession of Eastern Thrace, Gallipoli and the Aegean Islands. Smyrna was to be administered by Greece for five years, and the Straits and Dardanelles were placed under international supervision. Lloyd George had wanted terms more favourable to Greece. He urged on his colleagues that the Turks should be driven out of Europe. The Sultan of Turkey signed the Treaty under pressure, but Mustapha Kemal, leader of the Turkish forces, had retired on Angora and taken up arms against the Greeks.

with the fearful responsibility of letting loose the Greeks and reopening the war.[1] He renewed the attack on June 11th, inviting Lloyd George to demand of the Greeks that they replace their royalist commanders with generals of Venizelist[2] sympathies. The Greeks should also be required to evacuate Smyrna. Churchill predicted that another offensive would result in the destruction of the Greek army.[3]

When it appeared that the Greeks were likely to refuse an offer of mediation, Churchill suggested to the Prime Minister that Great Britain should definitely intervene to stop the war by blockading Smyrna against Greek ships. As late as September 26th, 1921, Churchill was arguing in favour of a blockade of the Piraeus if Greece should be unreasonable.[4] The Prime Minister made no effective response, and disaster did indeed fall upon the Greeks.

Further disagreement arose between the two men on domestic policy:

(1) Churchill supported Dr. Christopher Addison, Coalition Liberal, colleague and friend of the Prime Minister, whose failure to provide "Homes for Heroes" infuriated the Tories. Lloyd George was embarrassed because he intended to sacrifice his Minister and satisfy the Tory critics.

(2) Churchill attacked the failure of Government measures for dealing with unemployment.

(3) The Irish negotiations brought the Prime Minister and Churchill into conflict.

[1] Letter, Churchill to Lloyd George, February 22nd, 1921—Churchill: *The World Crisis—The Aftermath*, page 394.

[2] Venizelos, friend of Britain, had been defeated at a Greek General Election. He fled to France. His generals were dismissed and replaced by pro-German King Constantine's soldiers.

[3] See Appendix 4, Churchill to Lloyd George, June 11th, 1921.

[4] See Churchill: *The World Crisis—The Aftermath*, page 402.

(4) The dispute over Russia raged throughout the year. Churchill held that there should be "Peace with the German people, war with the Bolshevik tyranny". He accused the Prime Minister of following the opposite course.

(5) Then again there was a personal dispute of a serious character. Austen Chamberlain had been Chancellor of the Exchequer. With his promotion to the Leaderships of Party and House, that office fell vacant. Winston Churchill rightly believed that he was entitled to the job, which was looked upon as the highest executive post in the Government.

He had served as Secretary of State for War, and took over the Colonial Office on February 12th, 1921. He had demanded before taking office:

(1) Complete responsibility for civil and military affairs in Mesopotamia, then under the India Office and claimed by the Foreign Office.

(2) A Middle East Department under his control as Colonial Secretary.

(3) Egypt to be transferred from the Foreign Office to the Middle East Department after the meeting of the Imperial Conference in June 1921.

(4) The authority of the Colonial Office should extend to Palestine, Aden and Basra—"The Arabian Triangle"— which would of course include domination of the affairs of:

> Ibn Saud, King of Nejd
> Hussein, Sherif of Mecca and King of the Hedjaz
> The Imam of Yemen
> The Sultanates of Oman and Kuwait
> The Emirate of Bahrein
> The British Protectorate of Aden.

By early March Churchill set out for his new kingdom, where he exercised immeasurable authority over

Winston Churchill and Lloyd George
"The changes that are sure to come, I do not fear to see"

Kings and Countries, over High Commissioners and Ambassadors. His retinue was adorned by many important officials, and by Lawrence, Lawrence of Arabia, listed as an adviser.

Like Antony of Shakespeare's play, Churchill was engaged in dividing up the Near East. He proclaimed Feisal King of Mesopotamia. The crown of Transjordan was conferred upon Abdulla. Zones for Arabs and Zionists were mapped out in Palestine. British troops stationed in Mesopotamia were ordered to embark for England. The Kingdoms of Antony were distributed to his sons. Our own Colonial Secretary gave kingdoms to the sons of the Sherif of Mecca.

When he heard of changes in the Government in London, he hurried home. Chancellor of the Exchequer was his rightful post and he was quite certain the place would be at his disposal, along with the fringe benefit of residence at 11, Downing Street, just once removed from the Prime Minister's establishment at No. 10.

Lloyd George held different views. A rival too near the centre of power was not to his liking. He would not have three kings in Whitehall, himself, Chamberlain and Churchill. Sir Robert Horne had strayed just a night and day journey from London. He had wandered as far as the Casino at Cannes. He was summoned and on him the Prime Minister conferred the accolade.[1]

Churchill returned from his Egyptian conquests on April 10th. No Roman triumph for him, not even a laurel wreath. He was angry. He gave up his social contacts with the Prime Minister. No more dinner parties. No more intimate conversations. Formal relations only.

---

[1] Stanley Baldwin's name was mentioned and his appointment to the Exchequer was widely supported by Unionist Whips and many of the backbench Members. (See *Daily Mail*, March 22nd, 1921.)

Lloyd George and Churchill looked out on one another like two distant snow-clad mountain peaks.

The Prime Minister had the highest opinion of Churchill's intellectual qualities but decried and derided his political performance: quite often it seemed to me a demonstration of jealousy of which I believed there was a real big store, skilfully concealed. Rudeness was usually one-sided, though Churchill often made up for Lloyd George's aggressiveness in speech by his exceedingly embarrassing letters of protest over numerous policies. While discussing the plan for yet another Coalition, Churchill said: "If you are going to include all Parties (in a Coalition) you will have to have me in your new National Party." "Oh no," replied Lloyd George. "To be a party you must have at least one follower. You have none."

Strange that these slighting and wounding remarks by Lloyd George did not result in a breach of relations. But the Colonial Secretary was free from rancour. And, if offended, he would never conceal his hostility. It was not wise to give him secrets. He would often stumble into disclosure in one form or another and always without any intention of betraying a confidence.

I recall Lloyd George's description of his difficulties with Churchill and Reginald McKenna. He compared them to trees in the forest. Churchill, like the oak, he said, gave warning before crashing. McKenna he likened to the elm, the branch falls without any notice.

Mentally, morally and physically Churchill was of stouter build than Lloyd George. Churchill's firmness of purpose, right or wrong, made a profound impression on his colleagues and reinforced his power and authority. He worked harder and longer than Lloyd George and he had a wider vision. For countless years and in face of valiant efforts he was unable to capture and hold public confidence. Quite often he appeared to be popular, but never during the years between Wars was he regarded as a leader. He always walked in the shadow of kingship. Promise perhaps, yet the shadow never became the substance. He had a group of friends. He held them throughout. Lloyd George shed his friends like the ermine sheds its winter coat.

Miss Stevenson wrote in her diary two weeks and two days after the return of Churchill from Egypt:

Winston [is] still very vexed with the P.M. as a result of, as he thinks, having been neglected in the recent promotions. D. [David Lloyd George] says Winston fully expected to be made Chancellor of the Exchequer when all the changes were made, and he has not been to see D. since his return. D. has only seen him in Cabinets and meetings of the kind and Winston writes him "Dear Prime Minister," whereas it used to be "Dear Ll. G." or "My dear David" even.[1]

Lord Birkenhead, the Lord Chancellor, was the second Minister at odds with Lloyd George. He had no standing with the Prime Minister. They treated each other with every sign of distant and polite relations when they were together, but they showed distrust and even dislike when they were apart. A quarrel over legal appointments brought on a serious rupture.

The Lord Chief Justice, Lord Reading, was appointed Viceroy of India,[2] thus creating a vacancy on the Bench. Sir Gordon Hewart, the Attorney-General, was the proper, traditional and legitimate choice for the post.[3] Lord Birkenhead put Hewart's name forward. Lloyd George, however, did not approve. It suited him to delay the Attorney-General's departure from the Government for a year or two.

---

[1] Miss Stevenson's diary, April 26th, 1921.   [2] January, 1921.
[3] See Appendix 5, Miss Stevenson's diary.

Hewart was a brilliant Parliamentarian and Lloyd George's most capable Coalition Liberal colleague. If he had been allowed to go, Lloyd George would have had to put Ernest Pollock, the Solicitor-General, in his place. Pollock was a Conservative. His promotion would have disturbed the balance of representation of Parties in the Government, which would have been an embarrassment to Lloyd George at a time when he was seeking Liberal reunion. Hewart's constituency, East Leicester, if opened up, might be lost to Lloyd George's dwindling Parliamentary group.

Most Ministers are unwilling to go; Hewart was most unwilling to stay. To hold him, the Prime Minister was compelled to put him in the Cabinet and also to promise that the office of Lord Chief Justice would be at Hewart's disposal on the eve of the next dissolution of Parliament. That pledge could be implemented only if Lloyd George had in his possession the resignation of a caretaker Lord Chief Justice.

He put forward the name of Lord Finlay, a former Lord Chancellor, nearly eighty years of age and showing it. Finlay was willing to place his resignation in Lloyd George's hands. Birkenhead, the Lord Chancellor, was outraged by the plan, for he had a deep respect for the traditions of the Bench. Lloyd George's proposal was in defiance of all precedent and practice. Birkenhead made a lively protest.

There were two grounds for complaint. The Prime Minister had rejected the recommendation of Hewart by his own Lord Chancellor, who was the head of the Judiciary. But far more serious was the proposal that the Prime Minister should hold in his hand an undated letter of resignation from Finlay. That plan would make the Lord Chief Justice subject to removal at the will of the Prime Minister, thus depriving the highest judicial officer in the Kingdom of his independence of the political machine.

Birkenhead warned the Prime Minister:

The matter is, in my opinion, of the gravest importance both in relation to the future of our judicial system and to the credit and indeed the existence of the present Government.

Although it was a proper, reasonable and rightful dissent, Lloyd George replied to Birkenhead's written protest in anger, and contemptuously. He sent Birkenhead an insulting letter, distorting the facts. He referred in acrimonious tones to the Lord Chancellor's lengthy typewritten document. And he concluded the defence of his action by quoting Sir Edward Carson,[1] who was not a member of his Government and who was, of course, hostile to the Prime Minister's projects for an Irish settlement.[2]

The correspondence between the Prime Minister and Birkenhead took on a threatening form. They addressed each other as "My dear Chancellor" and "Dear Prime Minister" with a "Sincerely" instead of the usual "Yours ever," which is in common use among friendly colleagues in government.

Lloyd George was compelled to retreat from the Finlay plan because of the obvious physical weakness and failing mental powers of his nominee. However, he substituted Sir Alfred Lawrence, who was also nearly eighty, though in good health and full possession of his faculties. The Lawrence appointment was made in defiance of hostile opinion in Parliament and Press.[3]

Birkenhead was outraged by this incident, and his

[1] In the month of May, Carson was named by the Prime Minister as a Law Lord, with a seat in the House of Lords.

[2] See Appendix 6, Lloyd George to Birkenhead, February 11th, 1921. Also see Appendix 7, Birkenhead's reply, February 11th, 1921.

[3] See Appendix 8, George Younger to Bonar Law, April 13th, 1921.

personal relations with the Prime Minister became strained and embittered.

The strange conduct of Carson will come as no surprise to those colleagues who worked with him. He advised Lloyd George to appoint Finlay. He wrote to Hewart that Lord Birkenhead had told him the plan to appoint a stop-gap was illegal. He told Hewart it was a shameful thing if the Attorney-General was not at once appointed to succeed Reading. He said to Hewart that Lloyd George really intended to keep the Lord Chief Justice post warm for Reading and not for Hewart, thus unsettling the Attorney-General and disturbing the relations between the Prime Minister and his subordinate.[1]

Within a year Lloyd George acted on the Lawrence resignation. The Chief Justice was travelling up to town on Friday, March 3rd, 1922, to hear a case that had been adjourned from the previous day. He read an account of his resignation in the morning papers. He went into court, finished the case, and retired with a pension.[2]

Then there was Edwin Montagu, Secretary of State for India. He was bitterly and unalterably opposed to Lloyd George's support of Greek claims and pretensions. So was the Indian Government and also the Viceroy, Lord Reading. Montagu had strongly resisted the terms of the harsh Turkish peace treaty and had written to Lloyd George threatening resignation on that issue. He

[1] See Appendix 6, Lloyd George to Birkenhead, February 11th, 1921. See also Robert Jackson's *The Chief*, page 140.

[2] Lawrence took up the title Lord Trevethin in August 1921. Lord Trevethin on retirement received a pension of £4,000 yearly. He bought an estate on the river Wye, with fishing water which was in the end his undoing. On August 3rd, 1936, he fell into the river while catching a salmon and was carried away by the current. His chauffeur went to his rescue but Lord Trevethin called out, "I'm all right, I can swim." Unhappily after the chauffeur brought him out of the water he died of heart failure, thus bringing to a close at the age of ninety-two a remarkable life.

could not agree with the policy, advocated by Balfour and supported by the Prime Minister, of running the Turks out of Europe. He had demanded that a public announcement be made that the British Government did not wish to turn the Turks out of Constantinople.[1]

Then the quarrel exploded. Montagu wrote to Lloyd George, insisting on his right as plenipotentiary for India to send a memorandum in favour of Turkey, a Mohammedan power, to the Peace Conference at San Remo. Lloyd George was furious. He absolutely rejected this claim and Montagu gave way, accepting the Prime Minister's rebuff and rebuke. Personal relations were embittered by a written report[2] from the Tory Central Office that Montagu and Mrs. Montagu had voted against the Coalition Liberal candidate at a by-election in South Norfolk.

And, of course, there was Lord Curzon, who was continually falling in and out with Lloyd George. In April 1921, the occasion of dispute between them was the question of representation at the Lympne Conference.[3] Curzon, in a letter to Lady Curzon[4] on April 22nd, gave a vivid description of the quarrel. He wrote that the Prime Minister was troubling him with extraordinary tactics over the meeting at Lympne. With Briand, the French Prime Minister, Berthelot, the French Secretary-General of Foreign Affairs, would be present. But Curzon had not been asked to attend. Believing he might be the victim of a deliberate affront, he consulted Balfour, who promised, after lunching with Lady Cunard, to seek information.

[1] Now Istanbul.

[2] Memorandum from Sir Malcolm Fraser to Sir George Younger, October 11th, 1920.

[3] Talks between France and Britain on the question of reparations began at Sir Philip Sassoon's house at Lympne on April 23rd, 1921.

[4] See Appendix 9, Curzon to Lady Curzon, April 22nd, 1921.

"Girlie," wrote Curzon, "I am getting very tired of working or trying to work with that man. He wants his Forn. Sec. to be a valet almost a drudge . . ."

Balfour returned to Curzon with apologies from the Prime Minister: "A.J.B. protests most earnestly to me," Curzon wrote, "that it would be a calamity if I were to resign. . . . To me he discourses about the peculiarities of the temperament & character of L.G. [Lloyd George] which he regards with stupefaction. I wonder what he says to him about me!"[1] Curzon was always "being driven to resignation," but never reaching that destination.

Another source of weakness in the Lloyd George Coalition flowed from the disputes between Curzon and Churchill. These two Ministers quarrelled over many issues.

Curzon wanted a better place in the Government for Lord Crawford,[2] and a "big place". Churchill wanted Ormsby-Gore[3] as his Under Secretary in the Colonial Office. Curzon objected. He claimed the holder should be a Peer.

Churchill's insistence on taking over for the Colonial Office control of Egypt along with the Arab Kingdoms met with resistance from Curzon. The struggle persisted and was yet another source of weakness to the Government. It was on February 14th that Curzon secured a decision in favour of his Foreign Office. Although Churchill's claim was defeated it was not destroyed. The

---

[1] See Appendix 10, Curzon to Lady Curzon, April 23rd, 1921.

[2] 27th Earl of Crawford, formerly popular Chief Whip of the Tory Party.

[3] William George Arthur Ormsby-Gore, M.P., later Lord Harlech, allied to the House of Cecil by marriage. He declared in a public speech after the fall of the Coalition that his sole aim in remaining in politics was to exclude Lloyd George, Churchill and Beaverbrook from any office. Ormsby-Gore ultimately served under Churchill.

quarrel over Egypt became a continuing event and yet another cause of disintegration in the Ministry.

Many years after Churchill told me that he would have succeeded in seizing Egypt from Curzon's clutches if the Government had lived a little longer.

Curzon, in the hour of victory, wrote his wife:

... Then Cabinet 12-2, rather a long and worrying controversy between Winston & myself over the Middle East. He wants to grab everything into his new Dept., & to be a sort of Asiatic Forn. Secretary. I absolutely declined to agree to this, & the P.M. took my side. But it was hot fighting while it lasted.

Notes were passed during meetings between these two Ministers. In May 1921 the following exchange took place:

Curzon: I am against Ministers without portfolios.[1]
Churchill: I am afraid my own portfolio (although substantial) is sometimes only a frail defence against yr. displeasure.
Curzon: & vice versa.

On June 9th, 1921, Churchill wrote a letter to the Prime Minister, sending a copy to Curzon.[2] He proposed to meet the objections of the U.S. Government and the covetousness of Standard Oil of New Jersey by offering to transfer Mandates over Palestine and Mesopotamia to the U.S. Government. He asked permission to announce the offer in the House of Commons.

Curzon was angry, complaining once more that Churchill aimed at establishing for himself a separate Middle East Foreign Office. He wrote the Prime Minister on June 10th.[3] His complaints were vigorous

[1] Curzon referred to Dr. Addison, who in the Vice-Regal conception was a notorious bore.

[2] See Appendix 11, Churchill to Lloyd George, June 9th, 1921, and covering letter (Appendix 12) Churchill to Curzon, June 9th, 1921.

[3] See Appendix 13, Curzon to Lloyd George, June 10th, 1921.

and his rejection of Churchill's proposal went beyond a mere refusal. The following day Lloyd George sent a harsh and hostile letter to Churchill, addressing him as "My dear Colonial Secretary", and putting forward a very strong argument against Churchill's proposal.[1]

Churchill was not put off. He spoke again, impinging upon the province of the Foreign Secretary in Curzon's opinion. Another bullying letter was dispatched by Curzon to Churchill with, as usual, a copy to the Prime Minister:

... on two recent occasions you have made public references to the Egyptian question (which does not lie in your Department) which were without Cabinet authority, which in each case have evoked an immediate protest from Egypt, and which have rendered the already difficult task of the Foreign Secretary there more difficult.[2]

As usual Churchill replied at length, claiming liberty to speak on Egypt, dissenting from Foreign Office policy and asserting the right to present his views, alleging Cabinet authority.

I am not at all prepared to sit still & mute & watch the people of this country being slowly committed to the loss of this great & splendid monument of British administrative skill and energy. ... I can quite understand that those in Egypt who wish to see our troops relegated to "drinking condensed water on the banks of the Suez Canal" will not appreciate the reference.[3]

Curzon was now convinced that Churchill meant to seize Egypt from the Foreign Office, adding it to his Colonial Office Kingdom of the Middle East. He wished to administer all of the Arab territories, was the tale.

[1] See Appendix 14, Lloyd George to Churchill, June 11th, 1921.
[2] See Appendix 15, Curzon to Churchill, June 13th, 1921.
[3] See Appendix 16, Churchill to Curzon, June 13th, 1921.

Lloyd George wrote to Curzon and separately to Chamberlain on June 14th, criticising Churchill.[1] To Chamberlain Lloyd George wrote:

Curzon is going for Winston over his unauthorised pronouncement on questions of foreign policy. He has written him a strong letter on the subject. Curzon is undoubtedly right, but I hope there will be no flare up until I arrive.[2] Winston has always been in the habit of making these pronouncements on his own. He did it under the Asquith administration constantly whenever there was a chance of a real limelight effect![3]

His letter to Curzon on the same day approved in sweeping terms of the Curzon contentions with undertones of reflection on Churchill.

I agree with you that it is most improper and dangerous for any Minister to make a pronouncement upon questions of foreign policy, not only without having had previous consultation with the Foreign Secretary, but without actually a specific request from him to do so.[4]

The bombardment by Churchill continued. He wrote next day[5] to Curzon about the Greek offensive in Asia Minor. A mission should be sent to Kemal the Turk and if stated terms were agreed upon, pressure should be put upon the Greeks, "including if necessary naval

---

[1] On the same day that Churchill was attacked furiously by the Prime Minister in these two letters, Chamberlain wrote to Lloyd George—"Winston has had a great success both as to his speech & his policy, & has changed the whole atmosphere of the House on the Middle East question. Send him a line or wire of congratulation." Churchill answered the Prime Minister, thanking him in restrained though formal and courteous terms. He signed the letter "Winston S. Churchill."

[2] From Criccieth in Wales.

[3] See Appendix 17, Lloyd George to Austen Chamberlain, June 14th, 1921.

[4] See Appendix 18, Lloyd George to Curzon, June 14th, 1921.

[5] See Appendix 19, Churchill to Curzon, June 15th, 1921.

action off Smyrna or the Piraeus to compel them [the Greeks] to close with them [the terms]."

On July 4th, 1921, at a meeting of the Imperial Conference, an interesting and even amusing exchange of notes passed across the table between Curzon, Lloyd George, Chamberlain and Churchill. Curzon wrote Lloyd George:

It seems to me entirely wrong that the Colonial Secretary should on an occasion like this air his independent views on a F.O. question.

I would not presume on a Colonial Office question, either to intervene at all or to take a line independent of the C.O.

Lloyd George replied:

I quite agree. I have done my best to stopper his fizzing. Montagu, Chamberlain & Balfour would be entitled to join in —so on each item we should have six British speeches. It is intolerable.

The same day Austen Chamberlain pencilled a note to Curzon, while the Conference was meeting:

I think you are right to show Winston that you profoundly resent his constant & persistent interference. It goes far beyond anything that I at least have ever known in Cabinet even from the most important members of a Govt.

Unless you make him feel that it is a matter which you feel personally I despair of doing anything with him. To a *personal* appeal I think that he is nearly always open (I mean to an appeal on personal grounds).

Curzon wrote:

My dear Winston, I wonder what you would *think*[1] say if on a Colonial Office [question?] I felt myself at liberty to make a speech at this Conference—quite independent of the Colonial Office and critical of the attitude adopted by its chief.

Churchill replied:

[1] Word italicized is crossed out in original.

You may say anything you like about the Colonial Office that is sincerely meant: but there is no comparison between these vital foreign matters wh. affect the whole future of the world and the mere departmental topics with wh. the Colonial Office is concerned.

It wd. be impossible for me.[1]

In these g[rea]t matters we must be allowed to have opinions.

Although Curzon did not love Churchill, he hated Lloyd George. Gladly he would have helped to pull down the Welsh champion. Nothing could be gained, however, by seeking the support of the Marquis[2] in the movement against Lloyd George, even though he had always hankered after the Leadership of the Tory Party in Bonar Law's day, and his passion to become Prime Minister outstripped every other emotion in his chequered career. He would bite at any hook baited with hope of the highest office. He was a ready and eager rebel.

But, in the words of John Calvin—"There is no likelihood that these things will bring grist to the mill." Curzon always tried to take up with the winner when battle was joined. He changed sides for personal reasons and without regard for principles. His attitude to Protection varied between neutrality, indifference and hostility. He never took any part in the tariff campaign. But he was frequently criticising Salisbury, Derby and others for being opposed to tariffs. Of the powerful Tory leader he wrote: "Jim Salisbury has gone abroad & the Free Trade Conservatives are sulky & silent, except E. Derby [Lord Derby] who goes about trying to prove that he is both a Free Trader & Protectionist",[3] and of the popular Lancashire Tory leader:

[1] Words italicized are crossed out in the original.
[2] Curzon was created a Marquis on June 3rd, 1921.
[3] Letters, Curzon to Lady Curzon.

"... poor old Derby tries every night to loop the loop, as both a Free Trader and a Protectionist and only makes himself ridiculous." Again he wrote to Lady Curzon: "E. Derby gets back from Cannes tonight & has wired to come and see me at 10 p.m. about the passages in the King's Speech about Protection which he and I want to abandon. We shall have a tough fight over it in Cabinet tomorrow."[1]

The tariff supporters did not want Curzon. He was inconsistent, unreliable, untruthful and treacherous. Nobody wanted him.[2]

Lord Derby was a very different type, even though his conduct was unpredictable. He was honest and upright, highly regarded in the country—particularly in Lancashire. There was nothing mean or treacherous in him. He did not deliberately make mischief. His influence in the Conservative Party after the departure of Bonar Law possibly outstripped that of any other leader, not excepting Austen Chamberlain and Lord Salisbury.

Derby had refused to join the Lloyd George Coalition when offered the Colonial Office in succession to Milner.[3] He was hostile to the Government in the early months of 1921 and ready for any move that would detach the

[1] Letter, January 6th and 9th, 1924. The Earl and the Marquis won the tough fight.

[2] George Harvey, the American Ambassador, wrote to President Harding on December 9th, 1921. He gave an interesting example of Curzon's troubles with his servants, his valets and his chefs.

Harvey wrote that a coachman, who had served the Marquis for most of his life, was translated to chauffeur. Naturally, he was not very successful and Curzon dismissed him. Swiftly he repented of his harsh decision. In fact he decided that he could not improve upon him and would reinstate him. (In any case it was a Government car that was at risk.)

On the evening when Curzon made this decision, the coachman asked to see him. Being told that he was to be spared and reinstated, he informed his astounded patron that in seeking an interview he wished merely to inform His Lordship that he was the damnedest cad in England.

[3] Derby did not want office, he wanted power and popularity.

Tory Party from Lloyd George's coat-tails. In April, he was preparing to attack Lloyd George in a speech at the annual dinner of the Junior Imperial League. But the Prime Minister forestalled him. He had a conversation with Derby on April 15th and invited him to go over to Ireland in disguise to negotiate with the Sinn Feiners.[1] Derby at once changed his attitude. His speech at the dinner on April 16th was intended to be friendly to Lloyd George, but unhappily he muddled his role. He welcomed the Prime Minister as "the newest recruit" to the Conservative Party, thus embroiling Lloyd George with the "Wee Free" Liberals, whose support Lloyd George was also seeking at that moment. By the 18th of that month Lord Derby was rejecting his own past and defending Lloyd George against his critics. He wrote me:

On the subject of L.G. I do not think you and I quite agree. You think he is a spent force. I do not, and I am not quite sure that when it comes to this dumping bill that you and I won't find that he represents our views better than Austen Chamberlain does. I have got a genuine liking for the little man. I know his faults and they are many but at the same time I never can forget what he did in the War and be grateful for it.

Derby was never steadfast. In every controversy he was influenced by both sides, and nobody knew for certain where he would come down. He was like an eagle soaring through the sky, turning around and about, surely intending to settle, yet leaving everyone uncertain where he would find his perch. He would give encouragement to a movement for detaching the Tory Party from Lloyd George. But he would never be a convinced advocate of Protection and Imperial Preference. He hated Food Taxes.

[1] See Appendix 20, Beaverbrook to Bonar Law, undated but written in April, 1921.

Lord Salisbury, another enemy of Lloyd George, was bitter and unrestrained in his attacks on the Prime Minister. This nobleman had immense influence and authority. He persistently counselled the Tory members of the Coalition to break away from Lloyd George. He was, however, as hostile to tariffs as to Lloyd George. He regarded the fiscal issue as a disturbing and disintegrating force, which might split the Tory Party.

His opposition to Imperial Preference had reached full flower when the Welsh Church dispute occupied the attention of Parliament. He had held to the fixed belief that Tory resistance to the spoliation of Church funds would be ruined by Party differences over Tariff Reform. The Church funds came first and always over every other issue.

An early Easter (March 27th) brought political activities to a halt.

Lloyd George, joined by his friends Lord Riddell, Robert Horne and others, made up a jolly house party at Sir Philip Sassoon's home at Lympne. Lloyd George was always happy to take refuge with the young Member for Hythe.

Singing sessions at Lympne with many colleagues were a habit. The most interesting Chorus Minister was Churchill. He dwelt on old Music Hall songs with enthusiasm. But he was not quite successful in carrying a melody, and his voice did not justify his selection for the Westminster Abbey choir. Reading, who had served before the mast in his boyhood, sang sea shanties in a gentle, timid voice with much success. The robust Hewart's songs of the northern circuit made a favourable impression. But the leading performer whose efforts were respected—if not admired in secret—was the Prime

Sir Philip Sassoon—A most proficient private secretary. He had served Haig during the war—Geddes during the peace—and Lloyd George through the fateful years. He had many houses and most capable chefs

Minister himself. And his choice was "Glorious Welsh Hymns".

Sir Philip Sassoon, the host of the Minister Singers, was the grandson of a Rothschild. I remember his maiden speech in the House of Commons. It was an indifferent performance but it brought forth a flood of notes of congratulations—not because he had made a good speech but because he had big houses and even bigger funds to maintain them. North of London—Trent; London—Park Lane; South of London—Lympne: these were his headquarters.

He was a brilliant gossip and an habitual flatterer, indifferent to the status of his subjects. At my house in the midst of a large company I was asked, "Where is Philip?" I replied: "Flattering somebody somewhere." From behind a pillar nearby Sassoon cried: "Not you, Max!"

His advancement in political office was swift and sure after Miss Stevenson offered him the post of Parliamentary Private Secretary to the Prime Minister. He did not lack secretarial experience—first with Haig and then with Eric Geddes. It would be interesting to examine the guest lists of the young host who gathered the aged, the beautiful, the clever and over all the powerful at his dining room, wonderfully decorated by the Spanish painter Sert.

Two weeks after Easter, at "Trent", another Sassoon home near London, Miss Stevenson's diary gives an account of a "perfect Sunday":

Went down to Trent over Sunday after hectic week of unfruitful negotiations over coal strike. P.[rince] of Wales came on Sunday with Mrs. Dudley Ward. We spoke of Strachey's life of Queen Victoria, which had just been published and the Prince said: "That must be the book the King was talking about this morning. He was very angry and got quite vehement over it."

P. of W. had not seen the book, so we showed it to him and presently was discovered in roars of laughter over the description of the Queen and John Brown.

Had a perfect Sunday—ideal weather—and returned Monday morning.[1]

Over Easter other Ministers were scattered here and there. Newspapers dropped their political leading articles for essays on holy days and holidays.

Nothing had been accomplished in the design to substitute another for Mr. Lloyd George in the Premiership.

Miss Stevenson's diary, April 11th, 1921.

III

A HOUSE DIVIDED

Easter gave Lloyd George a short respite. The House of Commons met again on April 4th, 1921. The close season in politics was over.

Nearly three weeks had passed since Bonar Law had resigned from the Government. Speaker Lowther retired on April 25th and Lloyd George's speech on the resolution of thanks was praised by his friends. But his fortunes were ebbing away. Discontent prevailed and discordant voices were raised in criticism of the Prime Minister and the Coalition.

The raw ingredients of a real crisis were within reach. But how to make use of these materials had not yet been worked out.

The easy plan would be to enlist the help of Bonar Law, who was in Paris convalescing from his illness of March, though I believed him to be in good health by this time. His entry on the political scene at Westminster as the rightful leader of the Protectionist movement would give the necessary focus to a confused and perplexed Tory Party in the House. There was little or no hope of inducing him to make any decision which would involve him in hostility to the Government of which he had so recently been a member.

While he was staying in Paris, aloof from political issues and devoting himself to games of golf, tennis and chess, I wrote him several letters. In mid-April I gave him my version of the domestic situation.[1]   In politics, I told him, everything waited on the coal strike.   Churchill and Birkenhead were both angry with the Prime Minister.   Coalition Liberals and Protectionist Tories were quarrelling over anti-dumping legislation,[2] while Lloyd George hoped to rid himself of the Bill by criticism in Press and Parliament.   Even Asquith was failing to give a fighting lead to his Free Trade followers.

Bonar Law[3] sought more news, and nostalgically commented on the scene at Westminster.   He admitted that he wanted occupation, but was glad all the same to be out of the Government.   He would not come to London until the Whitsuntide recess.[4]   In mid-May another attempt to bring Bonar Law to London had no effect.[5]   An offer of a place on the Board of the Midland Bank, put forward by Mr. McKenna,[6] did not bring acceptance.

Sir Robert Borden[7] in Canada had been my correspondent over many years.   A letter to him of the same time[8] recorded the influence of the coal strike in warding off impending political crisis; the hostility of Churchill, and Birkenhead's intention to challenge the Tory Leadership of Austen Chamberlain.

Lloyd George, whose popularity in the country was

[1] See Appendix 20, Beaverbrook to Bonar Law, undated but written in April, 1921.

[2] A tiny infringement on the Free Trade front of Protectionist legislation in disguise.

[3] See Appendix 21, Bonar Law to Beaverbrook, April 30th, 1921.

[4] Whit Sunday was May 15th, 1921.

[5] See Appendix 22, Beaverbrook to Bonar Law, May 13th, 1921.

[6] Rt. Hon. Reginald McKenna, former Chancellor of the Exchequer under Asquith and in 1921 Chairman of the Midland Bank.

[7] For many years Prime Minister of Canada.

[8] See Appendix 23, Beaverbrook to Borden, May 12th, 1921.

declining with extraordinary speed,[1] delivered in early May an ultimatum to Germany. Reparations within a week, or a military occupation of the Ruhr—that was his cry. The Germans yielded and the announcement in the House of Commons was received with such enthusiasm that the Prime Minister was greatly encouraged. He told Miss Stevenson, his secretary, who wrote in her diary:[2]

. . . they [the Members of the House] were all very pleased—excepting Lord R. Cecil, who sat, D. [David Lloyd George] said, with a look of despair on his face. He saw the downfall of the Gov. further removed than ever! D. said he had the same look on his face when Bonar's resignation was announced—he realized what a mistake he had made in crossing the House, as he would have been Chamberlain's rival for the leadership.

Lloyd George, in his growing isolation and falling popularity, longed for the days when Bonar Law had protected and fortified the Parliamentary reputation of the Coalition. To Miss Stevenson he made a comparison of the old and new Leaders of the Tory Party.

We had dinner in D.'s [David Lloyd George's] room in the House again on Tuesday night. This is becoming an institution. He just asks one or two people with whom he can let himself go and it is a great relief for him. Since Bonar left, he [Lloyd George] has lost an ideal companion with whom he could laugh and joke and enjoy himself. He cannot do that with Chamberlain, who is pompous to the last degree, and has become increasingly so since he took Bonar's place. He is a vain man. He is very fond of relating an interview he once had with Bismarck, and what the great man said and what he said. Someone told me the other day—I think it must have been

---

[1] Briand and Millet when conferring with British Ministers over German reparations remarked on Lloyd George's declining authority over his colleagues—Miss Stevenson's diary, May 4th, 1921.

[2] Miss Stevenson's diary, May 12th, 1921.

Berthelot—that Bismarck also spoke of the incident but his comment was that nothing very great could ever come out of so poor a head!

In an attempt to meet criticism in commercial, industrial and banking circles over the failure of negotiations to end the coal strike, Lloyd George convened a meeting of the executive of the Mining Association (owners) and the Miners' Federation (workmen). The attempt failed and added to the growing confusion.

It was on May 13th that Lloyd George faced his House of Commons critics. Miss Stevenson, describing the scene, wrote:

D. [Lloyd George] made an amazing speech in the House on Friday. I knew it was going to be something out of the ordinary as he sent to get me up to the House and waited to begin his speech till I was there. He had fortified himself with a strong dose of port wine and just let go about Poland—and the French! It was a remarkably able speech—he was never in better form—full of the most sparkling passages and trenchant phrases. But I am afraid it will cause trouble! In fact the French press are already busy and beginning to howl. All the same, I think D. was right, though we nearly had a row after his speech about the things he said of the French. But they are certainly not playing the game in this instance. And the Germans will—and are—making the most of D.'s speech.

Again on May 18th he resorted to a statement to the Press:

D. [Lloyd George] has again attacked the French attitude towards Silesia in his statement to the Press. I begged him to make it less violent and succeeded in persuading him to omit a few violent words which would have made all hope of a reconciliation impossible.[1]

[1] Miss Stevenson's diary, May 20th, 1921.

The Irish issue was ever present. The misery and wretchedness of the Government's repressive measures gave much concern to the Liberal following in and out of Parliament, even though the Press paid only a restricted attention to the problem. The Irish Protestant hero, Carson, whose volcanic eruptions had subsided, was raised to the peerage on the recommendation of the man he hated, the Prime Minister. In the Cabinet the Irish controversy rumbled. The bitter hostility of the Prime Minister to his able Secretary for the Colonies, Winston Churchill, was the subject of an extraordinary passage in Miss Stevenson's diary.[1]

D. [Lloyd George] very annoyed at Winston, who is being difficult, as he has returned from his voyage very disgruntled. He was furious at all the changes which were made in his absence, and is making mischief behind D.'s back. He declared his intention this morning of opposing the Government's Irish policy, and D. told him he would have a chance of doing it immediately, as the question was coming up at once. This put Winston rather in a fix, as he must either go back on his statement to D., or else show his hand at once in the Cabinet and be no doubt in a small minority, since he has not yet had time to work up his Cabal.

Sir Robert Horne warned Lloyd George that Churchill was contemplating resignation and recommended an effort at reconciliation. Miss Stevenson's diary contained a clear and vigorous account of the Prime Minister's response:

Winston is going to prove troublesome and F. E. [Birkenhead] is half inclined to back him. Horne told me Saturday that Beaverbrook is getting hold of Churchill and Horne thinks we ought to keep C. [Churchill] in with the P.M. But D. [Lloyd

[1] Miss Stevenson's diary, May 25th, 1921.

George] is so sick with C. I don't think he cares if he does go. Horne says C. is criticising the Government on Finance and Ireland in the clubs and lobbies. H. [Horne] wanted to go to C. and have it out with him, but I advised him not to. I said the P.M. will give him "one on the nose" sooner or later and he is the best person to do it.

Lloyd George decided on a dinner party which he hoped would bring his Cabinet Ministers into closer and more friendly relations with himself and his plans. It was held at Sir Philip Sassoon's house in Park Lane, a frequent meeting place, where the Prime Minister was used to exerting his charms. That was the object of the Sassoon parties. Unhappily on this occasion the results were not at all satisfactory, though they gave pleasure to the Prime Minister, who rejoiced because he believed Churchill was embarrassed.

Geddes[1] stated that there was only one person that the people cared about and would listen to and that was D. [Lloyd George]. D. said that when Geddes said this, Winston could not conceal his anger and irritation and others noticed it too. D. says he is going to detach F.E. [Birkenhead] from Winston. He wants a general election in the autumn, as he thinks it would be useful then. But all the same he is a little worried at the way things are going, and would not mind at times, getting away from it altogether. Poor old thing, my heart aches for him sometimes.[2]

Lloyd George, alarmed at the signs and portents of rebellion among his colleagues, the discontent in the House of Commons, the discord between Tories and Coalition Liberals and the growing distrust in the

---

[1] Sir Eric Geddes, Minister of Transport.
[2] Miss Stevenson's diary, June 1st, 1921.

country, resolved on a campaign to restore his authority. He decided:

(1) To reject reconciliation with Churchill, while holding out the hand of friendship to Birkenhead.

(2) To hold a General Election in the autumn, so that every member of the Government would be compelled to "stand up and be counted".

(3) To make terms with Bonar Law for his return to the Cabinet, or to obtain assurances of his neutrality during the election.

One week after the Sassoon dinner party Lloyd George wrote to Bonar Law. It was his first message to his former colleague, though nearly three months had passed since Bonar Law left the Government and London.[1] In his letter the Prime Minister mentioned "Crises chasing each other like the shadows of clouds across the landscape. Miners, Unemployment, Reparation, Silesia, and as always Ireland." He declared that he missed Bonar Law's counsel more than he could tell, concluding, "I want to see you."

Bonar Law replied[2] that he was in better health than he had been in for four years; he was leading a lazy life, and if he were young it "would be perfectly disgraceful". He was sure that his sojourn would not amuse him indefinitely. He declared that Lloyd George had done "the best that was possible but even the best is not very good". And he promised to see Lloyd George on a visit to London planned for ten days later.[3]

Foreign policy, which gave rise to so much friction between Churchill and Curzon, occupied the Prime Minister's attention on June 11th, 1921. A meeting was held at Chequers, attended by Churchill, Curzon,

[1] See Appendix 24, Lloyd George to Bonar Law, June 7th, 1921.
[2] See Appendix 25, Bonar Law to Lloyd George, June 8th, 1921.
[3] Lloyd George hoped that the terms of Bonar Law's letter might mean a willingness to return to office.

Montagu and Sir Laming Worthington-Evans.[1] Lloyd George hoped to get agreement on Foreign Affairs in the Cabinet and particularly in relation to the Graeco-Turkish conflict. He failed. His own account of the meeting, set down in Miss Stevenson's diary, is a depressing record.[2]

D. [Lloyd George] said that every one of them was more or less hostile to him—Winston was obviously disappointed at finding the P.M. looking so well; Montagu always hostile and cynical; Curzon hopes to be the next Prime Minister and has just entertained the King and Queen lavishly. The latter by the way have dined this week with the Crewes, and lunched with the Asquiths. D. says it looks as though they were expecting a change of government, but I told him that he does not pay the King very much attention—he always gets out of going to the Palace if he can and has constantly refused invitations to Windsor. He cannot be surprised if the King is a little hurt.

D. is a little worried about the whole political situation. He says we have been on the crest of the wave—politically—and are now going down again into the trough and will have a bad time, it looks likely.[3]

There is no doubt he has a lot of enemies in the Government who will leave him if they think they can better themselves. Austen he thinks will stick to him. He certainly gets on with him much better than he expected to. Austen plays the game and he sees that he can trust the P.M. who conceals nothing from him.

D. has just had a letter from Bonar, who evidently does not dream of coming back to politics and commiserates with D. on

[1] Secretary of State for War.

[2] Miss Stevenson's diary, June 11th, 1921.

[3] Quotation from Lloyd George: "It was like the Battle of Dunbar, where after the battle was almost won, the clergy persuaded the Scottish Army to go down into the plains and fight. They did and were beaten." It was said by Bishop Burnet or another that Cromwell proclaimed, Glory be to God, the Lord has delivered them into our hands.

the bad time he is having—a thoroughly typical letter, not tending to cheerfulness.

The savage suggestion that Churchill was disappointed at finding the Prime Minister looking so well and the frank admission that "every one of them [the Ministers] was more or less hostile to him" was indeed a strange prelude to the contemplated General Election in the autumn.

Meanwhile on the same day Birkenhead wrote to Bonar Law, inviting him to return to the fray.[1]

He mentioned his step in the peerage:

I heard from Max that you had most kindly interested yourself in my promotion. I did not mention it to a living soul. I was too proud to go to L.G. and not prepared to recognise that Austin as leader in the H.C. had anything whatever to do with the matter. It was like you to remember it and kind as you have always been to me.

The coal strike was now over, he declared, but of crises there were too many to count. He mentioned neglect to take account of Bonar Law's prescience over agriculture and predicted very bad consequences in the agricultural constituencies. The Prime Minister in the last autumn had "rammed down our throats" bad arguments. Of the Graeco-Turkish situation he said "there is a devil of a fuss going on or brewing up . . . Winston seems to have become almost pro-Greek having always hated them. I suspect the explanation is that the Kemalists are being helped by the Bolshevists & W. will support anyone who attacks them." His anxieties over the loss of the agricultural constituencies and the "devil of a fuss" over the Graeco-Turkish conflict were well-founded.

With such disturbances in the Cabinet and with so

[1] See Appendix 26, Birkenhead to Bonar Law, June 9th, 1921.

many disintegrating influences at work[1] the Protectionist group began the preparation for election purposes of Protectionist literature for pamphlet and press. Mr. R. D. Blumenfeld,[2] the gifted and distinguished editor of the *Daily Express*, undertook this task, and with energy and ability performed his duties in a short space of time. Surely, the Cabinet so desperately divided could not stand even until the autumn.

---

[1] In mid-June, 1921, the Government losses in by-elections aroused anxiety. With five contests lost by the Conservative section of the Coalition and the fear of more to come, Chamberlain wrote the Prime Minister seeking authority to launch prosecutions against Lord Rothermere and me. We had certainly broken the election law, though unconsciously, by distributing free copies of our papers in by-election centres. The Attorney-General advised action. But Lloyd George was not so sure—his own *Chronicle* newspaper, which he had acquired out of Party funds in 1918, was in the same boat. Lloyd George, in a letter to Chamberlain, made it clear that any charge against the newspaper proprietors must go on without him.

See Appendices: 27, Younger to Chamberlain, June 10th, 1921; 28, Chamberlain to Lloyd George, June 13th, 1921; 17, Lloyd George to Chamberlain, June 14th, 1921.

[2] The only newspaper man, in my experience, who was the object of the affection and devotion of the entire political community.

IV

"THE PLOT"

Then suddenly an issue arose so seriously dividing the Tory Party from its Coalition Liberal allies that the death of the Coalition was expected almost immediately by its foes and friends alike.

The struggle turned on Dr. Addison. He had been Minister of Health, a post at which, in the opinion of his critics, he had made an utter failure of the building programme—"Homes fit for Heroes". Tory Members were violently hostile to his administration, and hoped to drive him out of the Government. He had few friends in the Coalition Liberal wing. On the last day of March, during the Parliamentary recess, the Prime Minister relieved him of his office and appointed him Minister without Portfolio at a salary of £5,000 a year.

The Prime Minister represented to Addison that the change was due to the departure of Bonar Law, and his presence in the Cabinet was urgently required in adjusting Government policy to the needs and sympathies of the new electorate.[1] The Tories were furious. The change in Addison's status during the Parliamentary recess was regarded as a trick. "Reward for incompetence" was their cry. But greater than any other grievance was the salary of £5,000, which cut straight across the current passion in Parliament and country for economy in public expenditure.

Criticism of the Prime Minister reached a rough and shrill note. Lloyd George was in a grave dilemma. If he retreated from the appointment of Addison, his leadership would be brought into contempt and his authority

[1] See Appendix 29, Lloyd George to Addison, March 31st, 1921.

would be damaged. If he held to his decision, the clash with the House of Commons would be a serious and grievous risk, perhaps with fatal consequences. After many days of procrastination and hesitation Lloyd George was forced to get ready to defend Dr. Addison in debate on the floor of the House of Commons.

It was not until the 9th of June, two months after Addison's change of office, that Chamberlain informed Lloyd George of bitter opposition to the Addison appointment. He wrote[1] that an undoubted majority of Unionists was likely to go into the lobby against the Government.[2] Next day Chamberlain wrote again, informing the Prime Minister that the Press was beginning to work up an agitation.[3]

By the 13th of the month Chamberlain reported that Charles A. McCurdy, who had succeeded Captain Guest as the Chief Coalition Liberal Whip in April, "is getting more pessimistic" and that Leslie Wilson, the Chief Conservative Whip, "says it is hopeless"—on Addison.[4] On June 15th Chamberlain wrote that Labour could not be expected to support the Government over Addison's salary.[5]

On the previous day Lloyd George had written to McCurdy, stressing that "As at present informed it seems to me that we are in for a bad defeat unless Addison realizes the position in time." "It would be folly for Addison himself to risk a personal defeat.[6] It does not

[1] See Appendix 30, Chamberlain to Lloyd George, June 9th, 1921.

[2] House of Commons' approval of Addison's salary, with a majority of Unionists voting against it, would have compelled Chamberlain to resign as Leader of the Party, because of loss of confidence and failure of loyalty of his followers.

[3] See Appendix 31, Chamberlain to Lloyd George, June 10th, 1921.

[4] See Appendix 28, Chamberlain to Lloyd George, June 13th, 1921.

[5] See Appendix 32, Chamberlain to Lloyd George, June 15th, 1921.

[6] "Personal defeat" meant humiliation of Addison if the House of Commons refused to vote his salary.

help him personally to bring down the Government over his own unpopularity."[1]

The storm clouds gathered and Chamberlain sent to Lloyd George a suggestion made by George Younger as a way out of the difficulty. Addison should not draw a salary. Lloyd George could make up the loss to his Minister out of his Party Funds.[2] It was no surprise to the Leader of the House that the Prime Minister did not answer this proposal.

Addison, meantime, considered himself a sacrificial offering to Tory intolerance. He declared in an *Evening Standard* interview on June 15th, 1921, that the attacks on him were directed by plotters, who aimed at excluding all Coalition Liberal Ministers from the Coalition Government. He denied any intention of resignation. He would not be driven out of office.

Thereupon Chamberlain wrote to Lloyd George that Addison was trying "to turn what was in part a genuine movement for economy & in part an attack on his own administration into a revolt of Unionists against Coalition Liberals". A majority of Unionists would vote against the Government, and he himself had written to Addison that he could no longer support him.[3]

The crisis was upon us!

Preparations for the critical division in Parliament went forward in agitated haste. Everyone believed that the impending debate would be a decisive event. Everything pointed to the defeat of the Government. Birkenhead, Churchill and Montagu were all of the opinion that the Government could not withstand the day of trial. So was Chamberlain.

Were a majority of the House to vote against the

[1] See Appendix 33, Lloyd George to McCurdy, June 14th, 1921.
[2] See Appendix 32, Chamberlain to Lloyd George, June 15th, 1921.
[3] See Appendix 34, Chamberlain to Lloyd George, June 15th, 1921.

Government, this would be followed by Lloyd George's resignation. Were a majority of Tory Members to vote against the Government, this would be just as disastrous to the Administration. For Chamberlain would, of course, announce that he had lost the confidence of his Party. His resignation in these circumstances would have the same result as that of Lloyd George—the fall of the Coalition Government.

In that event there could be only one possible choice for the place of Prime Minister. Tories everywhere would ask for Bonar Law. His selection would be the sure and certain solution. But would he accept? It was most unlikely.

In the midst of the turmoil Bonar Law arrived in London from his Paris sojourn. It was Thursday, June 16th, 1921. He listened with close attention to my complete account of the political situation, of the hostility among the Ministers, of their meetings at my house, of the divided counsels in Cabinet, and of the crisis over Addison. The survey conveyed the prospect and, indeed, the virtual assurance that the Government would fall.

He remained at the close of the recital unmoved by argument or persuasion. He would not return to the battle. He would visit Lloyd George at Chequers, the Prime Minister's country residence. But he promised that what he had learned of the intentions of the opponents of Lloyd George would not be disclosed to the Prime Minister. Neutrality was his decision.

Lloyd George meanwhile had decided on a dissolution and a General Election. He told Miss Stevenson that he had few friends. Austen Chamberlain would stick by him. The Coalition should commit suicide and rise like a phœnix from the ashes as a new party.

On Sunday, June 19th, at Chequers, Lloyd George told Bonar Law of his difficulties but failed to obtain

Lloyd George, Beaverbrook and his dog Tasso, fore and aft

any favourable response to his overtures for Bonar Law's return to office.[1] Miss Stevenson's diary records:

Today Rees of the *Sunday Times* rang up and told me that Bonar *had* come over last weekend with a specific purpose. When I queried it he said: "But we know for a fact and we know of course who was behind it (meaning Beaverbrook) but he found things unsympathetic." It is difficult to believe these things of Bonar but Beaverbrook seems to be able to make him do anything. I haven't told D. [Lloyd George] yet, but I know he will hardly believe the *Sunday Times* story. D. said to Bonar last Sunday: (knowing he would repeat it to Beaverbrook) "I may go out of office, but if I do go it will be because I want to go, and not because I am turned out."

Bonar Law came back to my house, The Vineyard[2] in Hurlingham Road, Fulham, on Monday morning.

[1] Lloyd George wanted Bonar Law to take over the Foreign Office from Curzon. The offer was repeated in specific terms in January, 1922, and refused.

[2] The Vineyard is a tiny Tudor house in Hurlingham Road. I took it over as a derelict after the first German war. Far from the centre of London I was relieved of casual callers and comparatively free of long-winded visitors. I provided facilities by means of private telephone lines without any direct contact with the Telephone Exchanges. Thus the political conferences held there were safeguarded against interruption.

The house is small, with only one sitting-room, a dining-room with an installation for the projection of cinema pictures, two bedrooms, as many bathrooms, and staff accommodation on the third floor. Outstanding features of this little gem of a house are three separate fireplaces on the Tudor scale, done in stone with oak chimney pieces. The foundations cover ancient catacombs where monks made wine for their monastery. It was in these ancient wine cellars that I kept the produce of France on which I drew most liberally. Lloyd George drank very little. Bonar Law smoked a lot and drank nothing but ginger beer and orange juice. However, there were other willing helpers. There is an acre of garden and, in my day, a tennis court where many politicians played, mostly badly. Mr. Balfour, an occasional visitor, was provided with a new set of balls for each set of games. He said that his eyesight was bad and dirty balls made it difficult to play the game.

I had a deep affection for that sure retreat, now owned by my sister who lives there in contentment.

The Times published on that same morning a letter from Lord Salisbury, urging Unionist Members of Parliament to withdraw their support from the Coalition. This was a development which was highly encouraging. True, the Marquis was a diehard Tory and a prejudiced and unreasoning Free Trader, who would resist any movement for Tariff Reform and Imperial Preference. His hostility to Lloyd George, however, was deep and bitter. He was not co-operating with Protectionists, but his contribution was most useful, adding to the clamour of the outcry against the Government.

Bonar Law, too, looked upon the Salisbury rebellion as an important political event. He had not been impressed by Lloyd George's conversations over the week-end. Unless the Prime Minister could find some rallying point which would bring together the quarrelling factions in the Coalition, the fall of the Government might not be far off. But he refused to have any share or part in the attempt to defeat his former colleague and leader, Lloyd George, and declared with emphasis that he would not attack Austen Chamberlain, his successor as Leader of the Tory Party. Nor would he consider succeeding Lloyd George even if the Government fell without help from him. He had resigned in March and departed on good terms with the Prime Minister. Nothing that had happened in the last three months could justify any attitude which placed him in hostility to the Government, even after its defeat. He regarded the "crisis" with deep anxiety, believing the Tory Party might be shattered by a dissolution and election. If that occurred, it would be a national disaster. His intervention would not help, but would rather hinder, the prospects of Party survival. Pleas which urged the importance of Protection, agriculture and unemployment left him cold. He forbade me to make mention of his name as a possible alternative leader, and pledged me to do and say nothing which could place him in an embarrassing and, as he believed, a humiliating situation.

Bonar Law's refusal did not come as a surprise to me. During his stay of five days in London, he had been keeping himself clear of any connection or association with the exciting events in politics. He turned his back upon the crisis. And to make quite sure that he would not be involved, he left me abruptly and fled to Paris on the afternoon train, with a clear intimation that he did not desire any further particulars or details of the "Plot".

It was a crushing rejection. A shattering and unnerving defeat! For years the hope that Bonar Law would lead the House and the country to a real and practical plan for uniting the British Empire in one economic unit had been my day and night obsession. The glittering prize had been dangled in our sight in 1914, when the Liberal Government of Asquith appeared to be on the edge of defeat. But the coming of war had saved them and quenched our hopes. Again, in 1918, hopes were deferred, when Liberal Coalitionists, on joining the Conservatives in a General Election, required and received a pledge ruling out Protection and Food Taxes. If Lloyd George were to fall over the affair of Addison, then another chance of obtaining the Empire policy would be offered us. But this prospect, which looked so bright, was seriously damaged by the refusal of Bonar Law to lead the movement.

Bonar Law's rejection of office brought up the name of Chamberlain. Some persons were under the impression that he could be separated from Lloyd George. It was nonsense. Chamberlain had given his allegiance to the Coalition and Lloyd George, and loyalty remained as always the guiding principle in his conduct.

Chamberlain, it was certain, would not be willing to join in the attack on Lloyd George and, indeed, would refuse to succeed the Prime Minister.[1]

Churchill would be the candidate whom Birkenhead and others would put forward for the Premiership. But he had not shifted his Party affiliation. He was still a Coalition Liberal, though he acted with Tory Ministers on most public issues, including the Irish troubles. Carson's influence might for this reason have been on the side of Churchill. But it was in this very month (on June 8th, 1921) that Churchill, speaking to the Manchester Chamber of Commerce, said: "I stand here as a Free Trader." He was greeted with rapturous applause. The following week, on June 15th, he welcomed the visitors of the Empire Development Parliamentary Committee at the House of Commons. He said: "When I came here last Sir Thomas Smartt [the representative of South Africa who was present] and I were much in disagreement. That was fifteen years ago, and we differed on an Imperial Preference, on which I have changed my views. . . ."[2] The declaration was greeted with loud cheers, but did not convince the Protectionist and Empire Free Trade elements. They would be opposed—and active in their opposition—to Churchill as Prime Minister.

Birkenhead had much better backing. If Churchill were ruled out, then he and his followers might be brought to support the Lord Chancellor. The Ulster Members would have accepted him. And that group, in those times, exercised authority and power, voting always as a unit.

[1] Chamberlain's attitude to Food Taxes had been undergoing change. He declared, in a moment of annoyance with me, that Food Taxes had been a millstone around his neck throughout his political career.

[2] See *The Times*, June 9th and 16th, 1921.

Lord Birkenhead: Lady Pamela Smith (now Berry)
He had firm friends
But a bad press

The choice of Birkenhead would have been acceptable to the Protectionist-Imperial Preference group. But could he be relied upon to stand up against the opposition of Churchill and other Free Traders? There was the terrible weakness—the dreadful uncertainty! Churchill would, of course, be an important member of Birkenhead's Government, and probably Leader in the House of Commons. Would Birkenhead show any real ardour for the Protectionist cause against the certain opposition of that determined Free Trader?

Birkenhead was a most willing starter and, in a contest for leadership, he hoped for a friendly nod from Bonar Law. But this he was not likely to get. Bonar Law intended to hold himself free from contact with Birkenhead and everybody else.

Birkenhead gave pledges of faith in the Empire policy, though unhappily qualifying his creed with the injunction that the Food Tax must not be mentioned during the crisis. The qualification was disturbing, but it was too late to make a stand. The crisis was upon us. In any case the prospects of an Empire policy under Lloyd George had reached a vanishing point. A new Government under Birkenhead could not be worse and might be much better. The first step must still be the defeat of Lloyd George.

Days and nights were given over to discussion on the prospects of the contenders. In the eagerness and excitement of the occasion policies and principles were sometimes forgotten. Personalities and relationships and associations filled the minds of politicians.

As the day of debate and decision drew near, everything turned on the Addison division. Friends called on Lloyd George to stand firm, and so also did his foes. Austen Chamberlain had told a story during a Parliamentary debate of a Jew in Spain, led slowly through the multitude of spectators after the Auto-da-Fe,[1] being solicited by the priests in attendance to renounce his faith and accept Christianity, thus escaping death by fire. The mob, determined not to be cheated of the spectacle, cried out: "Stand fast, Moses!" So it seemed that Lloyd George's enemies might have cried out: "Stand fast, Lloyd George!" Certainly there were important Ministers and others crying "Stand fast, Addison. Do not retreat. Leave the Prime Minister to sort out difficulties of his own making!" Churchill was actively supporting Addison. Birkenhead, though declaring he was no friend of the Minister without Portfolio, would give support. "He would play the game." Carson, though out of the Ministry, gave influential comfort and encouragement. The clash was at hand.

Then it was that on the morning of June 20th, having read the Salisbury letter in his newspaper, and with doubts and uncertainties aroused by the negative character of his conversations with Bonar Law, the Prime Minister decided to make a deal with Addison. He believed he had a solution which might pacify the House.

McCurdy, the Chief Coalition Liberal Whip, a man of ability and possessed of human qualities, carried on negotiations with the Doctor. McCurdy had given a memorandum to the Prime Minister, recommending that Lloyd George should defend Addison in the House of Commons. He should explain the need to retain a Minister without Portfolio during the Session. And he should announce that the post was never intended to be permanent and would end with the Session. Leslie Wilson, Chief Tory Whip, had agreed that Tory support

---

[1] The Auto-da-Fe was the ceremony during which the sentences of the Spanish Inquisition were read. Those who were condemned to the flames were sometimes burned on the night following the ceremony.

would be given on such terms. McCurdy concluded: "This does not drop Dr. Addison, nor does it commit the Prime Minister as to his future."[1]

It is not certain that Lloyd George accepted the McCurdy plan. Miss Stevenson's diary gives a somewhat different impression. She recorded:

The former [Lloyd George] says he cannot possibly persist in retaining him, especially as Addison has not been too loyal and is intriguing with Winston on Ireland. McCurdy had three hours with Addison this morning, and an arrangement was come to, whereby Addison is to go at the end of the Session and D. [Lloyd George] will defend this in the House on Thursday. McCurdy says Addison has no conception of the real position —says that the whole conspiracy is against him as a Liberal and progressive, and to separate D. from his Liberal colleagues. He has no idea how unpopular he himself is.

Whatever may have been the exact terms of the concordat with Addison, the Prime Minister had secured for himself a considerable advantage over his opponents, though danger still lurked in his path. His anxieties were recorded in Miss Stevenson's diary on the same day. She wrote:

Meanwhile intrigues are seething everywhere. Winston is very hostile but D. [Lloyd George] is watching him and F.E. [Birkenhead]. Beaverbrook is clearly engineering for a coup. Bonar Law came home for the weekend not for any ostensible reason, but I think it looks a little suspicious—he is so entirely in Beaverbrook's hands.

Miss Stevenson was misinformed. Bonar Law had already resisted efforts to induce him to move against the Government. But he had also resisted offers to rejoin

[1] See Appendix 35, McCurdy's Memorandum, June 17th, 1921.

the Administration and he had given no encouragement to Lloyd George's plan for a General Election in the autumn.

Lloyd George was frightened, alarmed and agitated. He discussed resignation with Lord Riddell. The decision to defy his critics was taken on the eventful Monday morning, June 20th. He would fight his enemies. He would destroy them.

Therefore he took the misguided course of directing an attack upon Bonar Law. He saw Lord Rothermere at the House of Commons. Next day Rothermere's paper, the *Daily Mirror*, carried an article purporting to disclose a Unionist plot by "conspirators" to put an end to the Coalition, with Bonar Law the choice for the new leader. Lloyd George evidently believed that these accusations would ward off any action by Bonar Law.

J. C. C. Davidson, former Parliamentary Secretary to Bonar Law until his retirement and serving Stanley Baldwin, President of the Board of Trade, in the same capacity, wrote to me:

10, *Barton Street*,
Westminster, s.w.1

My dear Max,

It is no news to you I suspect that Harold R. [Rothermere] spent an hour with the Big Beast[1] at the House on Monday— The enclosed[2] appeared on Tuesday in the *Mirror*. Funny isn't it?

Yours,
David
23/6/21

I replied:

[1] Lloyd George—not a term of derision—meaning Big Beast of the Forest.

[2] Cutting from *Daily Mirror*.

24th June, 1921

My dear David,

Many thanks for your letter. I am glad to know the source of the story. I suspected it as soon as I read it. None of the other papers take the slightest notice of it. I am going to pass the information on to "the Man across the Water" if you have no objection.

Yours ever,

Max

Tuesday, June 21st, was a day of intense excitement. Birkenhead proposed to make a speech in the Lords, which would have provoked the crisis. Miss Stevenson's report of the incident, told in her diary on June 22nd, praised Lloyd George for his skill.

He had heard that F.E. [Birkenhead] was going to make a statement in the House of Lords yesterday afternoon—he had also heard quite by accident that F.E. was going to make a sensational statement off his own bat on fiscal autonomy [for Ireland]. D. [Lloyd George] realized that the whole of the intrigue against him was centering round Ireland. F.E. and Winston had already in the Cabinet tried to engineer a crisis on policy, but D. had so turned the debate that if the break came, it would have been on *tariffs*—and the intriguers realized that this would not do.[1] F.E.'s coup was a new idea. But D. sent for him half an hour before his speech in the Lords, and in the course of conversation asked him what he was going to say in his speech. After that F.E. could not very well in decency have gone away and said something entirely different. Today however he has been asking *why* the P.M. sent for him, which shows that he realizes that D. must have guessed something and F.E. would doubtless like to know *how much* he had guessed!

Throughout these days of vigorous political activity Lloyd George acted with energy. He directed his Press

[1] Lloyd George believed firmly at this time that a tariff programme would lose another election for the Tories. Churchill and Montagu were of the same opinion.

Lieutenant, Sir William Sutherland, M.P., Lord of the Treasury, to give a story to the *Manchester Guardian* to the following effect: A rebellion by the Conservative wing of the Coalition was being organised under the leadership of Lord Birkenhead. Churchill had been involved, but at the last minute had refused to take the plunge, and the plot had been abandoned. The *Guardian* reported that Beaverbrook was deeply implicated in the conspiracy. Derby had been approached, but could not be relied upon.

Lloyd George was playing a skilful game. He hoped that the *Manchester Guardian* narrative placed his dissenting colleagues in the position of unsuccessful intriguers. He believed they would deny the newspaper accusations, thus compromising their meditated attack upon himself. Miss Stevenson gave this account of events:

An amazing article in the *Manchester Guardian* yesterday, exposing the whole plot with details. We don't know who wrote it, or how he got the information, but it is all correct. Last night D. [Lloyd George] had an emphatic letter from F.E. [Birkenhead][1] denying the whole thing—but "protesting too much". But no word from Winston, who is openly accused of treachery in the article. D. says that Winston does not tell actual lies, and that is why he will not deny it. But F.E. does not care what lies he tells. However the whole plot is exposed and the intrigue, I suppose, finished, for the time being. . . .

Then again another entry in the diary:

F.E. is *most* amiable to D.[Lloyd George] now. He keeps on denying that he had anything to do with the conspiracy against D. Said it was all Beaverbrook, and that he (F.E.) had seen him during the weekend and told him that it was no good

[1] See Appendix 36, Birkenhead to Lloyd George, June 23rd, 1921. Refer to Lord Riddell's account of a conversation with Lord Birkenhead in Lord Riddell's *Intimate Diary of the Peace Conference and After*, page 309.

trying to upset D. That if he did it, there would be no one to put in in his place, and that in any case he would not succeed. "No," was Beaverbrook's reply, "but I can *try*."

When Lloyd George went down to the House of Commons on Thursday, June 23rd, to open the Addison debate, he was a changed man. His confidence was restored. His courage flared up. In his coat pocket he may have carried the letter from McCurdy, giving in detail the settlement of the Addison dispute, and in his breast pocket the Birkenhead letter of submission and allegiance. He feared no foe.

The Birkenhead letter had removed that formidable figure from the list of his enemies, at any rate for a time. The pledges of loyalty therein barred any possible alliance between the Lord Chancellor and the enemies of Lloyd George during the Addison crisis, and probably for a long time. He had pulled out the lynch pin of the coach.

Lloyd George reflected on the success of the "exposure" of the "Plot". He had triumphed over his opponents by a simple device. Now he would put the hostile Members of the House of Commons to flight. The atmosphere of the House of Commons was charged with fervour and emotion. The Coalition had ceased to behave like a Coalition. Venom and hatred blazed up on the Government benches.

The Prime Minister opened the debate with an argument in defence of the post of Minister without Portfolio, which he declared was a necessity. Touching on the real crisis besetting the Government, which was of course the attempt to unseat the Prime Minister himself, he said: "We know perfectly well that when there are great issues shaking the country, those issues are very apt to be fought out on small incidents."[1] He then

[1] House of Commons Debates, June 23rd, 1921 (1594).

appealed to the House to decide the question on the necessity for a Minister without Portfolio and not on personal prejudice. "I shall invite the House of Commons today to vote only a sum of money that will enable us to retain and pay for the services of the Minister without Portfolio until the end of the present Session." Cries broke out: "Saved! Saved!"[1]

Interruptions persisted: "Why did you kick him downstairs?"

Lloyd George claimed that Addison at Munitions during the war had saved the nation hundreds of millions.

"Why was he not made Chancellor of the Exchequer?" Lord Winterton asked, and repeated his question frequently.

"He is sacked."

"You are intimidated."[2]

Lloyd George then made the extraordinary proposal that the salary attaching to the Ministry should be reduced by £500 in addition to the £2,000 demanded by his opponents, with several time-worn appeals to "the traditional generosity of the House" and to its "chivalrous nature".

He administered the customary Parliamentary spoon of honey about "the greatest tribunal in the world" and, asking the House, "as a question of confidence in the Government, to enable us to retain the services of this

[1] House of Commons Debates, June 23rd, 1921 (1599).

[2] In the course of the debate there were other observations and interruptions : "Instead of defending him to the death he has given him three months' notice." "Humiliated him before the House of Commons." At the bidding of the "Conservative bloc" Dr. Addison "had been thrown to the wolves".

And Lady Astor, M.P., defending Addison, "soared aloft into realms of idealism, away to a world where there would be no drink" (*Daily Express*, June 24th, 1921). It was the driest June since 1813.

LATE NIGHT SPECIAL.

Evening Standard

No. 30,230.   LONDON, WEDNESDAY, JUNE 15, 1921.   ONE PENNY.

DR. ADDISON ON HIS CRITICS.

" However this may be, the fact is that the movement against myself is largely animated by a desire to undermine the position of the Liberals in the Coalition Government. "

Addison's interview—Chamberlain wrote to Addison condemning the interview and declaring he could no longer support Addison

Minister until the end of the Session,"[1] he sat down. As the end of the Session was only a month or two distant, the House laughed. And there was no division.

Had he agreed to sack Dr. Addison? Or had he confined himself to disbanding the Ministry without Portfolio, retaining the Doctor in some other employment? Members of the House took one view. Dr. Addison the contrary. Relying on his engagement with McCurdy the Doctor believed that dismissal had been avoided.

In the Addison affair Lloyd George, intending to shelter his Government from the stormy blast of criticism over the failure of his housing programme, succeeded only in damaging himself. During his long career in the Commons he had excited many emotions; laughter and rage, admiration and fierce hostility. But always he had commanded respect for his powers and personality. Now he actually aroused derision, openly displayed. There was certainly laughter, but it was not laughter at the expense of his victims. It was laughter at the expense of himself, and from the benches of his own supporters. His performance was so inept that he gave many hostages to fortune. Instead of "scattering his enemies" as he claimed after the debate was over, he gave encouragement to those who wished to destroy him. His conduct displayed sure signs of a man who had temporarily lost his nerve. What made matters worse was the fumbling course of events which had put the Government in grave peril.

Then it was that many influential Members and groups of back-benchers declared that Addison had been treated shabbily. And it was said he had received his treatment from the hand of the man who owed him much and who had been his intimate friend. Addison, in December, 1916, had in fact given Lloyd George

[1] House of Commons Debates, June 23rd, 1921 (1602).

massive help to get him into 10 Downing Street. He had collected the names of more than one hundred Liberal M.P.s promising to support Lloyd George as Prime Minister. Lloyd George made full use of this loose promise of support from the Liberal benches. It gave him the right to claim that his support would not be drawn entirely from the Tory Party.

Yet this was the man Lloyd George rejected. The reason according to the critics was obvious. "Homes Fit for Heroes" had been Lloyd George's vote-winning slogan. But in 1921 there were many heroes and very few homes. The once inspiring slogan had become an angry catcall, and the man blamed by the public was Lloyd George himself. Did he try to shift the blame to Addison? Had he no higher motive than saving his own skin? His bitter enemies said the betrayal of Strafford by Charles I was the parallel.

Even after making due allowance for the bitterness of those extremely damaging attacks, there can be no doubt the Prime Minister made of himself an object of mockery. There was no Parliamentary vote at the end of the debate. There was no need for a vote. For the first time in the years of his downfall Lloyd George had made a fatal mistake. Two more incidents would follow, shaking faith and confidence. Then the deluge.

Within a week of the debate Addison was considering resignation. He wrote to his wife that two hundred Members of the House of Commons, under the leadership of Sir Thomas Robinson, a Lancashire M.P. supporting the Coalition, urged him to remain in office.[1]

[1] The following extract is from Addison's letter to his wife, June 29th, 1921: "I was greatly touched by Sir T. Robinson, a good Lancashire Liberal M.P., last night to whom I had spoken. He came back to me and entreated me to stay on. He said, 'Will you let me at my own expense get a couple of hundred members of the House to dine and pledge you support as I think I can. It would defeat these other fellows'."

The unhappy association was terminated within a month of the debate, when Addison resigned in anger over the Government housing programme, and thereafter joined the Socialists.

At Westminster and in Fleet Street it was said Addison was finished.

> *Of no man canst thou judge the destiny*
> *To call it good or evil, till he die.*

Within eight years Addison, who had joined the Socialists, held office again. Minister of Agriculture, Secretary of State for Commonwealth Relations, Lord Privy Seal, Paymaster-General and Lord President of the Council in succession. A Baron and then a Viscount. Leader of the House of Lords, and finally in 1946 the first Socialist Knight of the Garter.

In after years Lloyd George was to take the unusual decision of proposing Addison as a Trustee of his Political Fund. Unfortunately Lord St. Davids, his Chairman, objected. The prospect of Addison, a leading Socialist, administering Lloyd George's Fund would have given joy to many political writers.[1]

A place in Churchill's Coalition Government was offered to Addison and he declined. In good health until his eighty-second year, he died at eighty-three.[2]

When the House rose at the end of that beautiful June day of sunshine in 1921, and in the hours of darkness during the short night, and long before the morning newspapers appeared, Lloyd George told Miss Stevenson that he had "scattered his enemies". True he had escaped from those back-bench Members who were in "hot pursuit" of their leader with tomahawks in hand,

[1] See Appendix 37, Sir John T. Davies to Lloyd George, December 9th, 1936.

[2] Addison neglected to mention in *Who's Who*, that strange record of numerous suppressions, his many defeats at elections first as a Liberal then as a Socialist.

with hunting knives at the ready. But he had paid for his immunity and heavily. His prestige was seriously damaged. Could he resurrect his fortunes? On June 24th Miss Stevenson wrote in her diary:

D.'s [Lloyd George] speech on Addison in the House yesterday put the finishing touch to it [the plot]. He took the ground from under the critics' feet and there was not even a division! All the week, Winston has been trying to work Addison up in order to make him stubborn and so make things more difficult for D. Beaverbrook and Winston between them have been working the papers up against Addison, to try and make him take a stand and so have a fight in the House, where the Gov. might possibly have been beaten. But they failed hopelessly and D. was very pleased with himself last night.

On the same day Lord Riddell in his Diary gave an account of the attempts to oust Lloyd George with Churchill and Birkenhead succeeding him. Riddell mentioned Birkenhead's letter to Lloyd George disclaiming any part in the transaction.[1]

American Independence Day was drawing near and the Imperial Conference, then in session, was confronted with a demand for renewal of the long-standing Treaty of Alliance with Japan, bitterly opposed and deeply resented by the American Administration. Most of the Dominion Prime Ministers favoured renewal. But Meighen,[2] the Canadian, refused to approve. He would not accept any Treaty which would involve Canada in disagreement with the United States. He laid down the principle that Canada's advice should be accepted in all questions involving the United States.

Lloyd George was too much for his Canadian colleague. He worked up an argument that, under

---

[1] The Riddell Diary entry as published is May 24th. The actual date was June 24th, 1921. Other entries are also mis-dated.

[2] Arthur Meighen, Prime Minister of Canada.

League of Nations procedure, the Anglo-Japanese Treaty had never been legally terminated, as a year's notice was required. It was a subtle argument. Miss Stevenson reported in her diary:

D. [Lloyd George] very pleased with himself over the Japanese Alliance, which came up for discussion at the Imperial Conference last week. The question was as to whether the Alliance should be *renewed* and it would have proved a difficult question. It suddenly occurred to D. that under international law the League of Nations ruling probably did not hold good, and on looking it up found that instead of *renewing* the agreement this year, it had never been legally terminated and it required a year's notice to terminate it and no notice had yet been given. It would therefore leave a whole year in which to make up our minds. D. led the debate round in such a way as to leave it to the Lord Chancellor to make the point. The L.C. [Lord Chancellor] saw what D. was driving at and took up the cue—with great success, much to the disgust of Meighen who had just made a two hours speech against the renewal. F.E. [Birkenhead, Lord Chancellor] was much amused and passed D. this note—So the difficulty has been tided over for the present.

Out of the darkness over the disputes about Japan a bright gleam of sunshine shone out. Another conference! Miss Stevenson wrote:

Several places have been suggested and D. [Lloyd George] is very keen on Honolulu, but I am afraid it would be too far. Another suggestion is *Cuba*. It is to be in October and ought to be rather fun.

V

IRELAND

In the second week of July 1921 came a truce in Ireland. How or why it emerged no one can say exactly. It came out of the blue, and not as the result of any long fore-seen design. The only possible explanation is that Sinn Fein was exhausted and had been brought to the verge of collapse.

For months Lloyd George had accomplished nothing. He had been hammering away at the Irish problem with great adroitness, but his plans for a settlement met with the unbending opposition of the Conservative Party.

By mid-June, opinion among Conservative back-benchers was showing impatience with the ineffective military campaign. Sir Samuel Hoare, M.P., and a group of ten Members were working on an independent plan for a settlement with the rebels.[1]

But in July 1921 Conservative feeling was hostile to the Prime Minister. The Government's policy of repres-sion had been carried to a point where the country was reluctant to go any further. Three days before the truce was signed, on July 8th, 1921, Joynson-Hicks,[2] an

---

[1] See Appendices 38 and 39, Hoare to Beaverbrook, June 8th and 13th, 1921.

[2] He was the leader of the Puritans, and the enemy of "ungodly men", which included the Russians.

> "That man hath perfect blessedness,
>   Who walketh not astray
> In counsel of ungodly men
>   Nor stands in sinner's way."

important and influential member of the Conservative Party, who was to hold high office and aspire to the Party Leadership, wrote me a letter. The Conservative Party, he said, had silently supported the Government during the recent Irish troubles and had acquiesced in the negotiations then proceeding with the Irish Nationalists. He wrote: "It does, however, appear to me that this acquiescence in policy founded on no known principles cannot be asked of us much longer." It was time for Lloyd George to take note of the hostility of the Conservative Party.

On Friday, July 8th, Lloyd George went down to Chequers in the evening. Miss Stevenson's diary records:

Went down to Chequers with D. [Lloyd George] on Friday evening as he was very tired and wanted to get away but would not go without me. I went by train and he came on afterwards by car. He arrived in great excitement as while he was changing the telephone rang and D. on answering was told that it was a message from Dublin Castle for me. D. then spoke to Macready[1] himself and learnt that events have been happening very quickly in Dublin. De Valera[2] had agreed to come over this week, was going to issue orders for a truce, and had sent for Macready. The whole atmosphere was changed and Macready had been given a wonderful reception by the Dublin crowd. Naturally D. was very pleased, as it looks as though there is every prospect of a settlement.[3]

The following Monday, July 11th, the truce became a fact. The rebels may have regarded it as a temporary breathing-space affording an opportunity for recuperation. Certainly some of their leaders had no intention of

---

[1] General Sir Nevil Macready, Commander in Chief in Ireland.

[2] Mr. De Valera had been elected First Minister or President of the Irish Republic in 1919.

[3] Miss Stevenson's diary, July 11th, 1921.

conducting negotiations with the British Government which would lead to a final peace. But that the Black and Tan[1] policy had been effective in breaking down the rebel strength seems clear. Michael Collins,[2] a leading figure in the troubles in Ireland, expressed amazement at the British Government's proposal of a truce. In conversation with Hamar Greenwood, Chief Secretary for Ireland, he said: "You had us dead beat. We could not have lasted another three weeks. When we were told of the offer of a truce we were astounded. We thought you must have gone mad."[3]

On July 12th (Orangeman's Day) the Irish leaders arrived in London for meetings with the British Ministers. De Valera had talked with James Craig, the Ulster leader, who asked him: "Are you going to see Lloyd George alone?" De Valera replied: "Yes." Craig asked: "Are you mad? Take a witness. Lloyd George will give any account of the interview that comes into his mind or that suits him." But the warning, though indicating the measure of Tory distrust, made no impression on the Irish leader. He asked to talk with the Prime Minister alone.[4]

On July 13th Miss Stevenson wrote in her diary:

Just returned from looking at a lovely little house at Penshurst, but it has no view so D. [Lloyd George] won't consider it. He has just rung up from Chequers to say that De Valera has asked to see him alone, and naturally D. is delighted, as it is a great score after what the Irish and others have been saying

[1] A force of British ex-Servicemen recruited in London for service in Ireland and nicknamed "Black and Tan". Their stern and harsh reprisals were defended in and out of Parliament. They were never popular with the British public.

[2] Director of Irish Republican Army Organisation and Intelligence.

[3] L. S. Amery, *My Political Life*, vol. II, page 230.

[4] The account of the meeting with James Craig was given by De Valera himself on his seventieth birthday in hospital in Utrecht, Holland.

about his "not to be trusted." But D. told me on the telephone that his colleagues down at Chequers[1] are rather sticky about it and do not quite like the idea. Although they don't object to D. taking the responsibility, they hate to be left out of things —Austen particularly. However, D. is going to see him alone.

D. and I had dinner together with Philip Sassoon at Park Lane last night. He was saying what an extraordinary volte-face has happened during the last few weeks. It was not so very long ago that he was politically in deep waters, and in the trough of the wave. But now, as he said last night, we are riding up to the crest of the waves, and a very steep and sudden rise, too.

The following day the first of a series of talks between Lloyd George and De Valera took place. The same evening Miss Stevenson described in her diary what had passed between them.

De Valera just gone, after having been with D. [Lloyd George] nearly three hours. I have never seen D. so excited as he was before De Valera arrived, at 4.30. He kept walking in and out of my room and I could see he was working out the best way of dealing with De V. As I told him afterwards, he was bringing up all his guns! He had a big map of the British Empire hung up on the wall in the Cabinet room, with its great blotches of red all over it. This was to impress De V. In fact D. says that the aim of these talks is to impress upon De V. the greatness of the B.E. [British Empire] and to get him to recognise it and the King.[2] In the course of conversation today, D. said to

[1] Austen Chamberlain, A. J. Balfour and others.

[2] When the Irish delegates were refusing to incorporate the oath of allegiance in the Treaty a number of prominent Southern Protestants thought they could see a way round it. They asserted that the Irish were not republicans by instinct and that their real objection was not formal allegiance to a King, but to a King of England. So they proposed that the King be brought over to Dublin and crowned King of Ireland. They put this notion to Arthur Griffith and he agreed to support it. But when they put it to Shortt, Home Secretary, he brushed it aside saying, "I know these fellows. We can buy off the lot with two or three knighthoods."

De V.: "The B.E. is a sisterhood of nations—the greatest in the world. Look at this table: There sits Africa—English and Boer: there sits Canada—French, Scotch and English: there sits Australia, representing many races—even Maoris: there sits India: here sits the representatives of England, Scotland and Wales: all we ask you to do, is to take your place in this sisterhood of free nations. It is an invitation, De V.; we invite you here."

D. said he was very difficult to keep to the point—he kept going off at a tangent, and talking in formulas and refusing to face facts. And every time D. seemed to be getting him, and De Valera appeared to be warming, he suddenly drew back as if frightened and timid. D. says he is the man with the most limited vocabulary that he has ever met! When D. had put forward all the points of the invitation to Ireland, he (D.) turned to another tack and said: "I shall be sorry if this conference fails: Terrible as events have been in Ireland, it is nothing to what they will be if we fail to come to an agreement. The British Empire is getting rid of its difficulties; its industrial difficulties are being settled: Mesopotamia is settling down— we shall be able to withdraw our troops from Mesopotamia and Germany and other parts of the world. I hesitate to think of the horror if war breaks out again in Ireland." "But," said De Valera, getting very excited, "this is a threat of force—of coercion." "No, Mr. De Valera," said D., "I am simply forecasting what will inevitably happen if these conversations fail, and if you refuse our invitation to join us."

However they seem to get on well on the whole. All our information goes to prove that they are genuinely in earnest and the fact that outrages have ceased, shows that De V. has authority.

The following day, July 15th, another meeting took place. But De Valera was less friendly. Lloyd George told Miss Stevenson that the Irish leader had evidently been afraid he had gone too far the previous day and was bent on impressing on him the idea that he had proposed nothing and consented to nothing. Miss Stevenson gives an account of this interview in her diary on July 18th:

He [De Valera] insisted that what the people of Ireland wanted was a republic, and asked D. [Lloyd George] if the *name* of republic could not be conceded at any rate. D. replied that that was just what they could *not* have, that the people of this country would not tolerate it after all that had happened. "There must be some other word," said D. "After all, it is not an Irish word. What is the word for republic in Irish?" "Poblacht," was De Valera's reply. "That merely means 'people'," said D. "Isn't there another word?" "Saorstaat,"[1] said De V. "Very well," said D. "Why do you insist upon republic? Saorstaat is good enough." D. said that for the first time De V. simply roared with laughter.

The trouble however is simply going to be Ulster. D. has drafted a summary of terms which he will send De V. on Wednesday night and which De V. will reply to on Thursday. D. had the draft yesterday, but did not give it to De V., as he thought the time was not ripe. He saw De V. yesterday and arranged to let him have the draft. Smuts saw De V. yesterday morning and impressed upon him the great difficulty with Ulster, but S. says De V. doesn't really appreciate that the Gov. have any real difficulty and thinks that they are just using Ulster to frighten him. On the other hand, D. saw Craig[2] yesterday and the latter is quite obstinate and so are his Cabinet, and they think on their part that D. is trying to use Sinn Fein to persuade *them* to concede something. So the position is tightening a little and it looks very much as though Ulster would again prove a stumbling block in the settlement. D. is a little worried about it, but I can't help thinking that in his heart of hearts he is bent on settling it, but does not like to appear too confident in case anything may happen. There are lots of people who don't want a settlement and who would be very glad to see him fail.

[1] Saorstaat means Free State.

[2] Sir James Craig, Prime Minister of Northern Ireland. See Appendix 40, story on Sir James Craig.

Lloyd George was telling his intimate friends that he would resign from the Premiership if he could settle the Irish problem. He told Miss Stevenson that he was ready to go out of office after the Washington Conference[1] if a settlement was reached. "He will support Austen he says and if Austen is overthrown then D. [Lloyd George] can easily go into opposition which is what he would like," wrote Miss Stevenson in her diary on July 20th. "I think he really means it this time. If he did so he would destroy the remnant of the Wee Frees and gather the Liberals round him. If he settles Ireland, he can go no higher and the rest would do him good."

But the talks with De Valera were not progressing smoothly. On July 20th, Miss Stevenson recorded that on the previous day

De Valera had taken exception to a statement Craig had made and wrote D. [Lloyd George] saying that if D. took that view it was not worth while continuing the conversations. D. replied in a very curt note saying that he was no more responsible for Craig's views than he was for the statement De Valera had made to which Craig's statement was a reply. De Valera did not answer, but did not publish the letters and Smuts saw him this morning and reports that he is in a better state of mind and not nearly so obstinate. D. sends them the terms this evening and meets De Valera tomorrow: it will be the critical day and D. is getting very excited about it.

But the interview was not very satisfactory, and Lloyd George was very depressed.

After De V[alera] had read the terms he told D. [Lloyd George] he could not advise his people to accept them. "Very well, Mr. De V.," was D.'s answer, "then there is only one thing more left for us to discuss." "What is that?" asked De V. "The

[1] Disarmament Conference following pressure from U.S.A. to terminate Japanese Alliance.

:ime for the truce to come to an end," said D. D. said De V. went perfectly white, and had great difficulty in controlling his agitation. He then said that at any rate he would put them before his people and let D. know what their answer was. Although D. thought the meeting pretty hopeless at the time, . am perfectly convinced De V. was only bluffing and what we have heard since confirms this view. We hear that they are more than pleased with the terms, that they are more than they ever hoped to get, but that of course it is only policy to refuse at first in the hope that they may get even more.[1]

Lloyd George said: "Negotiating with De Valera is like trying to pick up mercury with a fork." De Valera's comment was: "Why doesn't he use a spoon?"[2]

Miss Stevenson wrote in her diary:

D. [Lloyd George] was very depressed. De V. had not even taken the terms away with him, but we now find this was a mistake, as he has since sent for them—How Irish![3]

The Prime Minister had had considerable difficulty in getting the Cabinet to accept these terms. Balfour in particular had "squirmed at the Cabinet when the terms were discussed, preliminary to sending them to De V. They were so contrary to all the views the old man had ever held on Ireland. But he gave in gracefully and in the end D. [Lloyd George] had an unanimous Cabinet, which was a great achievement. He took the terms along to the King himself late Wednesday evening. We dined together previously, after D. returned from the Cabinet. After D. had seen the King, Grigg[4] took the terms along to the Grosvenor Hotel."[5]

[1] Miss Stevenson's diary, July 22nd, 1921.
[2] See *Eamon De Valera* by M. J. Macmanus.
[3] Miss Stevenson's diary, July 22nd, 1921.
[4] Edward Grigg, Private Secretary to Lloyd George, M.P. (Nat. Lib.), 1922-25.
[5] The diary tells also of a Royal Garden Party. See Appendix 41, Miss Stevenson's diary, July 22nd, 1921.

Lloyd George was determined to reach a settlement, even if it involved further use of force before agreement could be reached. He told Miss Stevenson that if the Irish refused the terms there would be only one thing to be done—"to reconquer Ireland".

But the Prime Minister had many enemies in high political circles. Birkenhead was still strongly opposed to Lloyd George's Irish policy. Miss Stevenson wrote in her diary on July 27th, 1921:

F. E. Smith has been making foolish statements about Ireland and a general election in the Lords, much to D.'s [Lloyd George's] annoyance. F. E. is taking a good deal upon himself, but apparently he is aiming at getting the leadership of the Tory Party. He is in Beaverbrook's hands and the rumour goes round that he is doping, but we think there is not much truth in it.[1]

A few days later a great disturbance broke out over an interview Lord Northcliffe was reported as having given in the United States, alleging that the King disagreed with the Irish policy being pursued by his Government. His Majesty was quoted as asking Lloyd George: "Are you going to shoot all the people in Ireland?"

"No, your Majesty," replied Lloyd George.

"Well, then," said the King, "you must come to some agreement with them. This cannot go on. I cannot have my people killed in this manner."

Miss Stevenson's diary[2] reveals how the situation arose:

Great fuss over an interview Northcliffe is supposed to have given in the States, alleging a conversation with the King about Ireland. Apparently it was sent over here to Campbell Stuart, who refused to publish it, but it has appeared in certain news-

[1] Birkenhead was not taking dope and he was not drinking. In fact in 1921 he was a total abstainer.

[2] Miss Stevenson's diary, July 29th, 1921.

papers who have copied it from America.[1] D. [Lloyd George]
has obtained a statement from the King denying it, which he is
reading in the House this afternoon. D. however wanted to
prosecute for libel and got Poole from Lewis and Lewis here
this morning.[2] He then sent for Lord Stamfordham and found
out in the course of discussion that Lord S. had seen Wickham
Steed[3] and had obviously been talking to him in such a way
as to give him the impression that the King and D. had been
at variance and that is the explanation of the interview. D. was
simply furious and said to Stamfordham: "This means that the
King's secretary is seeing the Editor of the chief opposition
newspaper and give him the impression that there is a difference
of opinion between the King and his Prime Minister. I cannot
allow this to happen again." D. said S. was very frightened as
he is evidently the culprit. It will prevent the prosecution taking
place, but D. has secured a denial from H.M., and this will do
Northcliffe a lot of harm both here and in America.

Writing to Grigg on July 29th Stamfordham admitted
that he had seen Wickham Steed:

Windsor Castle
July 29th 1921

My dear Grigg,
    On my return to Buckingham Palace and reference to our
Journal I found that I saw Steed on Saty. 25th June, i.e. *after*
our return from Ireland—As I explained to the Prime Minister

[1] The interview, of which the King complained, was cabled from New
York by the New York correspondent of the *Daily Mail*. It appeared in the
early Irish and Scottish editions of the *Daily Mail*, but was cut out of all
subsequent editions. *The Times* did not publish it. The *Daily Express*
carried the interview on Thursday, July 28th.

[2] Sir Reginald Poole, of Lewis and Lewis, told me that on Lloyd George's
orders he had been almost dragged from Goodwood race-track. On hearing
Lloyd George's story insisting on prosecuting half the newspapers in
London, he advised caution. "What conversations had taken place between
Lord Stamfordham, the King's secretary, and Northcliffe or Steed?" he
asked. Poole advised Lloyd George to send for Stamfordham before
issuing a writ.

[3] Wickham Steed, Editor of *The Times*.

this morning the sole object in asking him to see me was to appeal to *The Times* to back up the government in their intentions to endeavour to give practical effect to the sentiments expressed in the King's Belfast Speech.[1]

Yours very truly,

Stamfordham

The following day a copy was received of a message sent by the Editor of the *New York Times* to his London correspondent:

Interview with Mr. Wickham Steed, Editor of the London *Times* published in the *New York Times* of last Monday, was written by a trustworthy reporter who believed that he reported accurately what Mr. Steed said. Mr. Steed has since told *The Times* that it contained matter that should not have been published. Mr. Steed did not have an opportunity of revising the interview.

As reported in England—in one of Lord Northcliffe's own papers according to the cable despatch—it appeared that the interview was incorrectly attributed to Lord Northcliffe himself.[2] It was not given to *The Times* nor has *The Times* reported him as giving any statement of a reported conversation between King George V and Mr. David Lloyd George.

(*Signed*) Editor of *The Times*

Lloyd George was infuriated by this attempt to discredit his Government by outrageous misrepresentation, as he regarded it. But his anger was calmed when the King issued a statement.

His Majesty the King has had his attention directed to certain statements, reporting an interview with Lord Northcliffe, appearing in the *Daily Mail* and reproduced in the *Daily Express* and some of the Irish newspapers. The statements contained in the report are a complete fabrication. No such conversations

[1] The King had made a speech at the opening of Parliament in Belfast on June 22nd, urging both sides to work for a settlement.

[2] Lord Northcliffe directed the *Daily Mail* reporter in New York to send the interview to London in Northcliffe's name.

as those which are alleged took place, nor were any such remarks as those which are alleged made by His Majesty.

His Majesty also desires it to be made quite clear, as the contrary is suggested in the interview, that in his speech to the Parliament of Northern Ireland he followed the invariable practice relating to Speeches from the Throne in Parliament.

July 29, 1921

Now that the crisis was over and all plans for libel actions abandoned, Lloyd George returned to preparation for the proposed peace conference with Sinn Fein. He decided to set up a committee of Cabinet colleagues, taking the precaution to include the names of Churchill and Birkenhead—both stoutly opposed to any concessions to the Irish deputation.

Although Birkenhead was a staunch supporter of Ulster and a long-time critic of Southern Ireland and of the rebellion, he wrote on August 10th, 1921:

Medea
Aug. 10th 1921

My dear P.M.

Whether the Conference with S.F. [Sinn Fein] comes off or not I am profoundly grateful to you for having asked me to be a member of it.

If it does I will do my best to be helpful & I shall not in any event forget this mark of your confidence.[1]

Yours ever,
F.E.

It was a strange message, giving an impression of confidence in Lloyd George, which was contrary to his real attitude. Then again, he promised to be helpful. The words may have impressed the Prime Minister but it was quite certain he would at that moment have hoped to rely on deeds instead.

[1] An impulsive letter. Lloyd George had selected Birkenhead and Winston Churchill as members of his Home Rule negotiating committee because they were too dangerous to leave out of it.

Meanwhile Lloyd George was using all his skill to gain the support of Bonar Law for his Irish policy. In mid-August Bonar Law, who was then in France, was asked by the Prime Minister to meet him at Sir Philip Sassoon's house at Lympne. Bonar Law wrote me on August 20th:

You will be interested to hear my news after I have seen the big man or big beast & some of his colleagues.

I think now that he wishes to see me not for any special thing but because he is going away to Scotland & if he did not see me now there would be no knowing when we should meet.

But at Sassoon's house Lloyd George spoke almost entirely of the Irish negotiations. He made no progress with Bonar Law.

Thereafter he went to Gairloch to recuperate under the advice of Lord Dawson, his physician.[1]

From there the Prime Minister wrote to Austen Chamberlain, in effect making out a case for a Conference with De Valera and associates even in the face of probable failure.[2]

Churchill disturbed the tranquil spirit of holiday Gairloch. He wrote a paper complaining of the failure of the Government Housing Programme and neglect of unemployment problems. Lloyd George fumed and spluttered. He claimed, "Churchill only does it to annoy." Never, never had the Colonial Secretary taken any interest in Social questions, and he was making mischief, Lloyd George declared. Sir Robert Horne was visiting Gairloch. As Lloyd George looked on the cheerful countenance of his Chancellor of the Exchequer, he may have thought, "Perhaps after all it was a mistake to reject the rightful claims of Churchill to that important

[1] See Appendix 42, Lloyd George to Lord Dawson, October 24th, 1921.
[2] See Appendix 43, Lloyd George to Chamberlain, September 21st, 1921.

place, with occupation of No. 11 Downing Street as a fringe benefit."

The Irish negotiations continued to drag on in argument and debate. Frequent letters and telegrams passed between Lloyd George and the Irish leaders. There were many rumours of hope and despair. Finally on September 30th De Valera accepted Lloyd George's invitation for the Conference to be held in London.

VI

Beaverbrook telephoned Tim Healy in Dublin asking, on Bonar Law's behalf, for news of the Easter Rebellion (1916):

> "Is there a rebellion?"
> "There is!" said Tim.
> "When did it break out?"
> "When Strongbow invaded Ireland!"
> "When will it end?"
> "When Cromwell gets out of Hell!"

WHEN CROMWELL
GOT OUT OF HELL

Early in October the Sinn Fein delegates to the Conference arrived in London. Arthur Griffith[1] had been set up as the Irish leader under the authority of De Valera, who remained behind in Dublin for tactical reasons. The other Irish delegates were Gavan Duffy, E. J. Duggan, Robert Barton,[2] and Michael Collins.

The British delegation consisted of Lloyd George, Austen Chamberlain, Birkenhead, Churchill, Sir Hamar Greenwood, Sir Laming Worthington-Evans[3] and Sir Gordon Hewart.[4]

Tim Healy, for long a Member of the House of Commons and later to become first Governor-General of the Irish Free State, had also come over from Ireland. He was staying, as he did frequently, in my house,

---

[1] Editor of the *United Irishman*, creator of Sinn Fein and Vice-President of the "Republic".

[2] A barrister, a solicitor, and a Protestant landowner.

[3] Secretary of State for War.   [4] Attorney-General.

The Vineyard. He was in London for consultations with his Irish compatriots. He would guide them in their political relationships with the British Parliamentarians, of whom he had such a vast knowledge and wide understanding.

Arthur Griffith said to him: "Give us your opinion of what we ought to do and what we ought to ask for." Tim Healy replied: "You have a fine chance. You can get a fresh deal for Ireland but you can only get as much as the Conservative Party can be persuaded to give you. The Premier himself is in chains to the Conservatives in this matter. Nonetheless, the great mass of sensible Conservative opinion will give you much if you handle the situation sensibly." Healy showed real prescience in his instructions to his Irish friends.

Yet the negotiations showed no sign of progress. Discussion went back and forth between the British Ministers and the Irish representatives. There seemed to be no issue out of all these afflictions. The British delegation, influenced by Sir Hamar Greenwood, became suspicious of the sincerity of the Sinn Feiners, believing that they sought only a period of repose to equip themselves for a new offensive. The Conference showed every sign of a disastrous termination. It was becoming more and more apparent that the negotiations would collapse and rebellion in Ireland burst out once more.

Lloyd George saw the emergency, and devised a plan whereby he might break off discussions with advantage to himself and his Government. On October 17th he presented the Irish delegation with an ultimatum. It was phrased in these terms:

The Irish Government confides the responsibility for the naval defence of Irish interests on the high seas to the Royal Navy and for this purpose as well as for those of general

Imperial defence places its ports, its harbours, and inlets unreservedly at the disposal of the Imperial Government in peace or war.

It was a test question. The ultimatum demanded in effect: "Do you concede to the British Admiralty the control of the foreshores and harbours of Ireland?" Defence was the dominating issue in the minds of the British politicians. Fear of invasion by a foreign power through a bridgehead in Ireland was an ever present reality, constantly canvassed in every political discussion on the subject of Home Rule. Shades of Roger Casement still hung over Downing Street.

If the Irish refused to give over facilities for the defence of their shores to British forces, the British Ministers would abandon the negotiations, giving as their reason the rejection of that issue, and of that issue only. Lloyd George fully expected a rejection. He had decided that he would then announce the refusal of the Irish delegates to make the necessary provision for defence and declare the Conference at an end.

On Saturday morning, October 22nd, 1921, the Irish negotiators consulted Tim Healy, asking him to discuss the ultimatum and the phrasing of an answer. Now Tim Healy was a wise man. He had far too much experience of public affairs to be embarrassed by the need for replying to any question. His Parliamentary knowledge was profound. So also was his knowledge of the Scriptures. The answer he returned was typical of the man, and of his devout attitude to the teachings of the Bible. Healy mentioned to the Irish delegates the attempts of the Pharisees to confound Jesus. "Is it lawful to give tribute unto Caesar, or not?" they asked, and Jesus, holding out a penny, replied: "Whose is this image . . . ?" "Render therefore unto Caesar the things which are Caesar's." Now Healy advised: "Ask Lloyd George what do you mean by the ports and harbours of Ireland? Or is your demand for control of the harbours and foreshores confined to a portion only of the island? What is Ireland? What will be the jurisdiction of the Irish Government?" Of course this response would at once open up the old dispute as to the exclusion of Ulster, bringing the Conference back again to the subject that had engrossed the attention of the delegates for so long.

Later in the afternoon I left Healy and drove to Wargrave, the home of Sir Edward Goulding,[1] where Bonar Law (by this time returned from his sojourn in France), Birkenhead and Churchill were guests together. Rain fell, turning gutters into lakes and rivers, and beating down furiously on the roof of my car as I made my way into the country. I arrived very late, and found the company engaged in earnest and argumentative debate. The subject, of course, was Ireland. It was almost the only topic of discussion in every drawing-room conversation. "Have you heard that Lloyd George means to bring the Irish negotiations to an end?" they asked.

I had not only heard, I said, but I could give the company the exact text of Lloyd George's ultimatum and also the answer now on its way to Downing Street. Where did you get your information, the assembled company asked. After considerable pressure I promised to disclose my source if I could have individual and collective pledges to respect my confidence. When the pledges were given, I made yet again the mistake of which I have been guilty so often, thus confirming my

[1] Sir Edward Goulding, Member of Parliament for Worcester, my faithful friend, Irish by birth, loved and trusted by his colleagues. In 1922 he became Lord Wargrave.

critics in some of their complaints against me. There was a most worthy Member of Parliament, formerly a Cabinet Minister and Minister Plenipotentiary to the Paris Peace Conference in 1919—Mr. George Barnes, who had preached many sermons from diverse pulpits. He lived up to every Pauline injunction. He obeyed the Ten Commandments as completely as obedience is given to mortal man. Thus it was that I seized on his name to make a good joke and I exclaimed "Barnes's mistress!" This was greeted with shouts of laughter and also perhaps another black mark against me because of my ribald conduct. But of course I was determined to conceal the details of what had taken place at the meeting at The Vineyard.

The atmosphere was distinctly controversial. Bonar Law was against the whole Irish negotiations—no good in his opinion would come of them. Churchill was prepared to carry out a policy of repression. Birkenhead was of the same view, though he was seeking after a compromise.[1]   Supposing, he said, we agreed to Dominion Home Rule either for a part or the whole of Ireland, what would happen? Why, the Tory Party, the only instrument by which we could hope to accomplish it, would break in our hands.

Bonar Law referred to income tax. As Ireland was to be relieved of all responsibility for the National Debt, it was a real issue in the controversy. Irish merchants would pay only 1s. in the pound, while Glasgow houses would have to pay 6s. People in England, Scotland and Wales would never stand for this difference; neither would their business activities. Irish trade would swamp them. The manufacturers of Ulster, though not seeking the benefits of lower income tax, must nevertheless

[1] Birkenhead's view was that without a vigorous assertion of force, you cannot cure the mischiefs in Ireland to-day.

Sir Austen Chamberlain
"He always played the game, and always lost it"

share the advantages with the manufacturers of Dublin and the South.

Only Goulding and myself made any attempt to stem this hostile criticism and to support a settlement. We believed that there would never be harmony within the Empire while trouble in Ireland was unsolved. Churchill insisted that my Irish views were disruptive of my much-canvassed conception of a united Empire.

Near midnight Goulding ordered in his Irish intonation "to roost, to roost", and his guests obeyed. Churchill followed me to my bedroom and continued his discourse on the conflict between my support for Irish Home Rule and my intense advocacy of a united Empire. As our voices were raised in controversy, our host appeared in his long nightshirt, carrying a lighted candle, and ordered us with some show of asperity to give over forthwith. "Silence!" he cried. "Silence!"

The Sabbath day at Wargrave was given up to tennis, with another resounding dispute in the evening, followed by a peaceful game of bridge.

It was on the following Wednesday, October 26th, that Birkenhead spoke with me. He said that the Prime Minister had sought him out and asked him to join in exploring all possible projects for an Irish settlement. Birkenhead was reluctant. He was asked to put his whole future with the Tory Party to the hazard, and in partnership with a man who up till then had shown him little trust or confidence. He was only willing to undertake such a task if Churchill, also without the Prime Minister's circle, was admitted to the negotiations. He demanded that Sir Robert Horne, Sir Eric Geddes and Sir Hamar Greenwood, who had become the close associates of the Prime Minister ever since the quarrel with Churchill in April 1921, should be expelled from his intimate political circle. Birkenhead and Churchill, supporting the Prime

Minister, would make up a triumvirate, thus reforming what is usually termed the Inner Cabinet. It is right to say that Birkenhead argued that all three—Horne, Geddes and Greenwood—knew nothing of nor understood the Tory temperament of the House of Commons, and that they were persistently misleading the Prime Minister through their ignorance of Conservative opinion.

Lloyd George consented to Birkenhead's requests. Henceforth all estrangement between Lloyd George, Churchill and Birkenhead would be a thing of the past; they pledged themselves that they would see this task through, and together.

It must be admitted that up to the dying gasp of the Lloyd George Administration, and beyond, this pledge was kept by both Lloyd George and Birkenhead. Churchill[1] joined the new pact, though by no means an enthusiastic supporter of Home Rule for Ireland, and in his case too for a time all coldness was wiped away.[2]

A few days later Miss Stevenson was to write in her diary: "He [Lloyd George] has successfully wangled Churchill and Birkenhead so that they are all out for it" —referring of course to his Irish plans.

The Ministers driven from paradise to outer darkness by the Lloyd George - Birkenhead concordat—Horne, Geddes and Greenwood—were no longer called to supper or to sing. It was as though a venetian blind had

---

[1] In his writings seven years after the event Churchill gave credit to Birkenhead for the Irish settlement, declaring that he himself played only a secondary part in the negotiations. He claimed that the Government should have persevered until dismissed from power. The settlement, he wrote, was fatal to Lloyd George and the Treaty was unforgivable by the most tenacious elements in the Conservative Party.

[2] An account of dinner conversations of the three leaders, usually at The Vineyard, written by Lady Lloyd-George (Miss Stevenson) appears in Appendix 44.

been pulled down. They could peek through the slats, but from without.

Sir Robert Horne, son of the Scottish Manse, was smooth and friendly. He was a competent Parliamentarian given to Scottish dialect stories, often twice told. He was a gay tennis player. When he attended a Conference with French Ministers in tennis flannels the charge of disrespect was damaging, though he survived the crisis, and still played tennis. A bachelor and swift in pursuit, he never consolidated his conquests. He had pleasant relations with the political hostesses. And there were many in action at that time.

With the downfall of the Prime Minister, Horne, after an interval, returned to his first allegiance to Bonar Law, under whose patronage he had entered Parliament, and then to Baldwin. Speaking in Parliament during MacDonald's era, Horne then said of Lloyd George's followers: "For their prayers they say 'We err and stray like lost sheep and the Leader of the Liberal Party is our shepherd and our crook.'"

Lloyd George was extremely angry and replied: "May I say just one word to him [Sir Robert Horne] about that. When the pastures were under my control he followed my crook."

Horne's directorships, gathered after the fall of Lloyd George, were of such importance or value that he never returned to the Front Bench.

Sir Eric Geddes, Scottish stock, was another singing Minister. He specialised in Scottish patriotic songs, rendering "Scots Wha Hae" with dramatic overtones. With sentimental effect he sang and acted "Roses of Picardy". His strong baritone delighted the Prime Minister. Geddes was much admired for strength of character and his frank expressions of his opinions. Lloyd George probably liked his earnest and aggressive agnostic outlook, though himself giving no countenance to such heresies. Miss Stevenson wrote of a visit Geddes made to Chequers in the first weekend of July 1921:

Geddes came to Chequers for the weekend. He has a most enervating effect on me—he is so insistent on what *he* likes and what *he* thinks and what *he* wants. He is, I think, the most aggressive and pushful personality I know and he doesn't appeal to me in the least. D. [Lloyd George] has persuaded him to stay on after his Railway Bill is through and take over an "economy campaign" in Gov. Depts. Geddes has agreed, but he will I know demand an addition to his long row of decorations in return.

Miss Stevenson's hostile opinion of Geddes was not confirmed. He was offered a Peerage by Lloyd George, possibly on this very occasion, and he declined the distinction.

Hamar Greenwood, Canadian born, was the most interesting member of the group. He came to Great Britain as a temperance lecturer. He made a success and reached Parliament based on the support of Sir Thomas Whittaker, M.P., and others. Lloyd George liked his high spirits and gaiety. He had a rasping though agreeable voice and he would do a gay song and soft shoe shuffle dance:

> *My name is Solomon Levi;*
> *At my store in Salem Street,*
> *That's where you'll buy your coats and vests,*
> *And everything that's neat;*
> *I've second-handed ulsterettes,*
> *And everything that's fine,*
> *For all the boys they trade with me*
> *At a hundred and forty-nine.*

Everybody joined in the chorus "*Poor Solomon Levi*".

Greenwood, as Chief Secretary for Ireland, was noted for his courage, which was in sharp contrast to that of some of his predecessors, and his brave conduct won him immense praise. He was not an enthusiastic advocate of the Irish Settlement though he went along with Lloyd George, who made no provision for him when the Irish office became a mere shell after the Free State Treaty. He embraced the Tory Party and was afterwards entrusted with the Party Honorary Treasurership. He spent his spare time in collecting funds for the 1935 election. And the Party won in a big way. He was elevated to the Peerage and I wrote him:

My dear Hamar,

Please accept my warmest congratulations on your elevation to the House of Lords. If any man in England deserves the honour, then you are entitled to it.

In the old days in France there used to be two branches of nobility—the Barons of the Sword and the Barons of the Robe. I may be termed a Baron of the Robe. You are certainly a Baron of the Sword. For you faced death with more courage than any man I have ever known and over a long time.

Yours ever,
Max

The triumvirate of Court favourites now suffered the fate of all Court favourites. They were swiftly and completely routed. Their influence was dimmed and extinguished. Churchill and Birkenhead entered upon the scene. These doughty fighters could not be described as Court favourites. They were equals.

The moment the arrangement with Birkenhead and Churchill came into effect an entirely new situation arose. Within six weeks a settlement was reached and an Irish Treaty signed. How did Lloyd George manage it? By the intervention of Birkenhead, who undertook the task of bringing the Conservative Party round to accepting the Settlement, and carrying Churchill with him.

Lloyd George cannot be criticised for this approach

to the Irish problem. Indeed, he must be praised. He decided with characteristic adroitness that the thing to do was to demobilise, as far as possible, opposition in that area where alone it could prove formidable—the Tory ranks. He may have talked with Chamberlain first of all. Of that I know nothing. But Chamberlain was the titular Leader of the Party. Looking round for rocks ahead, Lloyd George must have seen in Birkenhead a most formidable obstacle to his plans. Here was a man capable of rousing the great bulk of the Tory Party against a projected settlement by a single speech. Of course there was Bonar Law—but he could be "left to the last because he was the hardest task," said the Prime Minister.

Birkenhead told me on Wednesday, October 26th, that the Prime Minister wished for a conversation with me. He knew my views on Ireland and the treaty proposals, which were much in evidence in the leader columns of the *Daily Express*, but he wanted to have a clearer understanding of my future conduct in view of Bonar Law's hostility to the Irish negotiations.

As a result of Birkenhead's intervention, I met Lloyd George at dinner at Birkenhead's house in Grosvenor Gardens on Thursday, October 27th. It was my first meeting with him since Bonar Law resigned from his Government. The resignation had annoyed Lloyd George and he held me to blame. Churchill was there. I had suggested that Bonar Law be invited, but this proposal was ruled out. I took the precaution of telling Bonar Law beforehand of my intention to attend and also to support an all-Ireland settlement, with guarantees for Ulster. He made no objection though he regretted that I had adopted a political line he disliked, and indeed detested. He warned me I would lose some of my friends.

Lloyd George opened up the conversation by reminding me that at our last meeting he had offered me what Bonar Law had told him was "my heart's desire", as if he had conferred a favour on me and taking some advantage. But I knew well it was Bonar Law who would have done me credit.

It happened early in 1921. I was dining at the Criterion Restaurant, then the popular resort, occupying the top floor of a tall Piccadilly building. My guests were Sir Matthew Wilson and the Dolly sisters, famous theatrical stars from New York. They appeared in London with overwhelming success. It is right to say that the Dolly sisters also attained fame in Government circles when Lord Birkenhead referred, in the House of Lords, to the late Lord Salisbury and also Lord Selborne of that generation, who always worked together, as the Dolly sisters of the Tory Party.

During dinner I received a message to go to 10 Downing Street. On arrival I was shown to the Cabinet Room where Lloyd George was talking with Bonar Law. Lloyd George then offered to make me High Commissioner to the General Assembly of the Church of Scotland. The offer was indeed attractive to me, for my father was a Scottish minister serving in Canada under the Augmentation Scheme of that great institution of widespread influence in Dominions and Colonies throughout the Empire. However, I replied that I would not be suited to the office. It was my intention to continue my practice of sitting up late into the night. Indeed I had just come from dining with the Dolly sisters at the Criterion Restaurant.

Lloyd George then turned to Bonar Law and said, "Geordie gets it". Of course, "Geordie" was the Duke of Sutherland.

So I went back to the Criterion Restaurant intending to make the most of my freedom, which I had retained by paying such a high price. And there I found Geordie Sutherland—dancing with one of my Dolly sisters.[1]

Lloyd George asked me whether the opinions of the *Daily Express* on the Irish issue were also my own. I replied in the affirmative. He then asked whether I was prepared to fight for them and I said I was. But supposing a settlement with Ireland involved a defeat in the House of Commons and a dissolution, meaning thereby a Conservative revolt, was I still prepared to stand by the policy of settlement? Again I replied that I should stick to my opinion.

This conversation completely healed for the time being the breach between Lloyd George and me. It was easy for me to support his new Irish policy as I was convinced that Empire unity waited upon reconciliation of Irish elements in Canada and Australia, who refused co-operation with Britain until, as they believed, Irish wrongs were put right.

Both Churchill and Birkenhead argued vigorously against a resumption of the Black and Tan regime. But Birkenhead warned Lloyd George that there was grave doubt that the Conservatives could be won over to support an easy settlement. On October 28th Miss Stevenson wrote in her diary:

He [Lloyd George] had thrown a bomb-shell after questions when the question of Ireland came up and the "Diehards" were making trouble. They have put down a resolution for Monday condemning the Gov. for their action on Ireland, and D. said he would accept the challenge and treat the resolution as a vote of censure. This scared the enemy and though they dare not withdraw they do not seem eager to go on. D. is of

[1] His Grace the Duke of Sutherland has approved of publication.

T. M. Healy (right), William T. Cosgrave.
First Governor General of the Irish Free State with his distinguished
President, Cosgrave. Healy's sling was full of sharp and witty verbal
stones

DATE OF ARRIVAL	NAME.	ADDRESS.	DATE OF DEPARTURE
15ᵉ	Isabel Sykes —	Albany, Piccadilly —	
22	Birkenhead		
–	Winston Churchill	Sussex Sq. W.	
–	Beaverbrook		
–	A. Bonar Law	24 Onslow Gds S W	

Sir Edward Goulding's visitors' book

the opinion that anything might happen next week.[1] He even
talks of going out of office and is making preparations in order
to be ready for all eventualities. He has seen Bonar and the
latter says he will come in if D. goes out on Ulster.[2] D. would
prefer this. He says he is anxious to go out and that this would
be a good moment and a good excuse. It depends of course
primarily on the Irish, but a good deal hangs on how the Tories
behave. D. had Winston and F.E. to lunch today and impressed
upon them the fact that B. Law would come in if he went out.
This, he thinks, will make them loyal to him (D) for they will
not desert him in order to put B. Law in. Strangely enough no
one seems to contemplate the possibility of D. going out on
this Irish crisis. They simply think it means the failure of the
Irish negotiation. Carson came to dinner with D. on Thursday
and D. says he is quite obdurate—says he cannot possibly give
in on Ulster. Muriel Beckett met him in the Park this morning
and tried to pump him. He simply answered: "Isn't it a good
thing I am out of it all!"

Many conversations with Lloyd George throughout
the autumn strengthened my confidence in his determination to carry out a settlement of this dreadful curse
of Irish discontent. The ship of Empire, I held, must
not be wrecked upon the rocks of Fermanagh and
Tyrone, the centres of Roman Catholic population within
the boundaries of Ulster. Yet that was the plight confronting us so long as the clash of arms in the Irish
rebellion resounded through the Dominions, and particularly in Canada and Australia. I became an ardent
and zealous advocate of the Prime Minister's policy.

The immediate problem was how to win Bonar
Law's support, for he held such firm views on Irish

[1] The censure challenge ended in a triumph for Lloyd George. Only 43
diehard members of the Conservative Party voted for the motion. The
Government had 439 supporters.

[2] Lloyd George was threatening to compel Ulster to join an all-Ireland
Parliament. Bonar Law was opposing throughout any form of coercion of
the Northern counties.

questions and particularly on all issues relating to
Ulster. Lloyd George in his talks with me was expressing
an anxious desire that I should carry on frequent conversations with Bonar Law, giving him a full account
of the course of events and providing him with details
of the changing dispositions of important public men of
all parties.

Several meetings were arranged between the Prime
Minister and Bonar Law, with Lloyd George always
insisting upon my presence. Chamberlain and Birkenhead had come to the point where they believed that an
all-Ireland plan would be safer for Imperial interests,
providing ample guarantees could be set up for the protection of the Ulster Protestants. But Bonar Law
steadily rejected any attempt to win his countenance for
such a project. He firmly and rigidly insisted on the separate right of Ulster. He would not budge. Nor would he
show any willingness to discuss limitations or restrictions
of Ulster territory. And without Bonar Law the task
of persuading the Conservative Party to implement the
Irish truce in the form of a Treaty was indeed great.

On November 6th Miss Stevenson set down in her
diary a detailed survey of the position:

COLLEAGUES

Irish negotiations the whole week. D. [Lloyd George] has
hardly taken his mind off them for one minute. Divided into
three groups. He has successfully wangled Churchill and
Birkenhead[1] so that they are now all out for it. Strangely enough
and contrary to all expectations, Bonar Law showed signs of
proving difficult and D. heard that he was inclined to come out
and lead the Diehards if there was a break. D. saw Bonar on
Friday morning at breakfast and for his benefit drew a lurid
picture of what would happen if Bonar tried to form a Ministry.
How the Liberal, and Labour, and D. and his colleagues would

[1] See page 102.

all be opposed to him, while Bonar would only be able to get people like Page Croft[1] and Rupert G. . . .[2] to form his Ministry. D. added that of course they would always be friends, but it was inevitable that if this came to pass they would both say things for which they would be sorry afterwards. Bonar is influenced by Carson and also by the hope that this may be his chance of becoming Prime Minister. The extraordinary thing is that Beaverbrook is all out for D., supporting him most vigorously in his papers. D. says he will only be for him for a short run, but over a thing like this it is worth while taking all the support you can get. Beaverbrook is trying to influence Bonar Law, but unfortunately Chamberlain is seeing the latter this morning and D. says that he is so hopelessly tactless that he may do harm.

SINN FEINERS

The other group that D. [Lloyd George] has been in touch with the whole week and has been exerting his utmost influence to bear upon them, are the Sinn Feiners. And he has actually succeeded in extracting from them the conditions he was bargaining for, the chief of which is allegiance to the Crown. Having done this, he says he cannot possibly coerce the south. It now remains if he is to settle the Irish question, to persuade Ulster to make concession.

ULSTER

Yesterday D. [Lloyd George] saw Craig for the first time on the question of concessions. He had heard that C. was quite obdurate and would concede nothing and D. was rather hopeless about it. However he talked to Craig on and off all day and by the evening he had extorted from him considerable concessions, the most important being an all-Irish Parliament, which we believe will satisfy the Sinn Feiners. If D. succeeds in getting these confirmed, things will be extraordinarily hopeful. It is going now much better than he expected. He is still worried about Bonar, whom he wants to get on his side. Then Carson will be the only important person standing out. D. has

[1] Important and influential back-bench M.P.
[2] Rupert Gwynne, Member for Eastbourne.

repeatedly pointed out to Bonar that he (Bonar) will come in expressly to coerce the South. For D. will go out on the principle that he cannot coerce the South after the concessions they have made. Bonar jibs at this. He longs to have the great job but the risk is a great one and D. thinks he will funk it. Next week will bring forth great things.

Two days later Miss Stevenson wrote:

Ulster resistance appears to be hardening a little. Bonar Law still appears to be trying to collect forces to back him in his Diehard attitude. D. [Lloyd George] is going to try to get hold of Lord Derby as he thinks it important to have him on his side. Meantime D. has seen Craig again, but has not got much further. C. is apparently taking heart from the fact that Bonar is with him. D. thinks Ulster might agree to an All Ireland Council provided the "two countries" remain as they are. D. has sent a message to the Sinn Feiners telling them that he will stand by them and could never be a party to fighting them now that they have made the concessions they have, but pointing out to them that it is worth their while to bargain a little more in order to bring peace, i.e. in order to persuade Ulster to come in. Arthur Griffith sent back a message to say that they were willing to leave it in D.'s hands. D. says that they do not want to go back to fighting at any cost. Michael Collins does not want to be killed, any more by Craig's men than by D.'s.

Birkenhead was giving the Prime Minister his wholehearted support. An amusing misunderstanding took place as a result. An entry[1] in Miss Stevenson's diary reads:

Northcliffe, who apparently has not had accurate information as to what is happening here[2] and who evidently thinks that F.E. [Birkenhead] will not be backing D. [Lloyd George], but will be among the Ulster die-hards, has wired to Marlowe, the

[1] Miss Stevenson's diary, November 8th, 1921.
[2] Northcliffe was travelling in Japan and China.

Daily Mail editor. Northcliffe instructs Marlowe to give F.E. a message to the effect that he (N.) will give F.E. all the backing he wants. N. has further instructed the *Daily Mail* to take all further instructions direct from F.E. F.E. has taken N. at his word with the result that the articles in the *Daily Mail* for the last two days have been thoroughly friendly to D.'s policy![1] After all, D.'s policy is the one which *The Times* has been advocating all along as the only possible one for a settlement: but Northcliffe is quite unscrupulous if he thinks he has a chance of doing in D.

But Ulster resistance seemed to be defeating all Lloyd George's plans. On November 9th he informed his intimate colleagues that he wished to resign and to recommend the King to send for Bonar Law. His friends in and out of the Government opposed this project. Churchill wrote him on the same day:

> *Colonial Office,*
> *Downing Street,* s. w. 1
> *Nov.* 9, 1921

My dear Prime Minister,

The criticism will certainly be made that the Government in resigning have abdicated their responsibility. More especially will this charge be made if the reason given is "we are debarred by honour from coercing the North, & by conviction from coercing the South." It will be said, "here are men united in principle, knowing what they ought to do & what the interests of the country require, who are possessed of an overwhelming Parliamentary majority, including a majority of their own followers, who nevertheless without facing Parliament lay down

[1] On November 9th, 1921, the *Daily Mail* surprisingly attacked Bonar Law, who was demanding the exclusion of Ulster. More surprisingly, Carson was named among the supporters of Government policy, though the writer must have known the Law Lord's bitter opposition. The *Morning Post* described the story as a "frigid and calculated lie". The *Daily Mail* attack on Bonar Law was stepped up on the 14th and in more violent terms. Thereafter the newspaper returned to its attitude of sympathy and support for the claims of Ulster. The Birkenhead era was over.

the commission & declare themselves incapable of action in any direction."

I greatly fear the consequences of such tactics, no matter how lofty may be the motives wh. prompt them.

2. After this has occurred, Mr. Bonar Law will be invited to form a Government. Why should he not do so? Surely he wd. be bound in honour to do so, if the members of the present Govt. have declared themselves inhibited from moving in any direction. Why should he not succeed? Most men sink into insignificance when they quit office. Very insignificant men acquire weight when they obtain it. In the crisis under consideration, the Conservative party will have to rally to someone. Obviously they will rally to a Conservative leader, forming a Conservative Government, wh. has come forward to fill the gap created by the suicide of the Coalition; & wh. will be entitled to carry the standard forward against Labour at an imminent election, and to receive considerate treatment from ex-Ministers who have just thrown up the sponge. The delusion that an alternative Government cannot be formed is perennial. Mr. Chamberlain thought Sir Henry Campbell-Bannerman "wd. be hissed off the stage". Mr. Asquith was confident that you cd. not form an administration. But in neither case did the outgoing administration tie its hands in every direction by proclaiming itself honourably bound to do what the situation might require.

On these lines a very great public disaster might easily ensue, in wh. a reactionary Conservative Government might go forward to the polls against Labour, with the great central mass of England & Scotland remaining without leadership or decisive influence.

3. I wish to put on record that I consider that it is our duty to carry forward the policy about Ireland in which we believe, until we are defeated in the House of Commons, & thus honourably relieved from our duty to the Crown. Such a policy might well include the creation & recognition of an all-Ireland Parliament, subject only to the condition that no physical force must be used against Ulster from any quarter.

I hope these matters may be carefully considered in the light of the alternative of dissolution.

Yours vy. sincerely,
Winston S. Churchill

But Lloyd George had little intention of resigning. His suggestion of such a course may have been another skilful move in his campaign to keep Churchill and Birkenhead faithful to him. For on the very same day Miss Stevenson noted in her diary:

The note is being sent to the Ulster people who are coming to London today. D. [Lloyd George] feels that their resistance is hardening, but this makes him all the more pugnacious and determined to get a settlement *in spite of* Ulster if he can. He says he is inclined to get the S.F.'s [Sinn Fein] to accept Ulster's attitude of remaining separate and then point out to them (Ulster) that as they are not participating in the proposals which affect the South, they are not entitled to the lower taxation which Southern Ireland will obtain under these proposals. If the S.F.'s will agree to this, D. will put it up to Ulster and he thinks they will climb down.

D. is frightfully hurt about Bonar Law and the attitude he is taking. This is all the more extraordinary as Beaverbrook is fighting for D. and a settlement for all he is worth. D. says he knows he can only get him for a short run, but it is worth while. D. is seeing F.E. [Birkenhead] and Winston and Beaverbrook almost every night, so as to keep them on his side. F.E. is fighting splendidly but D. says that Winston is contributing nothing and he is just not going over to the other side.[1]

Bonar Law was still opposed to the Prime Minister's proposals.[2] On November 10th Lloyd George had another talk with him,

[1] Churchill was not really in favour of Lloyd George's plan for settlement.

[2] See Appendix 45, Bonar Law to Lord Rothermere, November 16th, 1921. Rothermere was then supporting Bonar Law's resistance to Lloyd George's plans.

but could not get much further with him. D. [Lloyd George] said Bonar would have to become P.M. B.L. asked what D. would do when Parl. met in February. "Well, Bonar," said D. "By that time I shall have been recuperating in the S. of France and shall be come back prepared to embarrass my friends in their difficulties." B.L. flushed scarlet.[1]

(Miss Stevenson had previously noted in her diary a rumour that Bonar Law had resigned in March 1921, not because of ill health, but to evade the Irish crisis. She wrote: "Rees, the *Sunday Times* Editor, came to see me this afternoon and told me of a conversation he had with Horder, B. Law's doctor, a little while ago. Horder is a friend of Rees. 'You know,' he said to the latter, 'Bonar's plea of illness and his sudden departure to the south of France, were due to one thing only—cold feet about Ireland. Some excuse had to be made, so I was deputed to give the excuse about illness. But there was really nothing the matter with him.' If that is true,[2] then B.L. is a double-faced hypocrite. There was no need for all the protestations he made at the time about his undying affection for D. [Lloyd George]. And in any case there was no need for him to come out and embarass D. now at this critical time.")

The following day was Armistice Day. Lloyd George was watching at the Cenotaph as the wreaths were being laid on—for Britain, Canada, Australia, India, etc.

Worthington-Evans[3] turned to him and said: "Next year perhaps a wreath of Shamrocks." D. [Lloyd George] told this to Arthur Griffith later in the day. A.G. was very moved and said: "If this scheme of yours goes through, you'll get it."[4]

Lloyd George was still struggling with the problem of Ulster. He had evolved another scheme for getting

[1] Miss Stevenson's diary, November 11th, 1921.
[2] It was not true.   [3] Sir Laming Worthington-Evans.
[4] Miss Stevenson's diary, 11th November, 1921.

a settlement even if Ulster refused the terms. Miss Stevenson wrote in her diary:

The S[inn] F[einers] are very doubtful of his previous one, in which they might lose the All-Ireland Parl., for which they are fighting. D. [Lloyd George] therefore suggests that an All-Ireland Parl. be set up for a year. If, after the first six months, or before the end of twelve months, Ulster wishes to withdraw, she can do so, but only by coming back as part of the U.K. and paying the same taxes as the U.K. D. says he knows the Presbyterians. They have their hand on their hearts all the time, but if it comes to touching their pockets, they quickly slap their hands in them. "I know," he said to me. "My wife is a Presbyterian!" D. says the Ulstermen, once having paid lower taxes, will not volunteer again for the higher ones.

On Saturday, November 12th, Lloyd George and Arthur Griffith had lunch at Philip Sassoon's house. Miss Stevenson was also there and records what took place.

D. [Lloyd George] first of all went to Philip Sassoon's for lunch and got Arthur Griffith along, to have a serious talk with him, so that he might know exactly where he was. The Ulster people had definitely refused the terms in the morning—refusing even to come into a discussion so long as it involved a question of an All I[reland] P[arliament]. D. therefore wanted to decide on his next move, for he is determined to pull this thing through. I do not think I have ever seen D. so excited about anything before. He talked to A.G. for a long time and D. came up from below very jubilant—but very excited and said that A.G. would agree to his new scheme, and that the Ulster people would be "done" in! Then F.E. [Birkenhead] and Chamberlain came along and they talked over the form in which this was to be drafted, and eventually we went off to Trent,[1] arriving in time for dinner. Horne came on Sunday morning. . . .[2]

[1] A home of Sir Philip Sassoon, Lloyd George's Parliamentary Private Secretary.

[2] Miss Stevenson's diary, November 14th, 1921.

That Sunday evening Lloyd George invited Bonar Law and me to dine with him. He wanted to have a final talk with Bonar Law in order to know where he stood. Later that night Lloyd George described this meeting to Miss Stevenson, who gives an account of it in her diary:

D. [Lloyd George] told me, however, that he had a talk to B.L. before dinner, privately,[1] and D. told him quite plainly that he was not playing the game. Bonar flared up and said if that was the case he would refuse to discuss the matter any further and for a short time there was real unpleasantness. However D. eventually talked him round and they sat up discussing till nearly one o'clock. D. *thinks* that Bonar has agreed not to oppose his new proposals for the all-Ireland settlement. But of course he has not told Bonar of the underlying scheme, i.e. the taxation part. D. says that if the Ulstermen accept they will do so in the hope that the S.F.'s [Sinn Fein] would refuse it. They (the Ulstermen) are quite ignorant of the fact that the S.F.'s have already agreed. It is a very subtle plan and I hope it will not have any hitch. D. is quite determined that it shall go through. Bonar has put his back up.

D. says the S.F. have behaved splendidly all through this fight. They have backed D. wholeheartedly and loyally; they have given nothing away to the press and have shown great courage in the face of difficulty and even danger, for they have plenty of extremists on their own side.

Carson was of course strongly opposing a settlement, in the interests of Ulster. Miss Stevenson's diary[2] records that

D. [Lloyd George] says Carson is animated by a desire to get back into the limelight, as well as by his passion for Ulster. Carson has not found Lord of Appeal a very exciting job, and F.E. [Birkenhead] is the principal figure in the House of Lords. Carson referred the other day to the H. of L. as a place "into which the rays of the sun never penetrate". Lady Carson, too,

---

[1] I was there.

[2] Miss Stevenson's diary, November 14th, 1921.

would like her husband to become once again the popular politician.

On November 17th a meeting of the National Union of Conservative Associations[1] took place at Liverpool. Here a strong attempt was made by a powerful group in the Party to break away from the Coalition and thus bring down the Government. But the motion was over-whelmingly defeated—partly by dexterous management, partly by the speeches made by Conservative leaders, foremost among whom were Birkenhead, Sir Archibald Salvidge,[2] and Sir Laming Worthington-Evans. Many versions have appeared in print over the years. Some writers hold to the view that the Party, though compelled to support the Coalition for want of guidance, never forgave their leaders. The brief account of the Conference by the 4th Marquis of Salisbury, to Bonar Law, is the best description of it:

Hatfield House,
18.11.21

My dear Bonar Law,

I am this moment back from Liverpool. You have no doubt had reports of the inwardness of the meeting but I may perhaps add a touch or two.

The meeting was I think so far at any rate as a great many of its members were concerned genuinely anxious for guidance as to its vote, but certain strong currents of feeling were quite apparent.

1. I should say a great majority disliked the Coalition. L.G.'s name was hardly mentioned; it certainly never got a cheer.

---

[1] The National Union of Conservative and Unionist Associations has no authority over the Parliamentary Party or the Central Office. The power to make policy really resides with the Leader of the Party. But this organisation has great influence. Policy makers are not willing to challenge its resolutions, though occasionally defying them.

[2] A brewer, Lord Derby's Sancho Panza, and under the influence of Lord Birkenhead.

2. There was a universal sympathy for the Irish Loyalists North and South and (probably) a predominant indignation at the way they had been left by the Government.

3. There was a determination to defend Ulster. On the other hand there was:

1. A very strong desire to avoid civil war and a general wish not to break up the Irish Conference until everything had been tried to secure peace with honour.

2. And there was the old deeply-rooted desire not to break up the Party—that is the Conservative & Unionist Party, not the Coalition.

3. The last argument that you must not come to a conclusion till you absolutely know the facts had some weight.

The result of all these currents of opinion was that if the division had come in the morning Gretton's[1] resolution would have been carried by an overwhelming majority, but when it appeared by Salvidge's amendt that the propositions of Gretton's resolution were not to be contested, and all that Salvidge added to them was a desire that, subject to these, the Irish Conference might succeed, the desire for peace and for the unity of the Party naturally prevailed. It is to be noted that Derby expressly said before the division that the moral compulsion of Ulster is nearly as bad as any other.

On the whole there was nothing to make me distrust the good sense of my countrymen.

Yours vy sincerely,

Salisbury

My own judgment of events leads me to the conclusion that the great majority of 1,800 delegates disliked and distrusted the Coalition. These delegates were determined to defend Ulster against domination by the Southern Irish. Civil war was looked on with abhorrence, and the Conference might be the means of avoiding it. Stronger than the desire to defend Ulster

---

[1] John Gretton, powerful back-bench Member of the House, Chairman of Bass Ratcliffe & Gretton Ltd. He left £2,362,000 at his death. But Estate Duties amounted to £234,000 more than the total value of the fortune.

or avoid civil war seemed to be the determination that the Tory Party should not be broken up and consigned to impotence like the Liberals.

The defeat of the Motion was, however, a great victory for Birkenhead and his supporters in the Conservative Party. The day after the Liverpool meeting a further hurdle was cleared. Arthur Griffith and Michael Collins were persuaded to accept in principle the exclusion of Protestant Ulster from the Dominion Free State.

But Lloyd George had another worry, though rather ridiculous. He presided during a whole afternoon on November 22nd over a dispute between Sir Alfred Mond (Coalition Liberal) and Lord Curzon (Curzonite) with the members of the Cabinet sitting as a jury.

Sir Alfred, upon becoming First Commissioner of Works, had found his brother-in-law, Goetze, completing murals for the decoration of the Foreign Office. Lord Curzon objected to the Goetze murals, claiming that he could not possibly subject the morals of his ambassadors to the scenes, which he described as Bacchanalian revels. Mond of course rushed to the defence of his brother-in-law.

The whole Cabinet group, intrigued perhaps by the Foreign Secretary's description of the decorations, moved over to the Foreign Office. There they inspected the works of art and decided unanimously, with the exception of Curzon, still protesting violently, that the decorations formed a suitable scheme for the adornment of the Foreign Office. After many years the paintings still hang.

The following day Lloyd George returned to the Irish negotiations which were perishing on the stem for want of attention. On November 23rd Miss Stevenson wrote in her diary:

Irish negotiations not going too well. The S.F.'s [Sinn Fein] have got scared. They say Ulster will concede nothing as yet, and they are being asked to concede their points one by one. They are asked to sign a document which has now been drawn up to agree to a status quo as far as Ulster is concerned, but giving them (U) the right to come in to an All Ireland Council (with reduced taxes!) at the end of six months or within a year. (D. [Lloyd George] says he thinks Ulster will come in.) The S.F.'s say however that if they sign this and it is shown to Craig, it will immediately become public, as everything that is shown to the Ulstermen does and they (the S.F.'s) will not dare to go back and face their people having given so much away without being sure of anything in return. They therefore yesterday sent an impossible reply, retracting practically everything they had conceded. D. sent back a message to them to say that unless they took it back, all negotiations would be broken off. They are seeing D. today and from what I hear, negotiations will not be broken off yet. But things seem shaky. D. is worried and irritable. There seems to be so many snags and he is almost worn out with these protracted negotiations.

The following day the situation had not improved and Miss Stevenson wrote:

D. [Lloyd George] has not yet seen Craig, but sees him to-morrow. Meanwhile the S.F. are being difficult and D. says tonight that it looks as though a break may occur at any moment. F.E. [Birkenhead] saw them this morning and apparently the interview was not very satisfactory.

But the period of uncertainty passed and the negotiations were not broken off. Yet it was the opposition of De Valera and his supporters which endangered and almost destroyed them, and it was in dramatic and exciting circumstances that the Treaty was signed late at night on December 5th-6th, 1921, at Downing Street. The closing scenes in the Cabinet Room on that bitterly cold and misty night have been often described by many writers.   Lady Lloyd-George (Miss Stevenson) in her autobiography gives a vivid picture of events:

I remember sitting in my room next to the Cabinet Room through the night of December 5th-6th when the last stages of the struggle were being enacted, and the signatures finally appended to the Treaty; wondering if even at this last moment the Irish representatives would not draw back, and all L.G.'s [Lloyd George] efforts be wasted.   L.G. has himself told how Michael Collins signed "like a man who was signing his own death warrant", as indeed he was.   Within a year he had been assassinated.   My colleagues, J. T. Davies, Geoffrey Shakespeare, and Ernie Evans came in from time to time for a chat and to report any progress which they had gleaned.

Just before 3 o'clock L.G. himself came into my room, exhausted but triumphant, and handed me the Treaty document with its historic signatures and seal.   "Lock it up carefully," he said, and I did so, in a despatch box.[1]   There it lay for many years, until I unlocked the despatch box on going through L.G.'s papers after his death, and discovered it again.

The achievement of the Irish Treaty revealed in full what it was that L.G. possessed which other men lacked, in the understanding of human nature, in the art of tenacious negotiation, to a degree which few men in history have exhibited.   If one way closed, he opened up another; he was, in the words of one of his friends, who presented him with a lovely piece of silver to mark the signing of the Treaty, "the solver of the insoluble".[2]

[1] Not locked up until the signatures were photographed and circulated to newspapers.

[2] The presentation was made by Captain Guest.

VII

ELECTION—YES! ELECTION—NO!

As the year 1921 drew to a close there was much rejoicing and many complimentary messages of congratulation and felicitation among the Tory group responsible for the triumphant conclusion of Britain's civil war.

Lloyd George was determined on seizing this opportunity to hold an election. And I was waiting and watching eagerly for a chance to incorporate a Protection and Imperial Preference policy in his election programme. Lloyd George was a good prospect. He was at heart a Protectionist, favourable to the farmer, therefore not unwilling to put a tax on foreign food. Churchill was the danger. He was always consistent in holding to the bitter and uncompromising doctrine of Free Trade. He was so powerful in argument and action that he might succeed in holding Lloyd George by "Stomach Tax" arguments and that sort of appeal to prejudice.

When Lord Birkenhead summoned a group of guests to his dinner table at his house in Grosvenor Gardens, for the purpose of discussing the General Election problems, I gladly accepted. Here might be the opportunity for persuading Lloyd George and his colleagues to adopt Protection and Empire as a sure winning platform. I would not neglect it. The guests were Lloyd George, Austen Chamberlain, Winston Churchill, Macnamara,[1] Charles McCurdy, Sir Archibald Salvidge, Sir Laming Worthington-Evans and me.

McCurdy, Lloyd George's Coalition Liberal Whip, opened the discussion with a clear account of the reasons in favour of going to the country at once. He did not mention any arguments against the election. Lloyd George followed with an excellent survey of his personal position and the need for solidifying his disparate support in the House of Commons through a General Election, with contests in the constituencies and the commitments of candidates on the political platform.

Austen Chamberlain opposed dissolution as an unnecessary interruption of Parliament and one entirely without justification. Churchill was indecisive and somewhat obscure in his statements. Plainly he was not in favour of an election. Lloyd George, who had relied on Birkenhead's support, was disturbed and distressed by the opposition of Chamberlain, the indefinite attitude of Churchill and the silence of Birkenhead. He decided to postpone decision until after his return from a meeting of the Allied Conference at Cannes, called for January 1922.

A few days after the dinner Lord Birkenhead led a small but congenial party of politicians to St. Moritz, Switzerland, where we stayed over Christmas at the Suvretta Hotel. The conditions indoors were excellent, but without there was no pleasure as the weather had turned against us. By the Friday night before Christmas I had enjoyed my full share of winter pleasure and decided to go off to the Riviera. But there was no outgoing train on Saturday. The next was Monday night. Churchill telegraphed me:

Dail [Irish Parliament] adjourned till third no decision likely before fifth hope escape for few days meanwhile wire condition

[1] Dr. T. J. Macnamara, Minister of Labour.

with you weather and painting possibilities P.M. goes Cannes Tuesday expecting you and Fred[1] early there what are your plans for moving south wire reply urgent.   *Winston*

I replied:

No sun, no snow, no ice, no train until Monday when I leave for the Riviera.

Lloyd George would be at Cannes. His passion for referring the Irish Agreement to the electors and all that went with a General Election was strengthened through opposition. And my anxious desire was to persuade him to put an Empire programme in the forefront, with Protection for agriculture at home and Preference for the farm products of the Dominions. It was my objective in public life at this time and always.

On Christmas Eve I received a second message from Churchill:

Revered[2] proceeds Monday daylight Grasse I go hotel Mon Fleuve Cannes with Freddie[3] by same train join me there at earliest if possible bringing plaintiffs counsel[4] who will be needed we can play about together for a week wire plans precisely seasonable greetings to entire troupe.

                                                    Winston

On arriving in Paris imagine my joy on hearing from Churchill that the Prime Minister was "very anxious" to see me. As the Prime Minister knew that my only quest was the Holy Grail of Empire and also the only condition of support for his plans, I read the Churchill telegram eagerly:

I expect to be here till fourth but surely you can get here by thirtieth Revered very anxious to see you and Fred[1] wire when you will both come.   *Winston*

---

[1] Lord Birkenhead.   [2] Lloyd George.
[3] Frederick Guest, Secretary of State for Air since 1921.
[4] Lord Birkenhead, Lord Chancellor.

By the New Year Lloyd George had set up his head-quarters at Villa Valetta in Cannes. There we gathered —Churchill, Horne, Worthington-Evans and myself. The only subject for discussion was Election—yes! or Election—no!

The Prime Minister's reputation, temporarily im-proved by the Irish Treaty, was again in swift decline. Without doubt the sale of honours for the benefit of Lloyd George's personal Political Fund had damaged his prestige and injured his standing in Parliament and in the constituencies. Moreover, the Tory Central Office and the heads of staff there were extremely hostile to the Coalition Liberal section, and most critical of the Prime Minister himself.

The real grievances of the Tory managers did not turn on the sale of honours but on the suborning by Lloyd George of their Tory Treasurer, Lord Farquhar, known to his friends and intimates as "Horace". Large sums of Tory money contributed by their supporters had been diverted by Lord Farquhar to Lloyd George's Fund. The danger to Lloyd George of publicity and also the menace to his future relations with Tory leaders might disturb and possibly destroy the whole structure of co-operation. What should he do? The decision was final: "After all there was the money."

Thus at the Villa Valetta it was an interesting and exciting moment when a parrot in a cage almost un-noticed intervened in the midst of the words of greeting addressed to the assembling company, crying, "Stop it, Horace!"[1] To those of us who knew of the dispute, still under cover, but likely to come to the surface unless blacked out by the events of an election, the interrupting parrot gave us a moment of embarrassment, amusement, and delight. Lloyd George was unmoved, though he

[1] Lady Lloyd-George's autobiography, not yet published.

did not show any cordiality to my outburst of laughter. We were to hear more of the talking parrot. "Stop it, Horace" should have been answered by the Prime Minister himself, "Stop it, Parrot."

Churchill would not declare himself in favour of an election. Plainly he required some further assurance as to the Prime Minister's policy in the event of a new Parliament. He was as urgently pressing an embargo against any traffic—political or economic—with the Russians as I was seeking increased traffic—political and economic—with the Dominions and Colonies.

Horne was interested in determining the wishes of the Prime Minister and giving support.

I was planning to hang on high my own goose—the Empire project. The decision in favour of election was my goal. Then I could say—support from the *Daily Express* and enthusiasm on my part with the possibility of interesting Bonar Law too. But only if the Empire banner was put in the forefront of the battle line. Lloyd George was giving me reason to hope. But any failure by the Prime Minister, any surrender to his Free Trade Liberals and, for that matter, Churchill, then I would be off in the opposite direction.

Worthington-Evans spoke out vigorously in support of an immediate appeal to the nation. Unless there was an election, he said, a split in the Conservative Party was inevitable and could not be postponed for long. A Conservative split, he argued, would put an end to Coalition. Sir Laming was the leading exponent of "Election at once". He concluded his statement by hurling defiance at all opponents. He claimed that immediate action would take the Tory candidates by surprise and leave them no time to bolt from the Coalition. With a deep, resonant, most attractive voice, he put his case with such force that the Prime Minister, who had the sole right to say the word "Dissolution", appeared to be readying himself for "Action this day".

When Evans concluded his intervention with a stirring peroration, silence fell upon the company. We awaited the pronouncement from the source of all power, the Prime Minister of Great Britain—Election—yes! or Election—no!

Then an inhuman, rough, and exceedingly harsh sound fell upon the company for the second time.

"You bloody fool! You bloody fool!" cried the parrot.

The company was shaken. The Ministers departed. I went off with Churchill. We drove into the night, and along the way we laughed over the parrot. Churchill was staying with Madame Balsan at her great Palace on the Hill. I was at that time putting up at the Hotel Negresco in Nice. I afterwards moved to the Carlton Hotel at Cannes.

At Lloyd George's request a pressing enquiry into election prospects in the North of England had been carried out by Lord Derby, the Conservative leader in Lancashire and occasionally a fervent supporter of the Prime Minister. Three separate written reports had been submitted by Derby to Lloyd George on December 22nd, 23rd and 24th, 1921.[1] Derby himself was against an early election.

Charles McCurdy, the Coalition Liberal Whip, had conducted a parallel enquiry in the North and had come down strongly in favour of an early election.

But Sir George Younger, Chairman of the Conservative Party, held strong opposing views on the subject. These were disclosed to the Prime Minister in a

[1] See Appendices 46 and 47, Derby to Lloyd George, December 22nd, 1921, and December 24th, 1921.

letter dated January 4th, 1922. He based his opposition
to dissolution on the grounds that in view of the fact
that there was no impending crisis necessitating an
election such action would be harmful to national
interests and would result in an immediate breakaway
of many Conservatives from the Coalition.[1]

With his letter to the Prime Minister, Younger enclosed a copy of Chamberlain's letter of December 28th,
1921. Here Chamberlain gave as further grounds for
opposing an election the inevitable dislocation of trade,
and the fact that the Coalition had not yet fulfilled its
1918 election promise of House of Lords reform. Also
attached was a copy of a report by Sir Malcolm Fraser,
Chief Agent of the Conservative Party, on the election
prospects of the Coalition, dated December 30th.
Among the arguments given in this report for post-
poning dissolution were the facts that an election would
be regarded as a tactical move and that the electors
would prefer a homogeneous Party with clearly defined
policies and would themselves be principally concerned
with standard of living and wages. Thus Labour would
have a strong appeal, and the Coalition, suffering from
a lack of satisfactory political organisation, would lose
seats both through the breakaway of discontented Conservatives and through lack of enthusiasm among the
electorate.

Lord Stamfordham, the King's Secretary, was informed by Austen Chamberlain on January 6th, 1922,
and in firm and strong terms, that he was opposed to a
General Election at this time.

I have done and am doing all I can to dissuade the Prime Minister
from advising a dissolution. If he persists, I shall have to sum-
mon my Unionist colleagues to decide what position we are to

[1] See Appendix 48, Younger to Lloyd George, January 4th, 1922.

take up. I am not sure that a dissolution would not destroy the Coalition.

Meanwhile, Sir George Younger had decided to launch public opposition to election projects. While Lloyd George and his intimate colleagues were engaged in Cannes in making plans for an immediate election with much speculation on a redistribution of top places in the next Government, Younger threw a bomb into Fleet Street. He informed the *Morning Post* (Conservative) that he was against an election. Though firmly opposing any appeal to the country, there was as yet no threat that Conservative candidates would refuse to stand in support of the Coalition. That frontal attack came swiftly.

Then Younger gave another interview and as a result declared that he and many Conservatives would decline to stand as Coalitionists. The election, he prophesied, would put an end to the Government. He was directing a rebellion against Lloyd George. By January 9th he was carrying on a high-powered campaign. He made a monopoly in newspaper speculation associating Chamberlain's name with his opposition. The Prime Minister was indeed embarrassed and he protested violently to Chamberlain.[1]

Younger issued a circular letter to the chairmen of constituencies to the effect that an election would split the party from "top to bottom". And on January 11th, he did most serious damage to election prospects by publication in the morning papers of a speech made by him in his own constituency.

Lloyd George was not influenced by all these objections to a General Election. He could not be persuaded to launch upon any project for reform of the House of Lords so urgently pressed upon him by Chamberlain

[1] See Appendix 49, Lloyd George to Chamberlain, January 10th, 1922.

and Younger. Lloyd George would say, "True, a pledge had been given but what is the method of fulfilment? You cannot table a plan that will be acceptable to the Coalition or even a majority of its supporters." And he quoted the text: "but God hath chosen the foolish things of the world to confound the wise."

Lloyd George, however, was convinced that the capture of Bonar Law would mean triumph even in the face of Younger's rebellion and Chamberlain's opposition. If Bonar Law joined the Government on going to the polls, the whole Tory Party would fall in line.

Lloyd George consulted Birkenhead, who replied that if Bonar Law joined all would be well. Churchill was also invited to offer advice. He replied in effect that Tory opinion had been made hostile to dissolution and the Tory press was unanimously opposed to a General Election. He did not approve of Bonar Law and his tariff notions and would not welcome him in the Government. Lloyd George declared he could defy Churchill's objections if he captured Bonar Law.

At the Prime Minister's request I arranged a meeting with Bonar Law, the Protectionist and Leader of Empire. He was just the right colleague for Lloyd George in his uncertain and shifting state of mind. We three met in my rooms at the Carlton Hotel in Cannes, where I had taken up residence. Lloyd George opened the conversation by stating his intention to dissolve the Parliament and appeal to the country. Would Bonar Law join him? The answer was in the negative even though the Foreign Office was at Bonar Law's disposal. It was just as well that Curzon, Secretary of State, who was the sitting tenant, staying at the Grand Hotel just down the street, was not consulted. He would indeed have disapproved.

By mid-January, Bonar Law's rejection of Lloyd

George's offer, and also George Younger's direction of the hostile newspaper publicity, meant that all hope of an immediate dissolution of Parliament with a Coalition approach to the constituencies must be abandoned.

Lloyd George had sustained a damaging defeat. True he was still Prime Minister in name. But authority no longer prevailed. His colleagues flouting him, his Cabinet friends showing hostility, and his enemies in his own inner circle rejoicing over his humiliation. First the Addison debate in June 1921. A most damaging exhibition of impotence in Parliament. Then in the opening days of the year 1922 an acknowledgement to his Cabinet colleagues that he was no longer their master, just a titular leader without authority or power over events or personalities.

My friend and political colleague, Lord Winterton, who was liked and respected by all Members of the House, awaited word from me and hopefully expected a favourable decision for the old and tried policy of Imperial Preference. Having entered the House of Commons at the age of twenty-one, the youngest Member since the days of Pitt, he knew the whole history of this movement. Indeed he had been Parliamentary Private Secretary to old Joe Chamberlain, the founder of it. He asked me for information. I wrote him on January 16th, 1922:

The situation changes with such rapidity that it is almost impossible to say from day to day what new condition will arise.

I spent several days with the P.M. at Cannes. He was strongly in favour of the election. I supported him in this view for reasons[1] which I will retail when I see you, providing we are both still interested in the election controversy. Since last night I have not seen him, but I have heard that he is off the Election.

[1] The prospect of an Empire platform

I cannot see how the Government will manage to survive the coming session if the House of Lords Bill is to be introduced in the Commons. It seems to me that an election and reconstruction is the only way out, even though the Government is unable to go to the constituencies until after the Irish Bill passes the House.

Winterton replied on January 18th:

It was very good of you to write to me and tell me the news.

I shall be in London permanently when the H. of C. meets and will suggest myself to come and see you.

If any coup d'état by L.G. or anyone else in the Govt. seems likely within the next fortnight in the direction of either a permanent coalescing of parties or the reverse—a complete split up, do get your secretary to 'phone or wire me here to come and see you, as I should like to take counsel with you in such a crisis. Our group[1] is a bit scattered at the moment, but those of us who are here might be able to do a certain amount by batting on as we did over Ireland.

Terrible about poor Jack Scott.[2]

Yours sincerely,
Winterton

Lloyd George was almost exclusively occupied in seeking a way out of his difficulties. He was compelled to abandon the plan for a Coalition election appeal. Yet he believed that the threatening and menacing attitude of the Tory back-benchers could only be met by an election campaign requiring a united front in the constituencies.

His mind turned away from Chamberlain and the Tories. He made an electioneering speech to the Coalition Liberals at a public meeting of 6,000 voters declaring, "Who started this talk about a General

---

[1] The Empire Group.

[2] A Secretary at the Air Ministry, he died of pneumonia contracted on the year-end journey to St. Moritz.

Election? I did not. I never started the idea and I certainly have not made up my mind about it." He was practising deceit. The election project was his own brain-child. His correspondence discloses again and again his ardent and indeed dominating desire for a Coalition election during this same month of January 1922.

His speech was the opening move of another stratagem aimed at achieving a reunion of the severed Liberal Party, with a Liberal programme and a return to Parliament with a true Liberal majority.

His hopes were raised by the possibilities of the Genoa Conference. It would be held in mid-April, and if he succeeded his prestige would be raised on high. His reputation would be enhanced. There were three principles which he hoped to establish at the Conference. One, to gain recognition of Russia. Two, the pacification of Europe. Three, an all-European non-aggression pact. All subjects dear to Liberal hearts.

In the midst of his worries, however, he was harassed by indecision. Would he go Liberal? Would he make another Coalition with the Conservatives?

At that moment the Prime Minister was summoned to attend upon the King. His Majesty did not like the idea of the Genoa Conference, called for mid-April. I quote Lloyd George's account of his interview with the King.

"I suppose you will be meeting Lenin and Trotsky?" the King asked.

"Unfortunately, sir," Lloyd George replied, "I am not able to choose between the people I am forced to meet in your service. A little while ago I had to shake hands with Sami Bey, a ruffian who was missing the whole of one day, and finally traced to a sodomy house in the East End. He was the representative of Mustapha

Kemal, a man who I understand has grown tired of affairs with women and has lately taken up unnatural sexual intercourse. I must confess I do not think there is very much to choose between these persons whom I am forced to meet from time to time in Your Majesty's service."

The King's only reply was to roar with laughter.

The following day Miss Stevenson's diary records:

D. [Lloyd George] has been in a very worried and restless condition all the week. He is always like this when he cannot make up his mind. He is undecided at present as to what is the best step to take in the political situation. There is no doubt that everything is in a seething state and anything may happen. D. is anxious to have a "go" at the Wee Frees and especially Grey. On the other hand, the Unionists are very disgruntled and there are rumours that some are making an effort to get rid of the Coalition. The net result has not been to improve D.'s temper, especially as I said before as he cannot make up his mind.

Lloyd George abandoned for the moment his Liberal longings and decided to await the meeting of the House on February 7th. A May election, he told Lord Burnham,[1] would restore to the Conservatives their unity of purpose. He could and would prepare a programme that would carry the approval of right and left, friends and foes.

Resignation and service under Austen Chamberlain was his last gambit, possibly not serious and not even sincere.

I was myself misled by Lloyd George when he told me that he intended to resign. In February I wrote to Dr. Herbert Bruce, Member of the Canadian House of Commons and staunch Empire leader:

---

[1] Proprietor and Editor of the *Daily Telegraph*.

Life is very exciting in politics here. Ll. G. may resign at any moment. His Conservative bedfellows are very uncomfortable. He is missing his touch with public opinion on account of his circle of sycophants who shut out the sensible advisors. Last January was the time for a General Election. George knew it but failed to seize the opportunity so that it is clear that he suffers too from the fault of indecision. It is always an early sign of declining powers.

Bonar Law is very strong. He has immense power and no responsibility. I think he is the only possibility if Chamberlain sticks to Lloyd George. F.E. [Birkenhead] gained rapidly last fall and declined swiftly this spring.

Then the fever for an election under his own leadership seized Lloyd George once more. By mid-March he was in Wales asking for my thoughts and I wrote him three letters, March 13th, 15th and 19th. I now believed that he would embrace the Empire programme, and I was convinced that our prospect of receiving this gift from the "Left" would be supported by the traditional programme of the Tory "Right". Let Lloyd George move to the "Left", if he wished, leaving Winston Churchill with his Free Trade friends. In my letter of March 19th, 1922, I wrote:

I would make one further suggestion. In the course of your speech the main object of attack should be the opposing newspapers. The Press is always unpopular with members of the Commons and you would rally a lot of sympathy. If you want some stuff on this line I will give it to you.

Lloyd George wrote me on March 23rd:

My dear Max,

I am back on Monday but leave for the country again on Tuesday. Could I see you during that interval? I mean to go wherever the policy of European pacification leads me. There is nothing else worth fighting for at the present moment. Office is certainly not worth a struggle apart from what you can

accomplish through it. It is the policy that matters and not the
premiership.   Ever sincerely,

$$D. \text{ } Lloyd \text{ } George$$

Although "European pacification" was his Genoa
programme, reconciliation of Russia gave rise to bitter
opposition in Britain.   Churchill, the leader of the
hostile hosts, was a consistent and a powerful enemy of
Russia. Lloyd George had decided to challenge and if
necessary part with his old comrade who had helped him
through many a ditch and over stile after stile ever since
the days of the Marconi scandal. Two old campaigners
who had fought together over the years were by this time
separated by many incidents.[1] Lloyd George wrote
Miss Stevenson from his keep at Criccieth:

The fat is well in the fire again. Austen writes to say that
Winston says he will resign if I am to recognise the Bolsheviks
at Genoa, and that he (Austen) cannot face the Tories on a
resignation over that issue. If that is the case then I go, and I
go on an issue that suits me. It puts Labour right on my side.
I have written Austen to say that I am not going to Genoa unless
I am free to recognise the Bolsheviks if they accept the conditions and that the Cabinet must decide between Winston and
me. The Cabinet which will settle my fate, will be held on
Monday. If the Unionists take Winston's view I go without
any hesitation.

I should like you to see Horne and find out what his view
is.[2] You may tell him it is a question on which I could not
recede without making myself the laughing-stock of Europe
after my Cannes proposals. He is of course in the same boat in
that respect. I am sending him copies of Austen's letter and of
my reply.

It is difficult to rest with all these "crises" hurtling about

[1] See Appendix 50, an interesting account of antagonism between
Churchill and Lloyd George over Russia.

[2] See Appendix 51, Lloyd George to Horne, March 22nd 1922.

your head. I have had today a return of those neuralgic pains that worried me.

The challenge to Churchill, which meant in effect— "Resign and be damned"—was a courageous act on Lloyd George's part considering the troubles confronting the Prime Minister. At that time Lloyd George himself recognised his own decline in influence.

Churchill, it is right to say, was willing and ready to resign. He was furious with the Prime Minister's Russian policy and remarked to me: "Tell me which way the little man [Lloyd George] is going and I am off in the opposite direction."

It is difficult for the layman who is not acquainted with the intricacies of political warfare to understand the curious and devious political shenanigans going forward. A record of the extraordinary intrigues of the year 1922 is not complete without a clear understanding of the amazing conduct of Lloyd George, who was actually secretly meditating from time to time abandoning the Tory Coalition. As early as mid-1921 he had been considering taking up with the Asquith Liberals, commonly called "Wee Frees". He contemplated the reunion of the Coalition Liberals and the Asquith Liberals. It was in March 1922 that Lloyd George decided once again that he had nothing to gain by uniting with the Wee Free Liberals, who were going to the country in a campaign in which it was obvious that even if he led them his defeat by the Tories was certain. Therefore he came to a decision. It is enshrined in a letter from J. T. Davies, Principal Private Secretary to the Prime Minister, written from Criccieth to Miss Stevenson: "Whether for good or ill I can see that he means to stick to coalition with the Tories."[1]

[1] See Appendix 52, Davies to Miss Stevenson, March 1922.

The truth was Lloyd George was determined to be on top. His colleagues for the future might be the reunited Liberal Party or a fusion of Lloyd George Liberals with Conservatives. One condition only was firmly and irrevocably fixed. He must be the Prime Minister. He did not seem to care which way he travelled providing he was in the driver's seat.

And I must admit for myself I did not care which way he decided to go providing Empire Free Trade was a leading feature of his programme. Lloyd George was of course a Protectionist at heart,[1] and he encouraged me to believe that at last he would become the leader of those who desired a united and economic Empire. He said that the document setting up his Political Fund would allocate the money for the purpose of securing: (1) Peace; (2) Empire unity;[2] and other objects. And indeed after his death his statement was confirmed. I was willing to take Empire Free Trade from any Government —Conservative, Coalition or Lloyd George Liberal.

At a dinner on Monday, March 27th, at my house, The Vineyard, in Fulham, the Prime Minister was really woolly in outlook, and confused in argument.[3] He would not come to any decision. He was drifting. So was our hope of Empire at his hands.

What was the reason for this want of decision? Why did he drift from one election project to another? There is only one explanation—infirmity of purpose. And that infirmity itself had only one explanation. Lloyd George knew that he should resign and leave his Government in the keeping of the Tories. He knew he was damaging

[1] Miss Stevenson wrote in her diary: "I have always felt convinced even before the war that D. [Lloyd George] would eventually become an advocate of Tariff Reform."

[2] See Frank Owen, *Tempestuous Journey*, p. 691-3.

[3] See Appendix 53, Lady Lloyd-George's (Miss Stevenson's) account of Lloyd George's taste in literature during this period of depression.

his own best interests by refusing to surrender power for a time. The glitter of his supreme office held him in chains and he could not bear to give up power and patronage, even for a few months or a year or even two, with the prospect of a return to his high office. It was weakness and he knew it was weakness. Hence the second failure.

Much damage followed from his first failure when he bungled over Addison. He was injured in his own House of Commons midst his own supporters. But the second failure destroyed his authority over his colleagues in the Cabinet. They beheld his weakness. They saw his indecision. Thereafter the Prime Minister was not even "first among equals".

Here was a man who had done battle with the most dreadful foe his country had ever faced. Great fleets and grand armies had moved at his command. The utmost perils had left him undaunted. He was ever fertile in inspiration and resource. He subdued not only the enemy without, but also the enemy within. He had to contend with recalcitrant colleagues, stubborn Admirals, treacherous Generals, who were quite ready to conspire behind his back, and even to involve the King himself in their intrigues. He looked on tempests and he was not shaken.

Now the same man showed himself as a faltering temporizer. The genius was still there, and so was the mental and physical vigour. But the will had gone. The great war leader who was capable of ordering armies and navies to advance into battle was incapable of ordering a dissolution of Parliament. Trying desperately to shore up a crumbling Coalition, he suffered humiliation. If he had had the power of decision, he could have forced there and then an immediate dissolution in the face of all opposition. For the sake of a few more months of power he pledged the future, a pledge that was never redeemed. He had taken the second step on the way to destruction.

Before the year was out he was ejected from the Cabinet Room and Downing Street he loved so much, never to return. Lloyd George in the days of his greatness commanded friend and foe and fate itself. Now he was himself the sport of fate.

VIII

GENOA AND RUSSIAN
RECOGNITION

The Conference was convened at Genoa in mid-April. Lloyd George had hoped for too much. He was receiving less than little—in fact nothing but disaster.

(1) Belgium resisted violently any recognition of Russia until foreign-owned property was restored. Russia refused.

(2) France under Poincaré supported Belgium, resisting Russian participation in the Conference except under stringent conditions.

(3) The Germans and Russians concluded secretly an independent treaty renouncing reparations and resuming diplomatic relations. Thereafter fear of war cast a shadow over the Conference and the nations shuddered. The treaty had in it the germs of another war.

The Conference collapsed on May 19th.

Poincaré had three reasons for blowing up the Genoa Conference—one, his support of the Belgians; two, his dislike of Lloyd George; three, his hatred of Britain, an old French custom. Maybe Poincaré's hatred had some of its roots in Lloyd George's friendship with Clemenceau and Briand. Both of them always treated Poincaré with contempt. Clemenceau, though spewing his humour over his British colleague, reserved his savage criticism for Wilson, who, he said, talked like Jesus and acted like Lloyd George. When Wilson was speaking Clemenceau pretended to be asleep. Wilson accused him and Clemenceau replied: "And it would have been better for the Peace negotiations had you slept instead of talking." Quite rough stuff for a man who imagined himself to be like unto a Greek god who had descended from Olympus to give peace to all the people.

While Clemenceau was a tiger, he had charm and understanding. He was a good tiger. Poincaré was also a tiger, but he had no charm, no warmth, and a rigidity of outlook that was quite inflexible. His memos show the limitations of the man, utterly hard, harsh, tiresome, uninteresting and without human sympathy. He was a stout little man, President of the Republic, hence a cypher, until after the outbreak of war. Then he led the Cabinet. When Clemenceau came to power, Poincaré became a cypher again. Cold to all mankind, hating his enemies always and not showing much consideration to his friends. He detested all foreigners, including the English. Russians were excepted. He had believed in the Russian steam-roller.

Though he married an Italian, he also hated Italy. And the marriage went very well, though he still hated Italy. When the Italians bombarded Corfu, shocking the civilized world, Britain, traditional friend of Greece, supported an appeal to the League of Nations. Poincaré[1] forgot his lesser hatred of Italy and seized the opportunity of supporting their cause solely for the purpose of embarrassing Britain.

The gallant efforts of Lloyd George at Genoa, his long struggle against some of his own colleagues who opposed recognition of Russia, his patience over French

---

[1] Miss Stevenson wrote in her diary, June 22nd, 1922 : "However D. [Lloyd George] will never like Poincaré. He thinks he is poor stuff. Someone said that it was quite possible that he had many sterling qualities. 'Well,' said Balfour, 'he has no business to look like that, then.' "

intransigence—all came to nothing. Another foreign expedition, and another failure. His prestige was low, as low as his spirits. A complimentary dinner did nothing to help him.

It was plain that Lloyd George had made a fatal error in January when he should have defied Younger, argued Chamberlain into agreement, and at once dissolved, notwithstanding Conservative machine disapproval. But he drew back at the critical moment and Conservative back-bench opposition to him hardened. The upshot was a complete set-back to Lloyd George, and a triumph of orthodox Toryism in the ranks of the Coalition.

He could have had the whole-hearted support and co-operation of the Empire Group if he had given us a Tariff Reform and Imperial Preference programme. Churchill would have joined in an election if Lloyd George had said no truck with Russia, and Empire tariffs might have been a fair price in payment. The anti-Russian platform might have been a bad dose of medicine, but we would have swallowed it. Thus he would have captured his most energetic colleagues. The Empire Group would have been quite as important to Lloyd George as the support of Churchill, for at that time Empire was a most popular cry.

By June of 1922 Lloyd George, defeated in his plans for an election, defeated by Tory colleagues in the Cabinet for the first time within public knowledge and humiliated by declarations of Sir George Younger and others, contemplated resignation again.

The control of *The Times*, arising out of the illness and approaching death of Northcliffe, attracted him. On June 23rd he dined with me at The Vineyard. He was deeply interested in discussing *The Times* and Northcliffe's illness, and asked if I was negotiating for the purchase of *The Times*. I could see that he did not accept my denial. The conversation was broken off when Churchill and Mrs. Churchill joined us. But it was evident that the Prime Minister would renew the discussion at a convenient opportunity.

Miss Stevenson's diary gives a vital account of the source of the Prime Minister's information, and also the reasons for his interest in the future of *The Times* newspaper:

And Northcliffe under restraint! Rothermere told D. [Lloyd George] that he had been queer for some time, but now he is really off his head. The day before yesterday he started telephoning first thing in the morning and continued for seven hours without ceasing. So yesterday they cut the telephone off. Northcliffe is cursing Rothermere and others, saying there is a conspiracy against him. He has made up the quarrel with Wickham Steed, and D. says the danger is that N. will sign over the control of *The Times* to W.S. [Wickham Steed]. D. would like to get *The Times* and if it is to be sold will try and get it bought by a friendly syndicate. He is very afraid that Beaverbrook may try and get control as B. is trying very hard to get at Northcliffe and pretends not to believe that the latter is mad. The whole thing is very complicated and it will be interesting to see what happens. D. says he would not mind resigning if he could become Editor of *The Times* at a decent salary and with a decent contract.

He was willing to exchange Downing Street for Printing House Square. His attitude was not surprising as his tenure of No. 10 was in any case increasingly threatened by growing disputes in the Cabinet and the Commons, and in the Press, and on platforms throughout the nation.

Sir Campbell Stuart had been for years the friend and confidential adviser of the newspaper Viscount, Northcliffe, who died in August 1922. Stuart was invited to lunch with the Prime Minister. There Lloyd George discovered that Campbell Stuart had negotiated the sale of the paper to Mr. J. J. Astor. For reasons I never understood Lloyd George there and then in his own hand wrote to Lord Stamfordham asking that Stuart should be given an opportunity of laying his plans before the King.[1] Stamfordham replied that the King was glad to hear of the project, but since it would be a commercial undertaking His Majesty ought not to identify himself "with the interests of any one particular journal".

Lloyd George, dining with me, and in the company of Birkenhead, discussed *The Times* again in the late autumn. Lloyd George in effect denied that he had ever had any interest in Fleet Street. He would leave that lane with many turnings to me—so he said. The *Times* ambition was not even a memory.

Lloyd George frequently dined at my home, Cherkley, near Leatherhead, often on a Sunday night. In mixed company he dominated the table talk. His Welsh nationality always shone forth. Describing the great men of Wales, he declared that Cromwell was a Welshman and his real name was Williams. H. G. Wells, sitting quietly under the spell of the magician, interrupted the monologue, adding "Williams the Conqueror" to the list of Welsh worthies.

The Government drifted with disastrous results.[2] They drifted on into the summer, with Lloyd George

[1] See Appendix 54, Lloyd George to Stamfordham, undated.

[2] One small disaster concerned me. For long I had been urging the Government to admit Canadian store cattle, then excluded by cunning regulations. On July 24th, 1922, a debate in the House of Commons by a vote of 247 to 171 in effect removed the embargo. The decision followed a by-election resulting in the defeat of the Minister of Agriculture, thus bringing the issue to public notice. The *Morning Post* took an unfriendly view of my activities. The journal printed a verse (*see overleaf*):

still urging an election, but not in very vehement terms, and with Chamberlain less inclined to resist as the inevitable end of the Government drew nearer. But that still seemed quite a long way off when the holidays began.

In Ireland the guns formerly aimed at Britain. had been directed against Irishmen by their brothers. Britain having escaped from civil war in Ireland was plunged into threats of being involved in the Greek war with Turkey.

Repetition of the position of Parties in the House of Commons may be desirable. In 1922, as in 1921, Lloyd George was in office with a following drawn from two Parties, but in fact the prisoner of the Tories. He had his supporters who were known as Coalition Liberals, relatively few in number, but holding many offices in the Administration. Then there were the Conservatives. These Members formed a majority of the House. But many of them believed themselves to have been returned by their constituencies with the aid of Lloyd George votes.

The Parliament was more than three years old. And there must be another appeal to the country in less than two years.

BENEFITS FORGOT

Lord Beaverbrook, your accents rude
Reveal a gross ingratitude.
'Tis true that hither none may bring
Canadian beasts for fattening.

Whoever may that rule arraign,
The last should you be to complain.
'Tis our affair, not yours, to rue
That, spite the law, they let you through.

The Times also, for the moment, surprisingly supported the Government, refused to print my name and referred to me as "a gentleman from Canada".

IX

GRAECO-TURKISH WAR

On August 5th, 1922, I went to Deauville with Winston Churchill. We travelled to Folkestone by motor, crossing on the Channel Packet. After lunching at an hotel in Boulogne, we motored to Deauville. On the way Churchill sang a series of songs, and I was much impressed by his dramatic rendering of the verse:

> *Splendid are thy courts below*
> *In this world of sin and woe;*
> *Joyous are thy courts above*
> *In that land of light and love.*

We arrived just after dark, staying at the Royal Hotel where we had engaged rooms.

That night I was taken ill. The hotel doctor was called, and prescribed two remedies, one for oral use and the other for internal application. The two separate parcels were endorsed with directions in French. Now much to my shame I am unable to read French, so I had to rely upon Churchill to give me the necessary directions. In one way or another through confusion the method of application was reversed. When the mistake was noticed there was much disturbance, but the remedies wrongly used had the desired effect and I was well again.

The Aga Khan was staying at our hotel. The Near Eastern peril was blowing up on the horizon. The year before I had spent some weeks in Germany, much to the betterment of my understanding of that country. Germany indeed appeared the storm centre in 1921. Con-

stantinople looked like it now. Why not go there? The
Aga Khan was at that time a strong friend of the British
Empire, an important leader of the Moslems, and an
advocate of a reconciliation between Turkey and Great
Britain. He was most emphatic in urging me to go to
Turkey and informed me of the receipt of a safe conduct
to Angora and a friendly reception by Mustapha Kemal.

My own ideas had always been utterly opposed to
Lloyd George's pro-Greek foreign policy simply on
grounds of expediency as far as the interests of Great
Britain and the British Empire were concerned. The
journey would be exciting and possibly an interesting
reminiscence. But as I became more deeply involved
I thought of nothing except Peace. Our soldiers from
Britain and from the Dominions had died for the sake
of Belgium, for the sake of the White Russians, for the
subjugation of Ireland. Why should the Empire give
yet another generation of youth to enable Greece to seize
territory from Turkey?

The Turks at that time had not achieved their
military success over a demoralised Greek Army. It
might, I thought, be possible to bring back from them
terms of peace which the British Government could
accept. For this purpose I was prepared to go up
country to Angora. The Prime Minister might be persuaded to give me something to go on. Accordingly I
wrote in August:

Dear P.M.

Now that you have joined the "Men of Property" where
Winston is a pillar of the Temple, I want very much to entertain
you at Cherkley on Aug. 26. The only poor man that will be
tolerated is F.E.—and he has a right to move in the company of
the rich.

I have been very ill for days. At one moment I thought that
I might at last get ahead of Lord Northcliffe. It all came from

drinking first and swimming afterwards—instead of the other way about.

Don't answer this letter. Let Davis [J. T. Davies] send me a telegram here to say that you will come on the 26th.

The French are fine cooks.

Yours ever,

Max

Lord Birkenhead accepted an invitation in reply to my telegram. Mr. Churchill also indicated his intention of joining us.

I spent three days with Lloyd George, Churchill and Birkenhead at my house in Leatherhead, Cherkley. My object was to negotiate myself into a position to come to a friendly understanding with the Turks. Lloyd George was not easily interested in the matter at all— his mind being occupied with the question of an election. When brought to talk on the matter he merely insisted that I must keep the Greek side of the case before my mind too. Churchill on the other hand thought the Greek pretensions ridiculous and Birkenhead was in much the same frame of mind, though he expressed himself with greater moderation. In fact, as was Wargrave before the Irish settlement—so was Cherkley before the Turkish débâcle! Mr. Lloyd George's prophecy to us was "tranquillity" in Turkey and "storm" in Berlin. "Why not go to Berlin?" he asked me. About Constantinople he was evasive and indefinite, though on the whole he encouraged me to go and promised he would listen to any proposal or argument I might bring back.

Finally Lloyd George and Churchill came to a fierce discussion but not over foreign questions. The former accused the latter of having opposed his plan for a January election "because you thought I would win". This accusation was met with great resentment, but not with a denial. In fact, Churchill thought in January that a new lease of life for the Government would mean a Lloyd George despotism. So violent indeed was the quarrel that when the party broke up I wondered if the two men could ever work together again. Next day, encouraged by Birkenhead, I left for Constantinople, little thinking that my three guests would be united over the "Chanak coup" which brought down their Government.

This is the political picture of the Graeco-Turkish war in the minds of men when Parliament recessed in the summer of 1922. On May 15th, 1919, Greek troops had made a landing in Asia Minor at Smyrna, in Turkey. They acted at the request of the Allied Supreme War Council, that is to say at the request of the Governments of Britain, France and Italy, holding Constantinople under an agreement of joint occupation. The Treaty of Sèvres, signed by the Sultan of Turkey, a prisoner of the Allies, on August 10th, 1920, assigned to Greece not only Thrace in the European territories of Turkey but the city of Smyrna and its hinterland in Asia Minor.

Lloyd George was a great partisan of Greek imperial pretensions. He believed that the Greeks were a strong people, prolific, and capable of establishing and maintaining a domination of the Eastern Mediterranean. He predicted years of peace for the Balkans under the leadership of the powerful Greek race. Miss Stevenson's diary for July 20th, 1921, recounts the Cabinet divisions and disputes on Greece and the Near East:

D. [Lloyd George] very interested in the Greek advance against the Turks. He has had a great fight in the Cabinet to back the Greeks (not in the field but morally) and he and Balfour are the only pro-Greeks there. All the others have done their best to obstruct and the W.O.[1] have behaved abominably. However, D. has got his way, but he is much afraid lest the Greek

[1] War Office

attack should be a failure and he should be proved to have been wrong. He says his political reputation depends a great deal on what happens in Asia Minor, though I don't think people care a hang what happens there. But D. says that if the Greeks succeed the Treaty of Versailles is vindicated, and the Turkish rule is at an end. A new Greek Empire will be founded, friendly to Britain and it will help all our interests in the East. He is perfectly convinced he is right over this, and is willing to stake everything on it.

But the Greeks asked for more. They were not satisfied with Smyrna. They were persuaded to insist upon Constantinople. This claim was supported by Balfour,[1] who demanded that the Turks should be driven out of Europe; but Cabinet opposition was too strong, even though Curzon, the Foreign Secretary, sustained the Balfour policy.

A head of resistance to the Greeks in Asia Minor, organised by Mustapha Kemal, with headquarters at Angora in the heart of Anatolia, was growing in strength and in military power. The Greeks were compelled to extend their lines in an attempt to consolidate their military positions.

Venizelos, Prime Minister of Greece, was an intimate friend of Lloyd George, and long-time faithful supporter of Britain and British influence. His principal strength flowed from King Alexander of Greece. A wicked monkey, captive in the Royal Gardens, one day when subjected to punishment, bit His Majesty, and brought his reign to an end on October 25th, 1920.

Constantine, father of Alexander, friend of the Germans and banished during the war, was recalled. He hated Venizelos, and in consequence the Government was heavily defeated at the Polls on November 15th,

[1] In 1915 Balfour, a member of the Committee of Imperial Defence, strongly supported a Russian demand for Constantinople.

1920. Venizelos fled the country and found sanctuary in a British destroyer which carried the fallen war hero to exile. Constantine was restored to the throne with Gounaris as his Prime Minister.

The French seized on this change in the Greek Government to abandon the Greeks. Franklin-Bouillon, the French envoy, made a treaty with Kemal on October 20th, 1921. French guns and airplanes were supplied to the Turks, thus firmly establishing the military strength and the morale of the Anatolian army.

In the following February (1922) Gounaris, the Greek Prime Minister, applied for assistance to the British Government. The Greek resources were exhausted, the morale of the Greek Army was smashed, the impending Turkish attack could not be resisted unless arms, airplanes and money were provided without delay. If help failed, the Greeks proposed to evacuate Asia Minor, leaving Smyrna to the Turks. Lord Curzon, British Foreign Minister, replied urging the Greeks to stay and fight. He said, "The remarkable patriotism and discipline of the Hellenic Armies, of which so many illustrations have been furnished in the campaigns of the last few years, will not fail them in any emergency that may arrive."[1]

While Curzon was placating Gounaris, he was attacking Montagu, Secretary of State for India. Lloyd George believed Montagu had been concerned in 1921 with Birkenhead and Churchill in the "Plot" aimed at destroying Lloyd George. And Montagu believed that Lloyd George had failed to carry out a pledge to appoint him Viceroy of India which Montagu greatly desired, pressing his claim without surcease for nearly a year.

Now Montagu had always been a stern opponent of the Prime Minister's Greek policy. In March, the Viceroy, Lord Reading, one-time intimate friend of Lloyd

[1] House of Lords Debates, December 7th, 1922 (343).

George, asked the Secretary of State for permission to publish a document cutting across the declared pro-Greek policy of the Government. He said that publication would calm the Moslems of India, who were concerned for their "brothers" in Turkey. Without consulting Curzon, the Foreign Secretary, Montagu approved the Viceroy's request and publication followed. Lloyd George dismissed Montagu and spared Lord Reading.[1]

When Montagu was dismissed, the Prime Minister offered the place to Lord Derby. From Cannes His Lordship showed a willing spirit. On the way to London he fell in with Lord Northcliffe in Paris. Lord Derby recorded in his diary that Northcliffe promised to support him. But Lord Northcliffe declared in a contemporary letter to his mother that he had told Derby that his newspapers would be hostile to the Lancashire Peer's joining the Government. Derby was pressed to accept by Balfour and Chamberlain. But Northcliffe's voice prevailed. Then the Duke of Devonshire was offered and refused the opportunity of taking a place on the perch with the glittering birds of paradise.

Now these firm refusals of place and power by men accustomed throughout their days and years to seeking and finding Government employment should have convinced Lloyd George that his fortunes were falling. Yet he was denied clear vision and continued to reign though not allowed at this time the right to govern. He held on, and in consequence weakened his power and authority.

Lloyd George, strange though it seems, favoured Baldwin for the vacancy but Chamberlain rejected this recommendation. Lord Peel was appointed. Difficulty arose over the Under Secretary's post. Lord Winterton refused, but was pestered into acceptance.

[1] See Appendix 55, Montagu to Beaverbrook, March 13th, 1922.

Chamberlain had a high opinion of Crawford, who had been an efficient and popular Chief Whip through tiresome years of Tory opposition. He was a strong favourite for the India Office in succession to Montagu. On March 21st, 1922, Chamberlain wrote to the Prime Minister:

I wrote a personal note to Crawford to tell him of Peel's appointment in the hope of mitigating any pain or disappointment that he might feel. He replied with a warm eulogium of Peel and an assurance that he felt no disappointment or surprise for he thought Peel the best of all the names that had been mentioned. In fact he behaved like the great gentleman that he is. His position in the Lords has been a very difficult one, for he has been deputy-leader and yet he has never been in our inner councils or had the knowledge and materials necessary for the efficient discharge of the duties of such a post. It would be a fitting recognition of his services and his loyalty if you would make him a Cabinet Minister without changing his Office. The First Commissioner has often been in the Cabinet before. The resignation of the late Attorney-General creates a vacancy and the appointment would, I think, be generally popular with our people. I beg you seriously to consider this recommendation in which the Lord Chancellor very heartily concurs. Indeed, he made the suggestion to me.

This can of course wait till you return to town, but please think it over.

But Crawford did not want the India Office nor Cabinet rank. He wrote in his diary:

Willie Peel goes to the India Office. I am delighted. He is an excellent man. Derby refused and talked about it. Victor Cav[endish—Duke of Devonshire] didn't want the post either, but has not been chattering. The papers on Friday said the post had been offered to me. Not a word of truth in it—but on questions of fact our Press is incorrigible. I am happy at the Office of Works—and should not have been any use at the India Office.

However, Lloyd George asked, through Stamfordham, for permission to add Crawford to the Cabinet. The King returned the letter with the endorsement in his own hand: "Quite unnecessary, too many in the Cabinet already but I approve." "God save the King," said Lloyd George.

By July 1922 the position was:

(1) Greece, backed by the British Government, had become bogged down and could not make any military movements.

(2) The Turks, backed by the French Government and strengthened by French arms and airplanes, appeared to be gaining domination of the battlefront.

(3) Britain and France, opposing each other with their kept Greek and Turkish Armies in Asia Minor, were acting jointly in the occupation of Constantinople, though failing to agree upon a common policy.

(4) Italy, the third occupying power—and with troops in Constantinople—invariably supported the French point of view.

(5) Greek troops in Constantinople, though of little importance, claimed to share the rights of the Occupying Allies and always sided with Britain.

The Greek military position in Asia Minor steadily weakened. Gounaris and his Ministry then declared they were willing to evacuate their Asia Minor positions and abandon Smyrna if they could get terms from the Turks, claiming at the same time from the Allied Armies occupying Constantinople a guarantee of the consolidation of Greek power in Thrace. They would abandon Asia Minor in exchange for a secure grasp upon Turkish territory in Europe, Thrace for sure, and if possible Constantinople too.

The defeat of Greece by Turkish forces in Smyrna would be damaging to Great Britain. The traditional good relations of France and Britain, though at the moment distant and somewhat chilly, would be shattered. A common attitude by Britain and France to both Greece and Turkey appeared to be the only path to tranquillity in Europe.

Arriving in Constantinople in early September, I was the object of curiosity to the Embassy and the Army Command. What was my purpose? Did I possess authority? And of what nature? Those enquiries arose from the displeasure of Lord Curzon, Secretary of State for Foreign Affairs, who was raising a storm of disapproval in London, supported, strangely, by the *Morning Post*. "Mysterious Mission" was the note of this newspaper criticism.

Meanwhile, Kemal's representative gave me an account of the changing military position. Victories over the Greeks had completely changed the outlook. They were confident of driving their enemy out of Asia Minor, and at once. A settlement carrying with it the evacuation of Smyrna by the Greek Army no longer interested the Turkish leader. There was now nothing for the Greeks to offer or to give. Their army was swiftly driven into the sea. The Greeks were eliminated from the scene in Asia Minor.

But since Turkey was victorious it was necessary to negotiate a treaty of peace between Angora and Britain, supplanting the Treaty of Sèvres, now in ruins. I had not even a fragment of authority to discuss the changed and utterly altered relationship. I at once set out on a journey to London, travelling through the Aegean Sea, where we encountered everywhere the terrible and dreadful tragedy of the flight of the Greek Army.

In the port of Piraeus, a few miles from Athens, the retreating Greek troops were arriving by every conceivable means of transportation. At the piers, soldiers were being required to hand over rifles and other arms. Many had unarmed themselves; they had thrown away their weapons in flight. The Government of Greece had prepared Athens for a revolution and the streets of the city were made ready for mob violence.

My journey to Rome by ship, motor and train was most uncomfortable. On reaching the hotel there I sent a telegram to Lloyd George asking for an interview. Lloyd George answered, inviting me to meet him at Geneva. My arrangements for the journey from Rome to Geneva were hardly complete when another telegram was received cancelling the Geneva meeting and sub-stituting London.

Now I could think of nothing but the Graeco-Turkish war. I rushed back to London determined to try to play the role of peace-maker between Britain and Turkey.

September 15th, 1922, was a day of grave incidents. Far-reaching decisions were taken. Two conclusions had most exciting reactions. Before the momentous Cabinet meeting of the day, Lloyd George wrote a letter to Curzon[1] who was then in complete accord with the "War on Turkey" programme of his Prime Minister. This letter contained the amazing proposal that Curzon should stir up some of the Balkan States to join in the fray.

An even more startling decision evidently approved by the Prime Minister's colleagues was embodied in a message to all of the Dominions. The Prime Minister asked for support of the Empire in rallying to the defence of the Dardanelles against the threatening Turkish Army. The Turkish threat, it was declared, required prompt action, and the Dominions were asked for assur-ances of representation by contingents of troops. It was,

[1] See Appendix 56, Lloyd George to Curzon, September 15th, 1922.

of course, an intimation of an intention to check the Turkish advance on Constantinople and would be looked upon by the victorious Kemal as an ultimatum.

The British Government had decided to mobilise for war against the Turkish Army! What a surprise! What a day! War against Turkey in the Balkans—war against Turkey in the Dardanelles! Possibly war against France! The end of a bewildering day.[1]

Lady Lloyd-George's autobiography records:

One morning . . . [September 15th] my door opened and L.G. [Lloyd George] and Churchill walked in from the Cabinet room. L.G. asked me to take down from Churchill the text of what I realised was to be a statement asking the Dominion Governments for their support in the event of a war with Turkey. I was horrified at the unwisdom of the message, conveying as it did the prospect of renewed warfare on a grand scale. L.G. and Churchill took the draft back into the Cabinet room, where the meeting was in progress. Shall I send L.G. in a note warning him against such an action? I thought. But then again, I thought, he will never agree to such a telegram being sent.

The next thing I knew was that the telegram had gone. It was one of the factors which helped to bring the Coalition Government to an end, and within a fortnight it had fallen.[2]

Lloyd George was in the country when I arrived in England on Wednesday evening, September 20th, 1922. I attended on Churchill and Birkenhead immediately.

When I left England at the end of August both took a friendly view of Turkey's national demands. Both were displeased with the Government policy of supporting Greece. Both were united in believing that pressure should be brought to bear on the administration to dampen down the ardour for Greek pretensions. They

---

[1] Lord Birkenhead was speaking of the bitter dispute with France "with a probability of a war against the Turks, and possibly France too".

[2] The autobiography has not yet been published.

claimed the British Government should modify its irreconcilable attitude to Turkey.

On my return from the East I was astonished to find Churchill and Birkenhead in complete agreement with the Prime Minister's Near Eastern policy. Birkenhead claimed that Christian minorities must be protected against the dreadful atrocities of the unspeakable Turks. Churchill declared the Turks were marching upon the Dardanelles, Constantinople and Europe. They should be stopped. He told me that he had written the message to the Dominions, which by this time had become the subject of much criticism in political circles and also in the newspapers. The Dominions, with the exception of New Zealand and gallant little Newfoundland, had rejected the appeal. Australia said "Yes" and "No". Prime Minister Hughes sent a complaining, hectoring and bullying dispatch of nearly two thousand words. The unity of the Empire, he said, was gravely imperilled. The League of Nations had neglected to intervene. Therefore his representatives would take immediate steps to rectify that omission. Then he mentioned that the Dominion would associate herself with Britain in maintaining the freedom of the Straits. But, he said, Australia would not risk one soldier's life. And finally, he declared, the Dominions ought not to be asked to associate themselves with Britain after the decision to go to war had already been taken. All this in one single, lengthy message.

Canada refused all overtures. Parliament must be called, said her Prime Minister, Mackenzie King. Churchill cabled: There would be no war. Contingents would not be required. A declaration of association was all that would be needed. Mackenzie King remained unmoved.

Now Lloyd George was to make his third and last

mistake. He had a fixed purpose. He would go to war. Being by this time a weak man, he had decided to be strong. And he would be strong at the wrong time and for the wrong reasons. Only this can explain Lloyd George's blind and stubborn rashness over Chanak. In his new-found energy and resolution—the energy and resolution of a man grown weak in judgment and decision, he was bolstered by the support of most of his Cabinet colleagues.

Lloyd George was like the strong man, Samson, also grown weak and exhausted, who asked God, "strengthen me I pray thee only this once". And God gave him strength but only to destroy him. So Samson pulled down the pillars of the temple and was buried in the ruins. "The dead which he slew at his death were more than they which he slew in his life."

There was much opposition in the country and no enthusiasm for any ventures abroad in the House of Commons, Press or Army. Though the populous Dominions had failed to respond to the call for contingents, yet the Ministers appeared to be fixed and settled in their purpose to discipline the Turks and if necessary to go to war.

On Thursday, September 21st, Birkenhead came to my house (The Vineyard) at Fulham. We argued at length and reached no conclusions. On Friday, September 22nd, I was joined at lunch by Birkenhead and Churchill. Meanwhile Saturday, September 23rd, had been fixed by Birkenhead for a meeting at The Vineyard with Lloyd George.

At lunch on Saturday I claimed that the Premier would find the Turks amenable to reason and I mentioned, with some little misgiving, the fact that Birkenhead and myself had already discussed the question of his being sent out to the East as a special Envoy. The Prime Minister negatived this plan quite definitely. And I must say that on the whole I was relieved since I now had reason to doubt Birkenhead in the role of the Angel of Peace.

But really, except for a little general discussion on home politics, Lloyd George would not listen to anything, and monopolised the conversation with a diatribe against the "atrocities" at Smyrna which he imputed without any special evidence to the Turks. We broke up late in the afternoon, with nothing accomplished.

The lofty sentiments in Lloyd George's letter to me of March last declaring, "I mean to go wherever the policy of European pacification leads me. There is nothing else worth fighting for at the present moment" had undergone a change and decay.

Lloyd George was now preparing for a very different type of fighting. Bombs and guns, marching soldiers and ships of war had taken the place of his programme of conferences and collaboration with former foes. Russian recognition was forgotten, the dangers of German resurgence ignored. The Conservative Party and their Coalition allies would be united at last. United in a war effort which always brought an unbroken front in the Government, in the House of Commons and in the country.

The military position in that month of September 1922 was an important factor in political discussions and decisions. The Treaty of Sèvres had laid down that the Dardanelles, the channel uniting the Mediterranean and Constantinople, was a demilitarised area, whose neutrality was to be guaranteed by the military forces of Britain, France and Italy. So, by September 1922, troops from those three Powers prepared to stem the flood of Turks coming from the sack of Smyrna and believed to be marching on Constantinople. These Turkish troops were approaching Chanak, on the Asiatic shore of the Straits. But both the French and the Italians complained that we were, in effect, sending ultimatums to Turkey. Then Britain invited the Greeks to take part in the defence of the Straits. This too was resented by France and Italy. The view taken by France and Italy was that the Government of Britain was taking a course of action that would lead inevitably to a clash of arms. On September 18th, therefore, the French and Italian troops were withdrawn from Chanak but not from Constantinople. This was a breach by France and Italy of the Sèvres Treaty. That Treaty was broken. And Britain was left alone to face the victorious Turks at Chanak, a point on the Asiatic shore of the Straits where the British troops had taken up their positions. It was plain that, notwithstanding the fact that the French and the Italians had withdrawn and in spite of the unwillingness of the Dominions to join in the expedition, the Ministers still meant to go to war.

Bonar Law, on hearing the story of the discussions of Saturday, showed no inclination to interfere with the course of events. He had, of course, been a party to the Treaty of Sèvres (August 1920) made by the Lloyd George Coalition when Bonar Law was second man in that Government. It was perhaps this fact that made him reluctant to listen to the new Turkish standpoint.

Yet, the severe terms of that Treaty were largely due to Lloyd George supported by Lords Curzon and Balfour.[1] The Treaty was extreme and unjust because a great portion of the Ottoman Empire had been stripped from Turkey. Adrianople had been handed over to the Greeks. Even the city of Smyrna in Asia Minor, far

[1] Balfour moved up from the Commons to the Gilded Chamber (House of Lords) on May 5th, 1922.

distant from Athens, had been ceded to Greece under the Treaty. Lord Balfour was very violently anti-Turk throughout and his strong memoranda were among the main supports of the Premier in pursuing his pro-Greek policy. He wanted to turn the Turk out of Europe.

Nonetheless, Bonar Law was not prepared to interfere with Government policy in the face of the crisis. He would abstain from criticising foreign policy, he said, as completely as possible. He showed a considerable interest in the opinions of Venizelos, and it was plain that this Greek statesman was in part responsible for Bonar Law's attitude. In any case, Bonar Law could not be moved to action.

The agitator for peace must never be at rest. So I spent my days and nights too in contact with Birkenhead, Churchill and Bonar Law. One or other was the constant subject of my attentions. On one occasion I tried to bring Bonar Law into personal contact with Birkenhead and Churchill in the hope that he would be influenced unfavourably by the course of their arguments for dealing firmly with the Turks. But Bonar Law himself refused to see them.

Bonar Law had his own friends in Lloyd George's Cabinet, and something might be hoped for on that account. Some of them were unwilling to pursue Lloyd George's courses in Turkey. The Premier had brought successful pressure to bear on these reluctant colleagues in the Cabinet, including Stanley Baldwin who was in close relationship with Bonar Law. Baldwin took two decisions at this time. When, in the Cabinet, they were face to face with war, he decided that the Government's policy was the correct one, though he longed for peace and advocated negotiations, particularly with the French. He contended we should never have gone to Chanak but, being there, we must see it through. Later on, he decided that it was time to part with Lloyd George because he was leading us into such situations.

On Wednesday, October 4th, at Birkenhead's house, with Churchill present, the Near East was discussed. The debate became bitter in tone. The accusation made against the Peace party was a charge of "scuttle"—a word thrown like a brickbat. Birkenhead referred to our duty to Christian minorities and showed a lively interest in the British Nonconformist Conscience. Churchill talked of the might and honour and prestige of Britain, which he said I, as a foreigner or invader, did not understand, and of how it would be ruined for ever if we did not immediately push a bayonet into the stomach of anyone in arms who contested it. He was always ready to fight England's foes. He was not departing from his honest and sincere convictions. Birkenhead was in a different position. Hard-headed, clear-sighted, free from any profound political faith, he was a team man, dazzled by preferment, and influenced by the mistaken belief that Lloyd George could get the votes.

Fresh from this encounter, I had the next morning (Thursday) what I intended to be a decisive interview with Bonar Law on the Near Eastern question. I was on the verge of despair, and I said, "Look here, this is the last time I shall speak to you on this subject. But I must say this: Lloyd George, Churchill and Birkenhead mean war—war against Turkey supported by France. War is unnecessary, and all we want can be obtained by negotiation. You alone can save us from war, and you alone possess the power to guarantee peace. If you will act, all will be well." Bonar Law made no reply, seemed in a sense unresponsive, and the conversation terminated.

This Thursday and Friday were the critical days. The Peace party in the Government consisted of Lord Curzon now and then, Mr. Baldwin always, and Sir

Arthur Griffith-Boscawen and Lord Peel. They met at Lord Curzon's house. The Marquis pretended that this group was prepared to act with him throughout and resign with him. It will be seen that this self-nominated leader, according to form, sat on the fence in the crisis awaiting the result. Would it be Bonar, or Lloyd George?

> *I'm sitting on the fence, Bonar,*
> *The place I've always sought,*
> *Until I see who's got the job,*
> *The Welshman or the Scot.*

Lord Curzon now insisted on going over to Paris to try to conclude a settlement with Turkey on the basis of agreement with Poincaré, i.e., by joint and not by independent action. The War party in the Cabinet tried to force Birkenhead on Curzon as a joint emissary, but Curzon replied he would go alone or not at all. His opponents were obliged to confess defeat, and Curzon left for Paris without any chaperon.

The reader may be confused as to the attitude of Lord Curzon. The reason for any such confusion would, of course, be the confusion in Curzon's own mind. Sometimes he was on the side of those supporting Greek pretensions. At another time he would show regret for the faded glory of Turkey. Sometimes he acted as the faithful colleague of Lloyd George. Then again, he would show extreme hostility to Lloyd George and also to the Greek policy.

At this time, while France and Italy had deserted Britain, the British Army and Turkish Army continued to face one another at Chanak, with the Turks frankly trespassing on the covenants of the Treaty of Sèvres which forbade them to enter the demilitarised zone.

On Friday evening (October 6th, 1922), when I had

almost despaired of Bonar Law's intervention, he came to my house at Fulham just at dusk. We sat in semi-darkness. He referred to the conversation between us at his own house. He said that he had made up his mind. He would send a letter to *The Times*.[1] He indicated the terms. Later, after writing the letter he told me the text. It was almost word for word as he had spoken earlier in the evening at The Vineyard. To my mind the dominating sentence in the letter was to the effect that we could not police the world alone. And I looked upon his declaration as a decisive statement. It seemed to me he was saying, in effect, "We must act with the French. Failing joint allied action, we must decline to do anything on our own account." In this letter Bonar Law not only declared that we could not police the world alone but said that, if we could not work with France and Italy, our proper policy was to withdraw from Europe and pursue a course which he described as "safeguarding" the more immediate interests of the Empire.

I was excited by this declaration of policy by Bonar Law because I thought it must lead to a peace with Turkey. I recommended him to send his letter to other newspapers as well as *The Times*. He agreed to do so. On Saturday morning (October 7th, 1922), the letter appeared in the Press and as I believed put an end to the prospect of war.

Birkenhead was dining with me that Friday night and with Bonar Law's consent I told him of the contents of the letter. He was greatly put out—declared Bonar Law's advice to be tantamount to "scuttle" and said that if Bonar Law challenged the Government in the House of Commons on such a policy the Government would be sustained. Bonar Law would be humiliated

[1] Bonar Law had informed Derby of his intention to write the letter.

and held up to public reprobation for dividing the counsels of the nation at a moment when we had plunged into bitter dispute with France, with a probability of a war against the Turks, and possibly France too. He added, with his usual shrewdness, that it was a new political situation. It implied the re-emergence of Bonar Law from retirement.

Birkenhead in turn communicated the news to the Premier on the telephone, pointing out how bad it was. Lloyd George then asked me to tell him the contents of the letter over the telephone. I did so, and Lloyd George, with greater pliability and acuteness, commented, "Oh! it's not so bad", meaning, of course, that the Government would be able to carry on all right but would have to alter course. Curiously enough, however, unlike Birkenhead he did not see that Bonar Law by the mere act of writing this letter at once became, for the first time since his retirement, an independent Conservative Leader and also an alternative Premier.

The people by this time were against war. The Government had failed completely in their efforts to stir up a war spirit. They could not engender any enthusiasm whatever for an adventure in the Near East. It is possible that if the Cabinet had persisted, some headway would have been made in the direction of securing public approval but, as soon as Bonar Law raised the standard of peace, around which people could rally, the whole enterprise was at an end. Some Ministers might still wish to go to war. They could unfurl the banners and beat the drums. But the nation would not march.

Lloyd George accepted the situation. He yielded to Bonar Law's warning.

X

BONAR LAW ENTERS

So we have the position that the Government has been frustrated in its policy. What would the Prime Minister do?

Bonar Law with his usual political prescience disclosed the position. He declared that the blows to the Government's prestige were so great that discontent in the House of Commons would grow and develop. He said that the Prime Minister would consider and deliberate on an alternative course. He would in all probability appeal to the country and, with a new mandate and disciplined majority, renew the pressure on the Turks and come to the defence of the Greeks. His position would be considerably enhanced in foreign countries and his power greatly increased if his Commons majority was sustained.

Bonar Law was alarmed. He declared that an appeal to the country by Lloyd George in the circumstances might—indeed would—break the unity of the Conservative Party. So the situation appeared to be gloomy indeed: either a Lloyd George majority with a renewal of foreign alarms and excursions; or the danger of serious, perhaps irreparable, damage to the Conservative Party, the only instrument for maintaining party government.

While the outlook might be gloomy for the Conservative Party which Bonar Law loved so much, it had tremendously improved the prospects of peace. There was every chance that an armistice would be arranged.

Lord Birkenhead and I were meeting regularly and, of course, by arrangement. I told him about Bonar Law's doubts and misgivings in relation to the future:

(1) Bonar Law foresaw that the failing prestige of Lloyd George would force an election.

(2) He was convinced that the Conservatives at the National Union meeting on November 15th would decide that their Ministers should withdraw from the Coalition.

(3) The alternative to a meeting of the National Union would be a General Election. But a General Election might give Lloyd George a majority. And that majority, he feared, might be used to renew a belligerent policy in the Near East. So the danger of a successful Lloyd George election began to loom up in the minds of men who wished a permanent policy of peace with Turkey.

(4) And Lloyd George was still encouraging the Greeks. For instance, when the Government at Athens begged him to arrange an armistice with the Turks, one of the Prime Minister's private secretaries telephoned back to the Greek Legation that "their Government should be very careful to avoid the mistake made by the Germans in 1918 and conclude an abject armistice in a moment of panic". In effect Lloyd George, though knowing his project for war had failed, was advising the Greeks to give up any idea of an armistice; if at an election he was sustained, he intended to reinstate his old bad policy.

Birkenhead asked me to inquire on behalf of Lloyd George if Bonar Law would join the Administration. Would he take the place of the Foreign Secretary— with the power of influencing and indeed deciding foreign policy? I knew very well that Bonar Law would not do so. It was of course the third time the suggestion had been made. The first time was in 1921 at Chequers, then at Cannes in the early part of 1922—the occasion when Lord Curzon, the Foreign Secretary, was sitting in a hotel not a hundred yards away, quite unaware that his job was on the bargain counter.

I told Birkenhead the offer, which was made with the intention of dressing up the Government for a General Election, had been rejected at two previous discussions.

Then he asked for a meeting between Bonar Law and Lloyd George. Bonar Law agreed. But he said that the Foreign Office was out of the question. His view was that if he undertook the task he would not be in the position to control foreign policy. And even if he were to become Foreign Secretary, Lloyd George's difficulties would not be solved. It was arranged that the two leaders should lunch at my house, The Vineyard, on Monday, October 9th.

My good relations with Bonar Law withstood the disagreeable controversy. Of late I had been pressing him much too violently and I had shown signs of impatience over his caution. Now that he had taken the decisive step by writing his letter of October 7th, our harmonious association had been completely restored. He had written that we could not act alone as policemen of the world. If we could not co-operate with the French, we should restrict our attention to safeguarding the Empire. Henceforth I worked under him and for him.

In the meantime, the Prime Minister had begun negotiations with his colleagues in the Government for an election. The Prime Minister did not think that the Conservative Party could come back as an independent Party with a majority in the Commons. He was certain that the result of a separate appeal must mean the inevitable defeat of a number of his followers who depended on Conservative votes. At best he would be left as a group-leader selling his votes in return for concessions instead of the head of a powerful Administration. The only alternative seemed to him the Centre Party—a conception always flashing before his eyes like an electric sign—in which his own followers would be reinforced and re-elected by vast numbers of Conservative votes.

The problem for the Premier, therefore, was this: could he persuade his Conservative colleagues to agree to an immediate dissolution? The problem for the colleagues was: supposing that they were agreeable, could they carry the Conservative Party into agreeing to or considering a manœuvre which, however defensible from a Coalition Liberal standpoint, was certainly a piece of sharp practice as far as the Tory rank and file were concerned? In a sentence, they were to be jockeyed into going down to the polls as a Coalition when the only reason for going to the polls in a hurry at all was the fact that the rank and file were so hostile to the Prime Minister and his policy that, as a consequence, they were fighting for independence. A swift election was the only way to destroy that independent movement, as it was hoped, for ever.

Thus stated nakedly, it seems impossible that Conservative Leaders could have contemplated such a policy. But quite apart from the question of personal loyalty to the Premier, Austen Chamberlain and his friends had a totally exaggerated view of the value of Lloyd George's assistance as an electioneering asset in the constituencies.

The position was, then, that Chamberlain was moving to Lloyd George's support. Churchill too favoured a prompt election; though a Coalition Liberal, he was acting in the closest relations with the Conservatives. Lord Balfour concurred in the election project, and gave unswerving support to Lloyd George. Birkenhead's position was still doubtful. He was doing nothing with Lloyd George to oppose the election but he showed that he appreciated the point of view held by Bonar Law. Curzon adopted a waiting and watching part. But the real risk of a manœuvre which offends the conscience of a Party is that some outstanding figure will rise up to protest. Those in power must secure every potential enemy.

The lunch meeting of Lloyd George and Bonar Law arranged by me took place at The Vineyard on Monday, October 9th. Bonar Law came early. He said that Lloyd George would make a deliberate attempt to square him on the General Election issue. Bonar Law declared that there would be a great danger to the country if Lloyd George received a renewal of his mandate. He outlined many objections, including the danger to the Conservative Party. And he emphasized that a Parliamentary majority for Lloyd George would be used by him and some of his colleagues to develop and extend their old bad policy in the Near East. Office under Lloyd George would be intolerable, he said, leading straight to war.

Bonar Law's conclusions were comforting to me. The declaration of Empire interests might lead to Empire Free Trade. Bonar Law then spoke sharply to me. He asked, "What do you want? Are you just playing the fascinating game of political intrigue?" He asked me what object I sought in arranging the lunch with Lloyd George. "What are you trying to do?" he asked. "Maintain the Coalition? Or do you wish to break it down?" I answered, "What do I want? An Empire programme, with Free Trade, or as nearly Free Trade as might be obtainable, with a tariff wall around the Dominions and Colonies."[1]

If Bonar Law had been willing to join the Government I hoped he would demand just such terms. But with Churchill and others against him, and Chamberlain no longer an ardent follower of his father, the founder of the movement for an Economic Empire, the several enemies would probably kill the project. Therefore I must work for the end of the Coalition followed by a Conservative Administration, with Bonar Law as Prime Minister, and an election with an Empire programme. Bonar Law remarked that he would not accept responsibility. He would not be Prime Minister. I must make my representations elsewhere.

My conversation with Bonar Law indicated clearly that he had made up his mind to do everything possible to destroy Lloyd George and the Coalition. This was a most dramatic moment. The two leaders would meet for the first time as rivals for public approval—their differences might turn a quiet lunch party into a very lively event.

For five years Bonar Law had held the stirrup iron while Lloyd George had mounted the steed, finally riding off to victory. In those days the Prime Minister had established a leadership coupled with authority which amounted to an ascendancy over his modest and self-effacing junior colleague. Here they would meet, not only on equal terms, but as rival leaders differing on essential and indeed vital public issues. How would it all work out? Would Bonar Law be overwhelmed by the dominating influence of his former master?

[1] Bonar Law believed in an Economic Empire with Food Taxes too. For at that time there could be no advantage to the Dominions unless Empire food was admitted to Britain free—and Britain imported more than half of her consumption of food. He could be relied upon, I believed, if he became Prime Minister to give us our policy.

It was a moment of high drama when Lloyd George entered the little room at The Vineyard. He came with his swaggering step—one foot thrown forward and leg slightly outward. His greeting was gay without any sign of patronage. Bonar Law responded with little enthusiasm but much dignity. He was no longer the courtier. He had a better understanding of the temper of the dominating Tory Party in the House of Commons— and Lloyd George knew it. From that moment Bonar Law was the master of the scene.

I had nothing to say. Lloyd George turned to me with friendly though distant courtesy. I was not "Max" to him that day. He called me "Beaverbrook", a sure sign of disfavour. The drawing-room at The Vineyard is small. It gives a feeling of intimacy when men sit and converse in it. When the first feeling of stiffness was over we got down to a more sympathetic basis. I was not in a hurry to go into the dining-room. I preferred that the conversation should develop a bit, and we had not yet sat down to lunch when Lloyd George asked Bonar Law if he was prepared to express his views on the desirability of a General Election under the Coalition banner.

As far as continuance of the Coalition and the General Election was concerned, Bonar Law said that Lloyd George was being misled, no doubt unwittingly, by his Conservative colleagues as to the temper of the Conservative Party. They did not want another Coalition. Lloyd George reminded Bonar Law that he had served in Coalition Administration for five years and they had joined in recommending a Coalition Government as early as 1910, when it was hoped by agreement to dispose of Home Rule, Disestablishment, Unemployment Insurance and the Land questions. True it was that, at a conference of the Tory group, Lansdowne, Chamberlain, F. E. Smith and others agreed to Coalition on just such terms. Balfour, then Leader of the Party, stood out. After three hours of deliberation he said: "I wish with all my heart that it were possible—but it cannot be. I *cannot* be the Sir Robert Peel of my party," adding, "though I cannot see where the Disraeli of the Party would come in, unless it were my cousin Hugh."[1] (Balfour always looked upon the Cecils as a family of political leaders set apart from the rest of mankind.) Bonar Law now replied to Lloyd George: "This time you have Balfour in your pocket—but not the Party."

The discussions then turned on the alternative of Lloyd George's resignation. Bonar Law advised him very strongly to resign and go into temporary retirement, and allow the Conservatives to form a Government. Birkenhead, who had joined the party, nodded approval to Bonar Law. The Prime Minister did not show himself by any means strongly averse to taking the advice proffered, but he said, "Suppose I do retire. What will happen to my followers [the Coalition Liberal Members and candidates]? Am I to desert them and leave them to destruction for the want of Tory votes?" Bonar Law made no response to this obvious effort to open up negotiations on personnel. But this difficulty was not perhaps insuperable so far as Bonar Law was concerned. Lloyd George had another objection at the back of his mind. He did not want to give up his place in the driver's seat.

At lunch that day again and again I deliberately turned the conversation to the Near East and the Government's policy there. Bonar Law encouraged me, but Lloyd George rode off. He would not talk about Chanak or discuss the future. A truce had been made with the Turks on October 4th. There was a good

---

[1] Lord Hugh Cecil.

chance that it would be resolved into an armistice which might lead to a negotiated peace with Turkey. There was general relief over this improvement in the situation, but men who looked ahead raised the issue: would the truce become a permanent peace? Or would there be a breakdown? Another rupture? More anxiety? Further fear? Bonar Law pressed again and again for some expression of the Prime Minister's future plans for the Near East. He could not get any satisfactory or even comprehensible answer.

Lloyd George made, I thought, a courageous and yet pathetic figure. He was no longer the man of the moment, striding on from triumph to triumph, scattering favours to his adherents as he advanced. He knew well the weakness of his own position—and that he held his associates to him only by past loyalty and the mistaken idea they had of his prestige in the country.

Birkenhead made the remark that if a Presidential Election on the American model could be held here, Lloyd George would be President by a vast majority— whereas it turned out that Bonar Law would have beaten him easily. On the whole I judged Birkenhead was an impartial observer, declining to take sides, and free in future to support either leader. Birkenhead, though saying little, was putting in a remark here and there, generally with a humorous turn and intention when the tone of the argument became tense.

The lunch lasted long, and at the end of it Lloyd George took Bonar Law by the arm, led him out of the dining-room into the little drawing-room, and then he said he would like to have another conversation with him before any definite action was taken. That conversation never took place.

I had been witness of a most memorable meeting. Lloyd George certainly acted with restraint. He did not behave as a tyrant on that day. His courtesy never failed, though sorely vexed again and again. Bonar Law behaved with such tact and self-confidence that his conduct shone forth so brightly, yet with a firm and unyielding attitude. I had never heard him to such advantage. Throughout the hours he was in complete charge.

Birkenhead and I stayed on at The Vineyard and continued our conversations. He was tired and possibly weary of politics, and anxious about the future. His life story was up to this time a tale of unbroken success, although crossed throughout by jarring notes of hostile criticism.

The lines of his face were cast in a rigid mould with the stiffness of a weapon or an instrument designed for some violent purpose. Yet when he was at his ease with friends, there was a delicacy and softness of features. As always his wit knew no brother.

I urged him to revert to his old faith and to join us in our cause, directed, as I believed, to secure peace abroad and, as I hoped over all, the development of the Empire. He listened to me with close attention while I unfolded an imperial policy and urged this programme on His Majesty's Government. I pointed out to him the immense difficulties attending on a continuance of the Coalition. I said that it was almost impossible for the Coalition to go on. Birkenhead replied by saying that we would find a way out. There need be no breach between us. I objected: how about the Near East policy? There is not much we can get from Lloyd George in that direction. Birkenhead replied that the Lloyd George Greek policy was wrecked and could not be salvaged.

We then entered into a formal compact. We agreed that neither of us would take a final and irrevocable decision. We agreed that we would try to work together with a common purpose. I was pledged to do nothing further to stir up hostility to a General Election under Lloyd George's leadership. Birkenhead was pledged to take no steps in the direction of such an election without first giving me notice which I in turn would convey to Bonar Law.

I reported my agreement to Bonar Law that same day. I argued that it appeared to me that Birkenhead had doubts of Lloyd George's policy in the Near East. That he had been dragged unwillingly into the war plan. That he had no real sympathy with Lloyd George's Greek policy and was not absolutely determined to follow him. That Birkenhead was the most formidable figure amongst the Conservative Ministers in Lloyd George's Coalition Cabinet. Let us try to bring him out in revolt against the Coalition and the Coalition Government's foreign policy.

Bonar Law raised no objection to the pact between Birkenhead and me, and directed me to keep in touch with him. I reported back again to Birkenhead that Bonar Law accepted the terms of the pact.

Now as a result of the lunch meeting on October 9th, Bonar Law appeared to me to be ready and willing to resist Lloyd George, and if called upon to form a Government ready and willing to consider an Empire programme. I was prepared to follow him to the uttermost. Shortly he faltered and it became as difficult to persuade Bonar Law to go into Downing Street as it had been to chase Lloyd George out of No. 10.

For the moment my hopes were raised very high. Here was a leader who would give us our policy. Here was a leader who would turn his back on Europe and his face to the Empire. Here was a leader with a cause justifying any sacrifice and stimulating every exertion.

And yet, Bonar Law's attitude was very difficult. He was keen to talk politics. He expressed an absolute certainty that the National Union of Conservative Associations would declare emphatically against the continuance of the Coalition. He said that the present position was impossible; that the Government must fall; that the country wanted a straight Conservative Government, and that such a Government would win at the polls. He foresaw a strong Conservative Administration, but he did not see himself as an element in it.

He was condemning foreign expeditions in strong and vigorous language. Already he had begun to talk of "tranquillity". And at every mention of an Empire programme he showed deep interest and paid close attention to all the arguments that I would advance in ordered array. I always emphasized the rich deposits of raw materials in many Empire possessions, offering vast wealth if properly developed.

There was no choice, he said, between these alternatives, a strong Conservative Administration or a Coalition Election. And the pursuit of a Coalition Election would result in breaking the Conservative Party into pieces.

And yet at this time he kept assuring me day after day that he himself would take no part in these events: that he was out of politics for good: that nothing would persuade him to come out against Lloyd George and hurl himself once more into the vortex.

It will be remembered that Birkenhead had said he would "find a way out". He tried. No doubt with Lloyd George's consent, the Premiership was offered to Lord Derby. Would he form a Government with Lloyd George as Lord President? He declined. Then the offer was made to Bonar Law. He was invited to meet

Birkenhead and Churchill; but declined the proposal, making it plain that he would not be caught up in these negotiations at all.

It was pointed out to him that this was a way of saving the Conservative Party. Bonar Law's reply was, "If that is on foot, let Lloyd George come to me; I will advise him how to save the Conservative Party."

Bonar Law was also being visited by Sir George Younger—an odd figure in politics, with an immense reputation. Sir George Younger possessed excellent political judgment. He was a man of pleasing manners, a charming companion, though somewhat taken up with the stories about his encounters in the past with one or other of the Conservative leaders. He would say, for instance, quite emphatically, "I told Austen exactly what to do, and, of course, he did it." Or, "Bonar Law, of course, acted on my advice."

Nor was he always clear in his public utterances. For, indeed, as late as September 29th he delivered a strongly pro-Coalition speech at the Western Division Council of the Scottish Unionist Association:

He [Sir George Younger] trembled to think what might happen if the Unionists had differences among themselves and if they had quarrelled with the friends [i.e. Coalition Liberals] with whom they had worked so long. He trusted that they would keep "on friendly terms with those with whom we have acted so long and will form in that case a bulwark against the Socialist party."

Churchill could have said no more. But, fortunately, in London Sir George Younger was pouring a totally different version of his views into Bonar Law's ears. But if what he said in the South was foresight, what he said in the North was folly. In any case, although he was inconsistent on the platform, he was a most useful

colleague in the parlour. At Bonar Law's house in
Onslow Gardens he was at this time a constant visitor.
And there he never faltered in his view that the Conservatives must now detach themselves from the Coalition and from the Coalition's foreign policy. Asked
about his speech of September 29th supporting the
Coalition, he said "the Coalition ought to be saved,
but even I cannot save it now."

In his conversations when I was present he showed
marked interest in the Empire plans which I would never
let rest for long. But he warned Bonar Law that he
should have no truck with me on any policy that involved the imposition of Food Taxes. That, he said,
would be disastrous to the main questions. Foreign
commitments, foreign expeditions, foreign conferences
were all to be swept away. There would be a new era of
peace at home and real progress in dealing with domestic
problems.

Sir George Younger has often been hailed as the
architect, patient and long-foreseeing, of the political
revolution which placed Bonar Law in power. He was
contemptuously referred to on all sides by the opposition.
Much abuse was hurled at him. More criticism was
directed to him than he ever expected. But he took all
things in good part.

But while Sir George Younger was meeting with
Bonar Law, the phalanx of Conservatives who were
prepared to stand for Lloyd George and the election was
increasing and solidifying. Chamberlain was now certain
in his support of Lloyd George, and this finally decided
Birkenhead. When I tried to persuade him to break
with Lloyd George he would reply confidently that
though there would of course be a Tory split the great
majority would go with Lloyd George and the Conservative Cabinet Ministers. Then a Centre Party would

be formed commanding Lloyd George's funds,[1] followers
and the *Daily Chronicle*—the Conservative Party funds and
organisation and the immense power of patronage. This
would secure a triumphant victory at the coming
election. When I spoke of the horrid shock Chanak had
been to the country he waved it aside as an episode
which would be overwhelmed in the new controversies
springing up out of the reconstruction of Parties—a fatal
and delusive dream.

When I talked of more foreign adventures under the
authority of a new mandate from the people, Birkenhead
declared that Lloyd George had learnt his lesson. He
would now apply himself to domestic issues. Thus
Birkenhead reached his firm decision to march with
Lloyd George. It was a fatal error from which he never
made a complete recovery.

Nonetheless we renewed our private agreement not
to act independently without consultation. The next
episode was, therefore, surprising. Birkenhead came to
The Vineyard on the morning of October 11th. He
stayed with me two hours and we discussed affairs in
detail—but he made no disclosure of the true position.

While I was still with Birkenhead, Bonar Law sum-
moned me. He fixed the meeting place at rooms in the
Temple I then occupied as an office. When I walked in
he asked if Birkenhead had given me notice of the
decision reached by the Conservative Ministers that
morning in favour of an immediate General Election.
I denied that any such decision had been taken. Bonar
Law replied that Birkenhead, Chamberlain, Sir Robert
Horne, and Lord Balfour had all agreed to support the
Prime Minister in an immediate appeal to the country.
I was astonished and asked for time to go and see

---

[1] About three million pounds at that time. " Gate Money," George
Younger called it. Meaning price for entry into Conservative pastures.

Lord Birkenhead before carrying on any further conversation. When I reached Birkenhead, telling him of
Bonar Law's information and further that he had himself taken the decisive action of throwing in his lot with
those Conservatives who would support Lloyd George
at a General Election, he made no concealment whatsoever. He said he had done the right thing.

I then accused him of breaking our understanding
about communication through me to Bonar Law before
definitive action was taken. I reminded him that he
had had every opportunity of telling me what he had
done when he visited me at The Vineyard that morning.

Birkenhead said at once that an explanation was
indeed required. He declared that Austen Chamberlain
at the conference when the decision was reached demanded a pledge of secrecy from Birkenhead. He said
that pledge was specifically made to apply to me by
name. He had, therefore, felt himself bound to keep
silence.

I returned to Bonar Law and received his approval
to set out on a campaign of propaganda against Lloyd
George and his Conservative colleagues. Thursday
morning, October 12th, marks the beginning of it. There
was to be no end for many a long day. Old friendships
were severed. Alliances were broken down. Com-
panionships were sundered, and relationships were
strangely altered.

Most of all I was personally to regret the breach
between Lord Birkenhead and me. And yet from the
start to the finish in this crisis he was in a most difficult
position. His reason told him that the Government was
taking the wrong course. His loyalty to Lloyd George
and his belief in the Prime Minister's strength in the
constituencies carried him along. He would have been
glad to have escaped conflict with Bonar Law. None-

theless when the breach came he did everything to prejudice our campaign. He made errors of judgment before the crash, and worse errors of temper after it. His election speeches were unjust and bitter to a degree. Yet my affection for him never perished. My gratitude to him for past kindnesses never died, and my memory of him is always with sincere and devoted attachment for a splendid and glorious figure in public and private life.

I began to see the position in a varying light. Hope is a candle that burns brightly. There is the possibility of (1) a new Government, and the policy of the United Empire with the chance of our getting the foreign Food Taxes which are essential to our programme. There is the possibility of getting (2) Bonar Law as Prime Minister—a Prime Minister who believes in the Economic Empire. With these two prospects surely much the best plan is to go for both of them.

At Bonar Law's direction I remained in touch with Lord Birkenhead, hoping to detach him from the foolish schemes of his colleague the Prime Minister. I continued my efforts to convince him that the future rested with Bonar Law.

The decision to go to the country was taken on October 11th. It was known to us on the same day. On the 14th of that month I arranged a conversation at The Vineyard with Bonar Law and Birkenhead, in the hope of detaching him from the Government group. Birkenhead showed plainly that he and his colleagues were counting on Bonar Law's bad health, his physical inability to fill high office. The conversation did not go pleasantly and I made no further advances to the Lord Chancellor. Bonar Law was quite well enough, and I was outraged by the suggestion that he was in bad health. I did not believe anything of the sort.

The prospects were glorious and the results would

be immense. Let us have Bonar Law for Prime Minister, with a Bonar Law Government, Empire Unity in the near future, Bonar Law's own tranquillity at home and no more foreign adventures.

On the same day the Near East policy which had been in the background was brought out of it. Lloyd George defined his position in unmistakable terms. In a speech at Manchester he attacked the Turks and, by implication, criticised the French. This was at a moment when his Foreign Secretary was about to enter the conference room with the representatives of these nations in an effort to turn a truce followed by an armistice into a permanent and lasting peace.

Why did he make that provocative speech sure to weaken his position? Lloyd George was of course misled by memories of 1916, when a nation obsessed by fear of German invasion, of Zeppelin raids, of bombardment of seaports, of long casualty lists, of sinking of Atlantic ships carrying precious food stuffs, rallied all men and women to their new leader (himself). Party dissensions were quelled and personal political quarrels were calmed.

He foolishly believed that a state of war against Turkey would unite Conservatives and Coalition Liberals, silence the two opposition Parties, and justify an appeal to the electors with a whopping majority for his leadership. But the nation could not be persuaded to fear the Turks or fight the French.

Chamberlain's attitude was influenced by memories of the Irish triumph of a year before. He took little notice of what was in reality a revolt of temper on the part of his own Conservative machine reflecting a similar uprising in the constituencies. The events of January 1922 had been forgotten.

Thus it was that the Prime Minister, sustained by

Chamberlain and his associates, moved steadily and firmly to a decision for an appeal to the constituencies and, as they believed, another mandate for the Coalition.

The Manchester speech of Lloyd George, of course, horrified Bonar Law. It was just the sort of folly that convinced him Lloyd George could not be trusted. Lloyd George himself by this oration had strengthened Bonar Law's opposition.

The whole question now turned on whether Lloyd George could capture a majority of the Conservative Party. By October 14th his confidence was high. He believed that he could carry the majority of Conservative Members and candidates with him. He thought that he could send them to their constituencies compelled to support him whether they liked it or not.

A dinner of Ministers, and including others, was held at Churchill's house on Sunday, October 15th, at which the Prime Minister, Birkenhead and Churchill met not only Liberal Coalition Ministers but also some of the doubting or hostile Conservative members of the Government. Earl Balfour was the chief stool-pigeon at this dinner—and much was hoped from the presence of Lord Fitzalan, Lord Lieutenant of Ireland. He had, as Chief Conservative Whip in the past, been a pillar of orthodox Toryism.[1] Stated briefly, the offer made to the recalcitrants was this—"Will you be satisfied not to resign if we hold a Party meeting?" The dice were, of course, to be loaded by calling only the Members of the House of Commons—believed to be the most favourable soil for the continuance of the Coalition. The Conservative Peers, save for those in the Government, were to be excluded since they were known to be hostile, while the Tories in the constituencies, equally hostile, would, of course, get no representation at all. In fact,

---

[1] Fitzalan made his position clear. He supported Bonar Law.

the whole Conservative Ministers-Lloyd George scheme
from first to last was based on the supreme necessity of
preventing the local Tory chairmen and agents, who
made up the National Union of Conservative Associations, destined to meet on November 15th, from expressing a view. By getting in the election before that date
they avoided the hostile National Union.

There was another scheme put forward by Churchill
and Horne: to submit the issue to the House of Commons and not to a Party meeting at the Carlton Club.
Lloyd George considered it, and rejected it.

In face of the offer at the Sunday night dinner party,
some of the rebellious Conservatives said "Yes." But
it was not made clear what "Yes" meant. One side
thought it meant acceptance of the Front Bench plan.
Others thought it meant that they could speak and vote
as they liked at the Party meeting, but would accept the
verdict of the majority.

The question of the date of the Party meeting now
arose. And but for the gravity of the issues involved
the story would take on a tinge of farce when we consider the extraordinary series of miscalculations and
uncertainties which attended and surrounded the Carlton
Club meeting.

The great urgency put forward for getting the election
over was the necessity for passing the Irish Constitution
through the new Parliament by December 6th.[1] The
Party meeting could have been held on Wednesday,
October 18th, but it was postponed until Thursday,
October 19th.[2] Why? Because Lloyd George (as he had
told Bonar Law) was absolutely convinced that the

[1] The Irish Treaty required ratification by the British Parliament before
December 7th, 1922.

[2] See Appendix 57, Lloyd George to His Majesty, October 16th, 1922.
And 58, letter in His Majesty's own hand addressed to Lloyd George.

result of a by-election at Newport in Monmouthshire would be to let the Labour man in on the split between a Government-supported Liberal on one side and an Independent anti-Lloyd George Conservative on the other—a triumphant proof of the necessity of the Coalition. The announcement of the return of Mr. Clarry, anti-Lloyd George Tory, on the very day of the Carlton Club meeting was one of the most exciting boomerangs in the long history of English political strategy.[1]

Between Sunday the 15th and Thursday the 19th the struggle became less like a battle than a series of single duels. Every man's political soul was required of him. Promises and promotions and honours were sprinkled from Downing Street on the green benches with a hose. The orthodox Tories appealed to the age-long traditions of a Party now caught fast in the house of semi-Liberal bondage. But all eyes turned to a single figure.

It was plain that with Bonar Law lay the decision. Either he would go to the Carlton Club meeting as the alternative Leader, or the malcontents must suffer defeat. Mr. Baldwin at that time, although a man of good reputation, whose subsequent record improved his status immensely, was an obscure figure. His talents had not been recognized. He could not carry the banner of leadership. Men would not have rallied to his side.

The final decision was taken by Bonar Law amidst much perturbation. But the struggle was internal, not external. On the one side stood a sense of duty of which Bonar Law had boundless store. On the other was a

---

[1] The morning of October 19th brought news which drove the final nail into the coffin of the Coalition. Mr. Clarry was returned by a majority of over 2,000, Labour second, and Liberal, supported by Coalition, a bad third. See *Life and Letters of Austen Chamberlain* by Sir Charles Petrie, vol. II, page 202.

fund of natural modesty, a love of well-earned ease, laziness and kindly feeling towards Lloyd George.

But his views of the situation had never changed. He was opposed to expeditions abroad. He was in favour of peace at home. He called it a policy of tranquillity. And he made increasing use of the word. He believed that Lloyd George was no longer suited to his high place. He was convinced that a further mandate to the Coalition would bring more adventures in foreign countries. Out of it, no doubt, would emerge a Lloyd George Centre Party, but that Centre Party would be disastrous to the Conservatives.

But the real question now was whether Bonar Law would attend the Carlton Club meeting of the Conservative Members of the House of Commons. A Carlton Club meeting is so called because it meets in the premises of the Carlton Club. It is, in effect, a meeting of the Conservative caucus. It is called by the Leader of the Party, and it consists of Conservative M.P.s with or without the Conservative Peers. It always deals with the question of the Leadership of the Party.

The Carlton Club meeting was the bull ring. The bull was the Conservative Cabinet Ministers who favoured the Coalition with Lloyd George. The matador was Bonar Law. But would the matador come into the ring? If he did so the bull might be killed. But no matador, no killing of the bull!

If Bonar Law went to the meeting he must speak. And if he spoke, he could say only one thing—that Conservative unity required the termination of the Coalition. No matter what the reasons might be. No matter what explanations were put forward. The end of the Coalition must be the real objective of the meeting.

But his reluctance to attend the meeting was real and he seized on every device to provide an excuse. First of all he sought out his doctor, Sir Thomas Horder.[1] He was convinced that Horder would solve all his difficulties and relieve all his doubts by advising him against any return to active life at all. But Horder told the inquiring statesman that there was no reason whatsoever against taking up again the burdens of public life. So it was that Bonar Law lost the first and best defence that he had erected against himself in the movement for a return to public life.

From Sir Thomas Horder, Bonar Law turned to Sir George Younger. He pointed out the need for acting in the best interest of the Conservative Party. What would be the result, he asked, if he attended the meeting and spoke against the Coalition? Sir George Younger made the surprising reply that Bonar Law would just win and no more. Leslie Wilson, who was Chief Whip of the Conservative Party serving under Chamberlain, then advised Bonar Law that no decisive result could be derived from the Party meeting even though Bonar Law put forward all his efforts and made use of every resource. So Bonar Law then developed his second line of defence. Would he be able to carry the meeting? If he failed to do so would he inflict more harm than good on the cause he sought to serve?

It was at this point that Sir Samuel Hoare[2] and his group of friends, including Walter Guinness and Lloyd-Greame, gave strong advice and vigorous counsel.

[1] Sir Thomas Horder was Bonar Law's doctor and he also attended Churchill in his attack of appendicitis, which came before the fall of the Coalition. Churchill's interest in his own case was second only to his interest in Bonar Law's case. "How's our ambitious invalid? What about our gilded tradesman?" he would ask. Bonar Law would inquire after Churchill too.

[2] Sir Samuel Hoare, afterwards Secretary of State Home Office, etc.; Rt. Hon. Sir Philip Lloyd-Greame, Secretary of Overseas Trade Department 1921-22 ; Walter Guinness, M.P., later holding several offices, including Leader of the House of Lords. Assassinated in Egypt in 1944.

Bonar Law—Gazing into the evening mists

Lord Derby—Pomp and circumstance

They were convinced that three-quarters of the Party's strength in the Commons was on the side of Bonar Law. This confidence could not be shaken and was supported by strength of argument and wealth of detail.

Meanwhile many of the Under Secretaries held a meeting condemning their Front Bench seniors. They met again the next day. Baldwin and Griffith-Boscawen, Ministers, Wilson, Chief Whip, and Younger, Party Chairman, joined them and approved of their revolt.[1]

At this moment a most immense attack was directed against me by the Conservatives who opposed Bonar Law, plainly for the purpose of weakening my influence with him. For it was foolishly believed that if I could be eliminated, Bonar Law would not continue the contest.

Sir Archibald Salvidge attended at Bonar Law's house at the request of Bonar Law with instructions from Birkenhead through Locker Lampson, Chamberlain's Parliamentary Secretary, to "spy out the land". According to *Salvidge of Liverpool*—by Stanley Salvidge —he appealed to Bonar Law for unity on behalf of "all the best Conservative brains":

One of the things being said was that much of the demand for a change of Government had been engineered by Lord Beaverbrook because, though he had till recently been a Coalition supporter, he had failed to exercise over the present Cabinet the influence he desired on behalf of certain oil interests in the East.

To Bonar's retort that surely I neither believed such a tale, nor suggested that he should for a moment consider it, I answered that I happened to know Beaverbrook did not possess any oil interests in the East.

Salvidge reported that he then said to Bonar Law that Lloyd George retained the unswerving support of every one of his Conservative colleagues in the Cabinet. Bonar

[1] October 16th and 17th.

Law replied, "I may as well tell you that Lord Curzon is here. He is waiting in another room." Salvidge retired at once, reporting forthwith to his friends at 10 Downing Street the news that Curzon had changed sides.

Birkenhead, when told by Salvidge of Bonar Law's answer to his gossip about my financial interest, "put his head back and laughed heartily." "Gentlemen," he cried, "hearken to my friend Salvidge, the blunt man from the North."[1]

One day an American newspaper, published in Paris, circulated a story that I advocated a policy of peace with Turkey on account of my control of Mesopotamian oil-fields. The libel came from Ministerial circles in London.

But a more subtle attack was developed by Lord Birkenhead. He subjected Bonar Law to ridicule. He told a story that Bonar Law was really abroad playing golf. That I had been dressed up in Bonar Law's clothes and disguised to look like him by Willie Clarkson.[2] That the Party meeting would be addressed by me masquerading as the real Bonar Law.

Then again, friends and colleagues working intimately with Bonar Law and sincerely supporting him reported that statements were being widely circulated and generally believed that I was "running" Bonar Law. These reports would have been annoying to the pride and self-respect of any other man—but not Bonar Law.

We were back again to the old days when Birrell[3] had said to Bonar Law, "You will go far if you will give

[1] Salvidge's text clearly shows that what amused Birkenhead was not Bonar Law's answer but the fact that Salvidge should have repeated the gossip to Bonar Law.

[2] A make-up expert for actors.

[3] Rt. Hon. Augustine Birrell, M.P., President of the Board of Education, for many years Chief Secretary for Ireland, pleasant and urbane critical essayist.

up your Max Aitken." Leo Maxse, stern Right Wing Conservative Editor and proprietor of the *National Review*, brother of Lady Milner, had written to Bonar Law:

As the Front Benches are crowded with political charlatans of proved incompetence who speak vastly above their ability, and whose ignorance of vital national affairs is only surpassed by their self-sufficiency, why not take this golden opportunity of looking outside into the larger world and associating the following elements with the War Government. (1) The Fighting Services, (2) the Dominions, (3) the business world. P.S. We are all terrified of having men like Max Aitken and F. E. Smith thrust upon us, or Winston Churchill. That way disaster lies as you start by chilling public confidence.

The Conservative Leader answered:

I never mind attacks on myself (and indeed considering your view you have been very generous to me through these trying times), but I really do not like what you say about Aitken. He is my most intimate friend. I know him as well as I know anyone and in my belief he is as honourable a man as I am and one of the ablest men I know.

So I had to meet these attacks, which were directed with rare skill. I should have been a simpleton if I had allowed myself to be overcome by any such tactics. I resolved to do everything in my power to dispel the suspicions which others were trying to sow in Bonar Law's mind. When I was summoned to his house, I would sit for ever so long discussing every conceivable subject except politics. In high spirits I would pour out fun and fantasy. But never a word on serious subjects.

Wednesday—the day before the Carlton Club battle. The hour of decision. In the morning Bonar Law spoke to me by telephone recounting his worries and his fears of destroying the Conservative Party. Throughout the day telephone messages reached me, from supporters of Bonar Law, urging me to go to Onslow Gardens and press for a favourable decision.

I heard from colleagues who had visited his house and from stout friends who were sound. But they all reported that there was a hardening of resistance. He was steadily repudiating the pressure to attend the Party meeting.

I held to a firm resolve. No effort to influence the decision until asked to confer.

All day I waited for a message. The hesitation of Bonar Law drove me to extreme anxiety. He knew I wanted him to go to the Carlton Club. If he did not send for me or give me news of his intention, surely he was rejecting the contest and refusing the Party conflict, and perhaps deciding upon retirement from public life and departure from the scene.

Tempted again and again to call him by telephone, or present myself at Onslow Gardens, I resisted. But would I get a chance to speak to him? Would I be consulted at all? Was I forgotten? After all, my home was quite near Onslow Gardens. I would wait until nine o'clock. If no word by then, urgency would drive me to action. It was such a long day. Impossible to turn my mind to any pursuit. Conversations with my newspaper colleagues failed to hold my attention. It was almost as though I had become obsessed by a single thought.

At last word came. It was nearly eight o'clock on Wednesday evening, and by that time, owing to a slight cold, I had developed a temperature. Away I hurried to Onslow Gardens. A curious and interesting company were gathered there. Bonar Law himself was agitated and in a state of high tension. There was his sister, Miss Mary Law, a woman of fine intellect, high character, and shrewd political judgment. But her attitude to her brother was then as always—"Tell me what you want to do, and I will tell you that you are right." There was also J. C. C. Davidson, who had been Private Secretary and afterwards Parliamentary Secretary to Bonar Law. He was then serving with Stanley Baldwin. He is a loyal man. He has ability and certainly strength of character. I have not always agreed with his judgments, but I have always accepted his sincerity. Davidson, at any rate, had no doubt. He wished so very earnestly that Bonar Law might attend the Carlton Club meeting. All his efforts were directed to that end. Every resource he could command was being used for the purpose of securing the Bonar Law leadership.

General Sir Frederick Sykes, Bonar Law's son-in-law, was present too, and held the view that the statesman should come out as the new Leader of the old Party. Then there was frank and warm-hearted support from Lady Sykes, Bonar Law's daughter. She was ready to take risks, and she would put everything to the test.

On my arrival, Bonar Law invited me to join him alone in his own library. It was a small room, over-heated, a bookcase standing against the wall with countless volumes of Carlyle, Hume, John Stuart Mill— all in orderly array.

Bonar Law opened up the subject at once, telling me that he feared that no good could come from his attendance at the Party meeting. An indecisive vote, he said, would be damaging to the very interests he wished to serve. He might do incredible harm and immense injury to the Conservative Party—the best instrument for good government, and essential to the well-being of the country now that the Liberal Party had been entirely destroyed. He produced a letter addressed to the chairman of his constituency in Glasgow declining to stand at the oncoming election. He contemplated mailing it forthwith and also issuing a copy to the newspapers. I remarked that he had only to send the letter to the post box in order to bring his political career to an end. It seemed an easy way to walk out and plainly the proper course to take if he desired such a result.

He then asked my opinion. I replied, "The letter is too long." Again he asked me for my opinion and said that he wished me to be serious. But I continued to dodge the issue.

It was then I reminded him of another occasion. He had shown me, years and years ago, when he was standing as candidate for Leader of the Conservative Party, a long letter to James Hope.[1] It was, in effect, a withdrawal in favour of Austen Chamberlain, an alternative candidate for leadership. I had read the letter and thrown it on the fire. Bonar Law had burst out in angry indignation and for a time our relations had been strained. So I said, I am not going to make such a mistake again. Your letter is your own affair.

My reluctance to speak began to annoy him. So I at once plunged into the arguments which I thought would be most effective in support of our cause. I had made ample preparation. I needed no notes, for I had prepared myself all day long for this critical quarter of an hour. I came to the end of my plea, concluding on a high Imperial note.

He calmly refilled his pipe and said quite simply: "I am going to the meeting." It was a dramatic moment. I was going hot and cold on account of my temperature. But it seemed to me I then went hotter and colder. I asked if I might make a statement to the Press Association that he would be at the Carlton Club. He concurred. I fled. Not a moment did I waste in reaching a

[1] Influential Member of Parliament and ardent supporter of Austen Chamberlain.

telephone. I called through to the Editor of the Press Association, gave him my name, and told him I was authorised to publish the statement: "Bonar Law will go to the Party meeting at the Carlton Club."

Then I returned home and to bed with two hot-water bottles and one of rum with a bowl of sugar. One last word of warning on the telephone to the *Daily Express* to make the most and the best of the great news. And then a night of sleep.

It was eight o'clock in the morning when I was called imperatively to speak with Bonar Law on the telephone. When I got on he told me that he had not slept all night; that he feared so much for the future of the Conservative Party; that he believed so greatly in the need for that instrument; that he worried so much lest it should be destroyed; that he would like to have another talk with me at once.

I replied, "Have you seen the morning newspapers?" which was a conclusive answer to his suggestion for more talk. The front page of almost every newspaper displayed the statement that Bonar Law was going to the Carlton Club.

Every political writer in Fleet Street knew that the announcement foreshadowed the fall of Lloyd George's Government that very day. And so it was.

XI

BONAR LAW—PRIME MINISTER

The Carlton Club Meeting was convened for the morning of Thursday, October 19th. Bonar Law arrived early, and was greeted with warm cheers. I joined the crowds on pavements and roadway. The wind was cold. A cold autumn wind.

Austen Chamberlain arrived with Lord Lee and Sir Robert Horne. There was some booing in the crowd, and a woman shouted "Judas!" There was a similar demonstration against Lord Birkenhead. Curzon was absent. He explained: "I would not speak against my colleagues." But he would intrigue against them. He was in fact waiting to hear who got the votes, Bonar Law or Chamberlain.

There were several incidents at the Carlton Club Meeting. M.P.s did not gather in solemn mood. They were genial and rather mirthful. As the meeting settled down, the Club attendant, on the direction of a Member of the House who was well known for practical jokes, hastened to the table and before Chamberlain and Birkenhead placed a couple of pegs of brandy and withdrew. Loud laughter from younger Members of the Party. Chamberlain eyed the liquid through his hastily adjusted monocle, gave a start and with a gesture he hid the tumbler behind a chair. Birkenhead took a perfectly sensible attitude.

Austen Chamberlain opened the meeting. In his

speech, he stressed the Socialist threat from Labour. He referred to a recent speech by Henderson, outlining Labour's policy: a capital levy, nationalisation of the great industries, and the right of work or of maintenance for every citizen. These were the issues raised by "quite the second largest Party in the State" at a time when the whole economy was still struggling in the aftermath of a great war. These were the real issues that had to be fought out at the next election, and not issues arising out of the old Liberal and Conservative policies. Loyal co-operation between the Coalition allies was essential if a strong Government was to be formed. The Government must go to the country as a Government, not trying to shirk their common responsibilities nor blaming any unpopularity on "a man who has led us through these troubles, who has acted throughout with a loyalty to us to which my friends will testify as warmly as I do. No man of honour would do that."

Stanley Baldwin, speaking for "the minority in the Cabinet, that is, myself and Sir Arthur Griffith-Boscawen", followed. He was much too cautious to mention Lord Curzon—which side would Curzon judge the winning side? He said that he accepted the Lord Chancellor's recent description of the Prime Minister as a dynamic force. A dynamic force was a terrible thing. This dynamic force had smashed the Liberal Party. Baldwin believed that in time he would also smash the Conservative Party. It was a measure of his disintegrating influence that Baldwin and Chamberlain, who held the same political principles, should be so divided that one was prepared to go into the wilderness rather than stay with the Prime Minister and the other to go into the wilderness rather than forsake him.

Bonar Law followed, and was greeted with a great shout of cheering. He made it clear that the Party ought to come out of the Coalition and go to the country on its own. He said:

I confess frankly that in the immediate crisis in front of us I do personally attach more importance to keeping our party a united body than to winning the next election.

The feeling against the continuation of the Coalition is so strong that if we follow Austen Chamberlain's advice our party will be broken and a new party will be formed; and not the worst of the evils of that is this, that on account of those who have gone, who are supposed to be the more moderate men, what is left of the Conservative Party will become more reactionary, and I, for one, say that though what you call the reactionary element in our party has always been there and must always be there, if it is the sole element, our party is absolutely lost.

Balfour spoke in support of the Coalition. Lord Birkenhead, although present, did not make a speech. A card vote, in which it was understood the names would be kept secret, was taken. About fifteen Members of the Government voted for maintaining the Coalition. They were supported by some Welsh Members, and by several Scottish Members, most of whom intended to retire that year. Bonar Law was supported by 187 votes against 87.

Lloyd George was waiting for news in Miss Stevenson's office. There they sat. Lloyd George was gloomy. Miss Stevenson was anxious and even alarmed. She tells that he was very quiet, but she talked of anything but the meeting, of which both were thinking.

At last a telephone message gave the word—Lloyd George was *out*.

Then Austen Chamberlain burst into the room, exclaiming: "We are beaten, we must resign." Lloyd George sitting distrait in an uncomfortable armchair completes Miss Stevenson's picture.

By two o'clock a Cabinet was summoned. Many Ministers who had voted with Bonar Law, instead of presenting themselves, presented their resignations. The King, who was at Sandringham, hurried to London, reaching Buckingham Palace at three o'clock. At quarter past four, Lloyd George submitted the resignation of his Government and advised His Majesty to send for Bonar Law.

There was, however, a final administrative act. The retiring Prime Minister recommended an Earldom for Lord Farquhar, who was Treasurer of the Conservative Party, friend of Royalty and famed in City circles as a financial genius. He was too an undisclosed bankrupt who had secretly diverted Conservative Party money to Lloyd George's Political Fund and also to his own purposes.

The explanation for this extraordinary promotion was, like Farquhar's undisclosed bankruptcy, quite shortly revealed. Farquhar had refused to sign a cheque for £20,000 drawn on his Trust account. The reason was obvious. The cupboard was bare. Inquiry led to further disclosures. £200,000 which the first Lord Astor[1] had given to Farquhar had been misappropriated. £80,000 had been paid to Lloyd George's personal Political Fund and according to the confession of the noble Earl £40,000 had been given to the King for one of his charities, or so said the Treasurer. The remaining £80,000, which Farquhar claimed had gone to the Tories, could not be traced.

The Treasurer was dismissed from his office and called to his Fathers all in the space of six months. His fortune had vanished and also his prestige in the West End as a friend of the Royal Family, and in the City as

---

[1] Lord Astor had been called to the House of Lords in 1916 as a Baron and promoted to Viscount in 1917. He died in 1919.

a burning and shining light in finance.[1] Shortly before this call to his Fathers, the new Earl was invited to dinner by Lord Birkenhead. There and then the bolting Tory Ministers, Balfour, Chamberlain and Horne, proposed to Farquhar that they should be regarded as the continuing Tory hierarchy, and the Treasurer's funds should be put at their disposal. The plan failed and the truth was—there were no funds. Horace had spent the lot.

The distribution of Lloyd George's departing honours was announced four days before the election that turned out the old and brought in the new. The press had reported that Marquis Curzon would get a Dukedom and Viscount Birkenhead would get an Earldom. Birkenhead did. Curzon didn't. The Marquis had changed sides, thus losing his chance of the coveted honour which never came his way. Several supporters of Lloyd George arose from the back benches of the House of Commons and made their way through the long corridor to the House of Make Believe. Salvidge did pretty well. He got a place on the roll of Privy Councillors out of his attachment and devotion to Lloyd George. Then he turned round and worked for Bonar Law in the month of November as generously and enthusiastically as he had served Lloyd George in the month of October. Hope for the future was "like the glimmering taper's light". Winston Churchill's name adorned the list as a Companion of Honour, along with the far-famed Dr. Jowett, Congregational Divine, minister to Westminster.

At ten past six, Bonar Law arrived at the Palace. There, he agreed to form a Government, subject to his being selected as Leader by the Party meeting.

[1] See Appendices: 59, George Younger to Bonar Law, January 15th, 1923; 60, Bonar Law to Lord Fitzalan, January 24th, 1923, and 61, Lord Fitzalan to Bonar Law, January 26th, 1923.

The Coalition had ended. It might be said—the Coalition had been brought to an end by a nimble monkey in a cage in the garden of Alexander, King of the Greeks. For the monkey bit the King—who died.

In consequence Venizelos, the Greek Prime Minister, was banished.

In consequence the French Government withdrew its support from the Greek Army and made a treaty with the Turks providing them with arms and supplies.

In consequence the Turks stood up against the British Government.

In consequence Lloyd George decided to go to war.

In consequence he lost the support of the Conservative Party.

And in consequence he fell.

> For the want of a nail, the shoe was lost.
> For the want of a shoe, the horse was lost.
> For the want of a horse, the rider was lost.
> For the want of a rider, the battle was lost.
> For the want of a battle, the kingdom was lost.
> And all for want of a horseshoe-nail.

"The King sent for Bonar Law." It was the second time in eight years. On the first occasion he stood down in favour of Lloyd George. On the second occasion he succeeded that statesman.

For me, of course, the sudden reversal of events brought the joy of new opportunities to secure the political objectives to which I had dedicated my public life. But there was also present a deep source of regret in the severance of association in politics with Lloyd George. I valued his friendship. I admired his strength, his courage, his high endurance.

Naturally, the war mentality was strong in him. Do not suppose that I criticised him for being filled with the emotions that misled him. I was too well aware of what he had accomplished. He had been through the long, pitiless crisis of the war from 1914 to 1918 when, by his own efforts, he had rallied the nation to face courageously the terrible military reverses in France, the frightening submarine campaign which threatened to cut off our food supplies, the niggling air raids on London which demoralised some portion of the population, and resulted in the popular cry of "Bomb Berlin" which harassed his Government.

He was hampered and vexed by the hostility of the Generals, particularly Robertson, Chief of Staff, and Haig, Commander-in-Chief. The King protected the Generals, and showed that he wanted to get rid of his Prime Minister, though afraid to strike lest a General Election should confirm Lloyd George in office.

Through these days and nights I saw Lloyd George continuously. Every depressing influence he encountered and surmounted. Some ex-Ministers who had served in Asquith's Government, and whose influence Lloyd George felt every day, became complete defeatists. Others, who had been Lloyd George's faithful colleagues through the years, joined, some furtively, some openly, the Lansdowne movement for an agreed peace, which would in effect be a surrender to the enemy. It was in these hours of trial almost beyond human endurance that Lloyd George's leadership shone so bright and so clear that he must remain for ever in our annals the pillar of a cloud by day and by night a pillar of fire.

The closing incident of the drama of the great war leader was a display of strength which was an extra-ordinary example of weakness. War on Turkey with the possibility of war with France too. Whatever may have been the motives of Lloyd George, the only possible benefit to himself would have been a united Coalition in the face of the enemy. Many of his followers deserted him at this hour because they believed his real object and purpose was that of personal advantage. I did not accept the view that this or any similar objective was the goal of the Prime Minister. Instead the mistaken display of strength after months of weakness appeared to be the real reason for the final schemes which brought to utter failure and complete oblivion the glittering career of the great Prime Minister. He carried all before him in the first German War. He led us to victory and his strength was our shield. He gave us peace. His Treaty of Versailles, if carried out, would have given us a long peace, and certainly protection against a second German War during our time, and possibly throughout the century.

The Party crisis was over—but not really. Forthwith excitement gave way to anxiety. Could Bonar Law win the General Election? Had Austen Chamberlain been right when he said that only a Coalition could win a majority over the Labour Party? Could any man in politics set up a Government without the help of Lloyd George?

The new Prime Minister's opponents had no doubt of the answers. They were certain that Lloyd George and only Lloyd George could appeal with success to the constituencies. How could such a man as Bonar Law, who for years had been holding the stirrup iron so that Lloyd George might more conveniently mount the steed, hope not only to secure the return of all constituencies held by Conservatives in the dying Parliament but to gain an additional twenty-five seats, without which he would not have a Parliamentary majority? It was in their opinion a foolish supposition. And the group of ex-Ministers who had been defeated at the Carlton Club in the morning were in high spirits in the afternoon. Bonar Law's Government would be just a company of caretakers—in for a month perhaps, and then compelled to turn to Lloyd George and to them for help against MacDonald, the leader of the tiresome Socialists.

The crash of Bonar Law seemed to these men a certainty, the return of Lloyd George inevitable. Had not Bonar Law himself declared a short while before that Lloyd George, if he wanted to, could be Prime Minister for life? Well, Birkenhead, Churchill and their friends would now show that Bonar Law had been right. They would bring Lloyd George back— more powerful than ever. Bonar Law they would treat with respect and even with favour. He and his circle would all be given places, and important places, in the Lloyd George coach. But the old gang were the bold gang. And the triumvirate of Lloyd George, Birkenhead and Churchill would soon be taking up the load which Bonar Law could not carry.

That was the picture of the Coalitionist side on the afternoon of October 19th. There was no sense of defeat in the Lloyd George camp, only of delay. Back they would come, stronger than ever—the proven indispensable.

Altogether different were the emotions of the victor of the morning. Bonar Law was plunged in gloom. He had not wanted the Premiership. Events had compelled him to the position. He disliked the idea of opposing former friends. He conjured up imaginary accusations of bad faith. Since there was no alternative he would run a straight and honest race, but it seemed to him very likely that his mount would throw him possibly before the winning-post was reached. Twenty-five seats in addition to the present constituencies held by the Conservative Party. Twenty-five seats were a lot to win. And there was neither confidence nor joy at future prospects in Bonar Law's house in Onslow Gardens.

Lloyd George and Bonar Law
"We twa ha'e paidl't i' the burn"

The Cabinet of Noblemen—seven Peers, four Baronets and Knights

But the burden must be shouldered, the appointed task carried through. Bonar Law must start at once to form his Government.

Gloom and foreboding in the Leader of the victors— strange indeed. The ranks of former Ministers who had been defeated were rejoicing at their future prospects. The triumphant Leader of the Tories looked on the future with pessimism.

Now came the task of forming the Bonar Law Ministry. No invitation was given to any of the Conservative Ministers who had stood by the side of Lloyd George. And, I am bound to say, none was sought.

Where would the new Prime Minister find a Chancellor of the Exchequer? McKenna, a life-long Liberal? He had a high standing in politics and a big position in the City. Would he join? Bonar Law sent for him, meeting at the house of his son-in-law Sykes. McKenna declined the offer. He gave me two reasons for his decision: (1) He did not believe that the Conservatives under Bonar Law could win an independent majority; was he then to endure all the tempest of an election in order to become Chancellor for a day?; (2) Failing an independent majority, he wished to negotiate a Coalition between Asquith and Bonar Law, thus eliminating the danger of a return to power of Lloyd George and his associates. He enlarged on this argument by declaring that if he accepted office from Bonar Law in advance he would be hampered in his relations and limited in his influence with Asquith and the Asquithian Liberals.

Socially and intellectually Asquith considered himself above Bonar Law and Bonar Law held to the same opinion. No doubt rightly on many counts. Asquith read widely and well; Bonar Law confined himself to detective stories and tales of mystery. When he became

Leader I presented him with a collection of histories and biographies selected for me by Tim Healy. Bonar Law said, "If I must read your books to equip myself as a competent Leader of the Party, then I would rather be an incompetent Leader and I prefer to resign." The detective stories were not displaced. Yet the same Bonar Law had studied Carlyle in his youth and constantly drew upon the Scottish historian for illustration and example.

McKenna, after the election, asked Bonar Law, "If you had failed to get a clear majority, would you have been willing to make a coalition with Asquith?" "No," said Bonar Law, "not through any lack of respect or regard for Asquith; but the Tory Party out of office for a time would not have suffered on that account."

It came to me as a surprise that McKenna should refuse the office. He desired very much to return to public life. He afterwards accepted an offer of the same office from Baldwin. In fact, it is clear that if McKenna could have been persuaded at the time that victory would rest with the followers of Bonar Law, he would have joined the Ministry. In that case he might have been Bonar Law's successor. The whole course of political history would have been diverted.

When McKenna refused the place, Baldwin was selected as the Chancellor of the Exchequer. He had no hesitation in accepting this high office though he had strongly approved of the offer to McKenna.

Other offices were parcelled out in the usual way. Many seekers were disappointed. None was over-pleased.

It was from L. S. Amery that Bonar Law received the suggestion that Neville Chamberlain should be offered a place. Bonar Law gladly concurred. For the name of Chamberlain would add strength to the new Administration. To his surprise, Neville Chamberlain willingly accepted the office of Postmaster-General.

It was a happy moment for me. Empire Free Trade on the way. Only one more river to cross. The General Election. Then Glory Hallelujah. But my happiness was shortly and suddenly blown to bits like rock on a hillside under a charge of dynamite.

And I was plunged into despair and misery. The tragedy was launched by Lord Derby. True I had taken such detailed precautions to divert any trouble from his Lordship. Every argument had been used to persuade Derby to support our Empire programme. So I took care to have the last word at the moment he went into Bonar Law's room. Haig wrote, "Derby . . . like the feather pillow, bears the marks of the last person who has sat upon him." Haig's pillow failed me. Instead of triumph or even a stalemate, complete defeat was the result of that fatal interview which took place after ten o'clock at night on Thursday, October 19th, following the Carlton Club meeting. Bonar Law opened up the conversation by suggesting tariffs on imports including agricultural products. And as his Lordship was reputed to be a patron of agriculture, though with no farming experience, this bait seemed attractive. The new Prime Minister added that the revenue would be used for reducing the price of beer. It was my thought that Lord Derby's friend and political manager would swallow this concession like a glass of lager, for Salvidge was a brewer. Derby made his position quite clear. He would not tolerate Food Taxes and if proposed, he must at once retire.[1]

Lord Salisbury was of the same mind and with clear expression of the same intention other Ministers took

[1] See Appendix 62, *Lord Derby* by Randolph Churchill, pp. 454 and 455.

fright at the threatened departure of these important colleagues.

A committee of Derby, Curzon, Amery, Douglas Hogg[1] and Cave[2] prepared the election programme. It was on October 20th that Bonar Law was handed the fatal document. They recommended that the election should be fought on the simple issue of "a change of government". No Tariffs. No Food Taxes. The recommendation was unanimous.

That Amery, the constant and faithful advocate of Empire, should have agreed to it I own amazed me. Surprisingly in his account he tells that he took the initiative and that "all agreed, some of them, I suspect, relieved at my moderation".

Then Bonar Law informed me of the disaster. He would accept the recommendation. I had climbed beyond the clouds into bright sunshine when sudden darkness swept over me. And the darkness was very dark. What would I do? What could I do? Faithful to my friend I must stay. He had tried, and failed. There would be no recriminations from me.

In going in and coming out after a short space of time with Bonar Law, Derby had done this Empire, now referred to as a Commonwealth, and the whole world an irreparable sum total of harm. Misguided, it is true, but all the worse for that.

With the Government formed and the policy fixed, the appeal to the country was launched. Mr. Lloyd George and his Conservative supporters adopted election tactics which gave every appearance of meeting with

---

[1] Mighty lawyer who appeared for the first time in the House of Commons and on the Front Bench. He was a Parliamentary success and for many a day possibly a future Prime Minister.
[2] Lord Chancellor.

success.[1] They hoped that their supporters would be returned to Westminster in sufficient strength to compel the new Administration to rely upon their votes. Birkenhead and his friends counted confidently on securing this position of advantage for a mixed Conservative and Coalition Liberal following. Their strength was greatly increased by a decision taken by Bonar Law to do nothing to encourage contests against his ex-colleagues in the Lloyd George Ministry.

This immunity from official attack was to cover not only the Conservative ex-Ministers who clung to Lloyd George, but also the Coalition Liberal colleagues, including C. A. McCurdy who was Lloyd George's right-hand man, his Chief Whip, and Mr. Churchill. Those who had been Under Secretaries were also included in the favoured list. Sir George Younger approved of the arrangement, declaring that he wished to attract as much Coalition Liberal support as possible in those seats where Conservative candidates faced the Asquith Liberals.

Now this whole arrangement savoured too much of the novel "A Change in the Cabinet". It was a case of the old Coalition all over again under a new name. The critics would declare that nothing had happened except "Changing the Guard". The old bad policies would be continued. The sins of Mr. Lloyd George and his colleagues would be visited on Bonar Law and the new Administration. It was certain that Asquith and his candidates, along with the Labour Party, would pin on to the coat-tails of Bonar Law and his friends the unpopularity attendant upon the last days of Lloyd George. Here was Bonar Law with his lenient survey

[1] Lloyd George's Tory ex-Cabinet friends and out of office: Birkenhead, Lord Chancellor; Balfour, Lord President of the Council; Horne, Chancellor of the Exchequer; Chamberlain, Lord Privy Seal; Worthington-Evans, Secretary of State for War; Lee, First Lord of the Admiralty; Crawford, Transport and First Commissioner of Works; and others.

of Coalition politics and his kindly consideration for Coalition leaders helping to reinforce the charges.

At once I detached myself from the Central Office policy, and on my own authority[1] launched candidates in some constituencies where Lloyd George supporters were being given a free run. In many divisions local Conservative Associations made it unnecessary to take any measures. Included were most of those who had served on the Front Bench with Lloyd George. In some cases I paid election expenses. Here and there I took the course of arousing local sympathies and giving countenance to local efforts. The plan worked very well. Out of fifty-six seats where Conservative candidates were launched against Lloyd George's party men, only two of the Lloyd George candidates were successful. These hybrid Liberals, when they faced Conservative opposition, broke out everywhere in angry indignation, and with denunciations. They did not blame Bonar Law himself for their misfortunes. They believed, rightly, that he wished to protect them.

At The Vineyard in Hurlingham Road another meeting, attended by Birkenhead and Captain Guest, Minister for Air in the fallen Government, was disastrous to old and treasured friendships. They complained that though Bonar Law had declared he would not favour or support Tory opposition to any persons who served in the last Ministry, there were signs of a developing movement of opposition in several directions. Would I pledge myself to observe the Bonar Law promise? Their colleagues had agreed if no opposition was launched against them that Lloyd George followers would give full support to Tory candidates in constituencies where there were no Coalition Liberal candidates—in fact an offer of a "saw off".

[1] I told Sir George Younger of my intention.

There was nothing doing. Tory candidates would be launched against the lot. "What! Against Churchill too?" Yes, against Churchill too. The visitors became angry. How could I go against my old and trusted friends? The reply that the public interest overruled friendships brought from Guest the declaration, "You don't deserve any friends." Birkenhead joined in. The going was rough. The argument was bitter and acrimonious. Others in the house listened with surprise and curiosity to the violence of the language and the cries of unrestrained hostility. Presently Birkenhead and Guest departed. It was long before friendly relations were restored.

At this moment I made another futile attempt to persuade Bonar Law to adopt a progressive Empire policy —to lay it down as his platform. He could not be drawn. He feared too much the hostility of the Tory Free Traders and the evil effects on them of a Food Tax. Besides, he had many determined Free Traders in his Government, including Derby and Salisbury, all against Food Tax, which they called "Stomach Tax".

I then asked for a declaration banning our costly adventures in Mesopotamia as an indication of our intention to withdraw from the meddle and muddle in Near East politics. In Mesopotamia we were carrying a mandate of the League of Nations at immense cost to ourselves. In one year our expenses there ran to more than £40 million. There was no prospect of getting any trade from Mesopotamia. There was nothing for us in the occupation but worry and trouble. The land was far distant. It was not easily defended. And it was not worth defending, for it was a barren desert incapable of commercial or agricultural development. Its frontier was constantly being menaced by the Turks. In fact we had given a hostage to our enemies in Mesopotamia.

Bonar Law appeared to be impressed by what I said on this subject. So I reduced my recommendations to writing. In the end he declined to take action, declaring that he must have time to consider his programme in relation to Mesopotamia and the East after he had had the advantage of considering the whole situation while in office.

One splendid result flowed almost immediately from the new spirit of asperity that had been introduced into the campaign. Birkenhead and Lloyd George assailed the Bonar Law Ministry on every platform. Lloyd George described Bonar Law as "Honest to the verge of simplicity" and in attacking the Government programme said: "It is not a policy, it is a yawn."

Birkenhead spoke of "The Second Eleven". Of Sir George Younger, who had announced that he was not standing again, the ex-Lord Chancellor had said, "When the tempest raged, and when the Captain would naturally be on the bridge, I would not give any particular encouragement to the Cabin Boy to seize the helm. And I am more than ever of that opinion when the Cabin Boy has announced that he does not intend to make another voyage." Then again during the campaign Birkenhead declared: "Since the day when the proverbial Frog swelled itself up in rivalry with the Bull until it burst, no man had ever been in such grave physical danger as Sir George Younger was."

Bonar Law reacted vigorously. He spoke out in condemnation of the Lloyd George Government which had just been destroyed. He criticised with vigour their policy in the Near East. He declared that we had been threatened with war on account of it. He criticised the speeches of Lloyd George, which showed an attitude hostile to France and Turkey. He condemned in general the extent to which Lloyd George had embroiled us in foreign affairs.

Under the changed attitude of asperity, the situation improved greatly and our prospects of victory at the polls were enhanced every day.

It is true we had inadequate newspaper support. The *Daily Mail* would do nothing for us. Lord Rothermere appeared to be holding the scales. He regarded himself as a timekeeper or a referee, giving equal space to Lloyd George and his colleagues, along with Bonar Law and his friends. I was able to persuade him to allow me to write articles in his papers in support of Bonar Law. But nothing more could be got from him just then. Later on, however, we were to get timely and valuable support.

As the day of trial drew near, the anxieties of those who had put these grave issues to the test increased and multiplied. And then Election Day was upon us. It was November 15th. The big guns of oratory all up and down the country had fired their last salvoes. Most of the more powerful pieces of election ordnance had been directed against the Tories. Lloyd George himself was unexcelled in the demagogic art; and Birkenhead too with his gibe that Bonar Law was leading a team of "second class brains".

Opposed to all this oratory, all this talent, was only the plain honesty of Bonar Law and the solid-seeming arguments of the persuasive voice of a newcomer to the big league of politics—Stanley Baldwin. For the first time in his career Baldwin had been called upon to play a major part in an election. On previous occasions he had been no more than one of the rank and file who confined their activities to their own and perhaps a few neighbouring constituencies. In Bewdley, his constituency, he could be assured of a friendly welcome and dutiful applause. But now, in a new position, as second man in the Government, he had had to venture forth throughout the land. He spoke with success. He said nothing sensational. He made no spectacular promises. He went before the electorate as a plain business man representing a plain business Government out to do a solid job of work. And the electorate liked it.

But the campaign was all over now. The fate of the politicians rested with the men and women who were making their way to the polling booths.

The Coalition Liberals had launched 131 candidates in carefully picked seats. They believed that at least 100 of them would be elected. If so, it would be the end of Bonar Law. The new Premier himself was not quite sure of his own position. In Bonar Law's camp that day all was nervous anxiety.

All through those voting hours there was no time for thought—no opportunity for reflection. Nothing but work. The tasks might be small and the results negligible, but the sense of duty was uppermost in our minds. I spent my day taking voters to the polls and making sure that all in my immediate circle who supported Bonar Law candidates went to vote. That sort of task has a peculiar reaction. You find yourself spending hour after hour dragging out voters for a candidate whose seat is safe and safe over. Yet as your ardour grows, these tasks multiply. The time limit set on your activities results in a spirit of feverish haste and impetuous activity. There never was an election, up to 1945, when I did not perform these duties and never a day after the election when I did not upbraid myself when exhaustion followed my zeal.

That night, when the polls were closed, the reaction set in. I sat through a late dinner with my family and

Mr. and Mrs. McKenna, beset by fears, distressed by foreboding and filled with anxieties. Shortly the election results were to roll in. The first return that reached us was from Oxford where the sitting Conservative Member, who had held the seat for years, was overwhelmingly defeated.

After the Oxford defeat, the results came in slowly, slowly. How could we get nearer to the returns? How could we manage more quickly to have the results at our disposal? The *Daily Express* office would be a better centre. So off we went, only to find the editorial staff gloomy and depressed. The results were being marked up on blackboards. Forebodings of disaster distressed me.

It looked as though we would have a hard passage, although it was perfectly plain that Lloyd George and his colleagues would be of small influence and of little consequence in the new Parliament. There was a certain morbid satisfaction in being relieved, at any rate, of a menace which had been uppermost in our minds for days and even weeks. As the night wore on there came grave doubt of Tory victory. In the boroughs the Labour Party was winning many seats.

Meantime the Prime Minister sat in his own office in Downing Street. He was still living in his house in Onslow Gardens, but the Downing Street office that night was the centre of activities. Here were gathered the intimate friends of Bonar Law—the colleagues anxiously waiting for the results, and the personal friends too.

A curious wave of depression and anxiety swept over the Prime Minister. He appeared to fear most of all his own defeat in Glasgow, and he repeated over and over the difficulty his Government would have to face if, after the election, the Prime Minister himself should have no seat in the House of Commons. Who then would lead when the House met?

When he was asked if he had any doubt about the victory of the Government, he seemed to show little confidence, and he was in despair about his own personal position. His reasoning was this—the boroughs were going badly. Could the balance be redressed by the counties? But the boroughs going so badly meant that Glasgow would show results unfavourable to him.

The hours dragged on. Midnight struck, then one o'clock. At last, at two in the morning the Glasgow result was announced. Bonar Law was in—his majority 2,500. A fall of 10,000 and a minority vote taking Labour and Liberal votes together into account. At once the Prime Minister went off to his own home wondering what the next day would bring, quite convinced that the Government would not get a clear majority. What would the return of tomorrow bring? Good fortune? Bad luck? Davidson and others believed in good fortune. Bonar Law led the pessimists.

And the optimists were justified in their predictions. The next morning the results from the counties began to roll in and the brightening prospects, as the tale of the Tory victories was unfolded, widened through the day until in the evening triumph was assured—absolute and complete. Agriculture had spoken. And we rejoiced.

On election night Lloyd George, Birkenhead, and several other ex-Tory Ministers gathered together at Sir Philip Sassoon's house in Park Lane along with intimate supporters, including wives. The dinner was good, and the arrangements for the receipt of returns admirably worked out. Sir Philip, who was Parliamentary Private Secretary to Lloyd George, was a wonderful provider. Churchill had said of him, when asked why Sassoon had got one of his many jobs,

"When you are leaving on a long journey for an un-
known destination, it is a good plan to attach a restaurant
car at the tail of the train."

That evening their host's dining car was very merry.
The brandy flowed around and around. Then the news
from the constituencies also flowed. Gaiety departed.
And gloom entered.

Sir William Orpen, painter of portraits and writer of
amusing verse and letters, was also present. He described the scene in his own style:

> Gee it was late—that raw black night
> And we were almost all quite tight
> "Mid beauty" and the flowing wine
> With clouds of nicotine divine
> We sat
> And watched
> And waited
> Till lo! The small machine began
> To "Tic, Tic." Then the little band
> Ran smoothly out in Philip's hand
> Curling, curling like a snake[1]
> Till Philip's hand began to shake
> Impossible!
> 'Twas like the writing on the wall
> That told of old King Nib's sad fall
> When in the dawn we learnt it all
> Old England's choice, we clearly saw
> Was Max!
> I beg pardon! Mister B. Law.

(Copyrighted in Ireland or any other Free State)

Little did Sassoon's revellers—who were plunged into
despair that stormy night—know that I too had suffered

---

[1] Special ticker machines with tape had been installed in Sir Philip's
dining-room.

my day of defeat and humiliation over the Empire Policy. The Earl of Derby, the Marquis of Salisbury, the Marquis Curzon and my own colleague and Empire fighter Amery had all joined together in giving me what the Americans call "the air". But I made no complaint, no yattering, no tears or lamentations. Orpen's line about Max was therefore not even good satire. But my spirit was not broken, I would try again. And I did. And I failed again.

The results when the last returns were in gave Bonar Law and his Conservatives a clear majority of over 70 seats, more than Lloyd George's total of Coalition Liberals with only 57 seats. Labour and Socialist members with more than 140 seats became the Official Opposition. It was a tough result for Lloyd George.

Now the election had been fought with much bitterness. There were hard feelings between supporters of Lloyd George and his Tory colleagues on the one side, and of Bonar Law and his friends on the other. The leaders made tough speeches. But when most of Lloyd George's colleagues, including Churchill, Greenwood, Walters, Kellaway and Freddie Guest, lost their seats, much fiercer resentment was voiced, with charges of bad faith. Lord Birkenhead was responsible for many witty comments, thus increasing the asperities of party politics already too bitter and violent.

Austen Chamberlain was an exception. He did not nourish or cultivate animosities and hostilities. Besides, during the years of co-operation with Lloyd George, they never became close friends. Their association after the defeat was not intimate. When Lloyd George was talking of Liberal reunion, Chamberlain made his position clear. He also would move off in the opposite direction.

As long as the Coalition Government existed Chamberlain's loyalty to Lloyd George never faltered. Leadership, popularity, livelihood, all thrown away in the hour of trial at the Carlton Club meeting, when men were counted. At that moment of crisis it was not easy to judge Chamberlain at his true worth. But as the years pass, the consciousness of his grand character, and steadfast devotion to honour and integrity is made manifest to all those who worked with him. "Excellence of character rather than capacity," said Lloyd George.

Others would engage in ordinary conversation with their old colleagues who had joined Bonar Law, but hatreds and animosities persisted. Lord Birkenhead had formerly given deep offence to Sir Robert Houston, the Lancashire Member with a red beard, plainly dyed, bright and ever brilliant in hue, by referring to him as "the original dye-hard". Now Baldwin spoke of Birkenhead, who was given to good living, as "the original drink-hard."[1]

It was when the Coalition group realised the fullness of their disaster that bitterness against the men who had contrived their downfall broke forth uncontrolled. They had dreamed such bright dreams of their return to power. Now they saw themselves for five long years perhaps deprived of any share in the conduct of affairs. They turned in fury against those who had driven them into the wilderness. Against Bonar Law they held their fire. He had not contrived their defeat. And besides he was a man too deeply respected, too obviously sincere of purpose. Baldwin was another matter. He was a man they declared who had betrayed the citadel from within. They would not lightly forgive him. But the man against whom at this moment their attacks were above all directed, their bitter jests discharged, was me.

[1] Carson, when criticising Birkenhead early in 1922, had said that he preferred diehards to livehards.

It was known that I did not seek a place in the Government. The inference was clear. I wanted power without responsibility. I wanted to fill that position altogether alien to the traditions of British politics, so it was said. And falsely said. The charge against me was that I wished to be a power behind the Prime Minister. Such was the burden of the attacks made upon me at this time. And it must be added that their anxieties and opposition were shared by one whom I had not harmed. Stanley Baldwin was becoming anxious. He was number two in the Government but who was to be number two in Bonar Law's private counsels? Was it to be Beaverbrook? If so, there would be trouble ahead. Differing from the Coalitionists in all else, Baldwin agreed with them when they cried out against what they thought would be my influence in the new Government. From that day of conflict the mistaken opinion persists that I seek after power without responsibility. It is not true. There have been times when I have taken too much responsibility.

My first conversation with Bonar Law after the victory took place at Cherkley, my home near Leatherhead. I praised Bonar Law's judgment and discretion. The public had shown strong approval and immense confidence. The way was clear, the path was plain. He must now determine his policy and follow it resolutely. He would, I knew, suffer reverses. He would encounter difficult situations. Sometimes the course of discretion would appear to be best.

He spoke of the difficulties standing in his way. He foresaw many troubles, and much worry. Then he emphasised his Near Eastern policy. He had come to power on its success. He must be driven from office on its failure. The country wanted peace and he must give it peace. He knew the temper of the people and that war was averted by popular will. He said that he must deal with the French and with their Prime Minister, Poincaré. Relations were strained. The quarrels of Lord Curzon and Poincaré during the last Administration added to his difficulties, since he must continue to carry Curzon as his own Foreign Secretary.

For Curzon had deserted Lloyd George and Lloyd George's Conservative colleagues and joined the Bonar Law movement in plenty of time. It is true that he failed to escape charges of double-dealing when he deserted his old friends. It is true that he was looked on with doubt and misgivings by some of the new colleagues he made. But there he was, an impeccable Conservative, a great aristocrat, a hallmarked Tory leader, born in the purple, believed to be in possession of a big American bank account.[1] Just the sort of material with which the Conservative shop window has always been dressed.

Bonar Law need not use him but the habit in Tory circles of always selecting the Curzon type is too strong. So there was his lordship, who had been pro-Greek and pro-Turk, pro-Lloyd George and now for Bonar Law! At the moment he was on the side of his Prime Minister. But not for long. The day of betrayal will come when Bonar Law is least able to resist betrayal.

Bonar Law looked out upon a stormy scene. Troubles were many. His burdens were heavy. I mentioned the Empire and the prospects of an Empire policy. I reminded Bonar Law that the Imperial Conference would meet in a few months and I developed once more, in conversation, the plan that has since come to be known as Empire Free Trade. The policy that would provide for unrestricted Free Trade between Britain and the

---

[1] There was no big bank account. It was said that Curzon was penniless at his death and owed the Government £80,000 in tax.

Crown Colonies, a partnership with the Dominions. A limited partnership, it is true, but as near as may be approaching the great ideal of a united Empire, with all the hopes and all the expectations of an endless and uninterrupted peace.

His spirits rose. He looked into the future more hopefully. How much can be done? How far can he go? He has no mandate, it is true, to impose taxes on foreign foodstuffs—or even duties on foreign manufactured goods. The making of a new platform has many difficulties and presents much trouble. But it is a constructive programme. And it is a programme for which Bonar Law himself has striven during his whole parliamentary career. He has advocated it consistently and continuously. He had seen it upheld by a triumphant and delirious Party meeting when he became the Conservative Leader. He had seen it destroyed in 1913 by the timidity and the folly of his own supporters.

Now he is a Party leader in power. Now he is the choice of the country. The first Minister. Installed by public acclamation.

What high hopes! What great expectations! What mighty prospects! What glamorous adventures! What splendid results!

But disaster pursues us. Disaster pursues us with a step as steady as time and an appetite as keen as death.

XII

EVENTIDE

Christmas was drawing near. I was called to dinner at
10 Downing Street by Bonar Law. I was told that the
discussion would turn on the situation facing us over
Germany.

France and Britain are now at issue over German
reparations. The British point of view—that is the point
of view of Bonar Law—is that Germany must be granted
a final settlement with a moratorium in order that she
may re-establish her credit. If this is not done, the
Germans will collapse. They will declare for bankruptcy. The French, however, are enraged at what they
regard as Germany's fraudulent bankruptcy. They
demand solid guarantees of future payments and are
preparing to march into the Ruhr valley and hold it, as
a pledge, along with its coal output.

Lord Grey is at Downing Street that evening. Bonar
Law has asked him there to talk on the position that is
developing over the Ruhr. He and Lord Grey discuss
foreign policy at length.

I did not make any record of the conversation at the
time, but my recollection is that Lord Grey supported
Bonar Law strongly in the course he was taking in
relation to France. Just before we gave over, I raised
the issue of Food Taxes for the next election. Lord Grey
rejected any such venture. Stomach Taxes, he said,
and certain destruction at the polls.

After dinner we played bridge. Lord Grey was troubled by his eyesight but he managed to play, though slowly and with difficulty.

On my departure from Downing Street that evening, although Lord Grey had spoken strongly against Food Taxes, I felt that Bonar Law was making real progress in the intention to launch an Empire policy. Moreover, I rejoiced to see him in better spirits. The dinner had done him good. It had helped him in the decisions he was making.

At Christmas time we were together again. Bonar Law came to stay at my house at Leatherhead. He was oppressed by the difficulties of our relations with the French and determined not to be dragged at the wheel of their chariot. The divergence of view between Bonar Law and the French Government was weighing heavily on his mind during the Christmas days which he spent with me.

His illness was not apparent, save only in his voice which for a time he lost entirely. And he never complained. But for him Christmas was grey or even black. As usual when he was worried he would eat almost nothing but milk puddings and rice, swallowing his meals with even more than his customary rapidity. And as soon as the last mouthful was eaten, he would light his cigar. This haste to be finished with eating, and desire to begin smoking was an invariable sign with him of nervous tension. Plainly he was feeling considerable anxiety about the Ruhr prospects.

He was much interested in a game of chess which his son, Richard Law, and Lord Castlerosse were playing. As he looked down on the board he said that either of them could win if he knew anything about the game. Then he went on to make a comparison between nations and chess players. He thought that either France or

Germany could win the game that was going on at that time on the chequerboard of Europe. But both France and Germany were playing badly.

After Christmas was over, Bonar Law returned again to the strife and turmoil of Downing Street. He was not happy. His tasks were bearing heavily on him. His responsibilities oppressed him and he had become gloomy and sad.

After spending a few days in town he set out for Paris, to carry on negotiations with Poincaré's Government. But it was soon plain that there was no reconciling the British and the French points of view. On January 2nd, Bonar Law tabled his proposals—for the re-establishment of Germany's credit by means of a final settlement. On January 4th, the conference broke down. Within a week, the French had occupied the Ruhr.

But Britain was not involved in that occupation. Britain, thanks to the action of Bonar Law, had cut herself away from the occupation policy of France. It was a long step.

Meanwhile the *Daily Mail* was making a stand for France and the French point of view. It was carrying on a strong propaganda on behalf of a continuance of association with France. "Hats off to France" was its slogan.

On the second day of the New Year I arranged with Lord Rothermere to meet at The Vineyard. Up till then he had done nothing to support Bonar Law. What is more, he was being urged to join Lord Birkenhead and the rebel Conservatives in a general campaign against the Government.

I opened up to him very frankly, asking support for Bonar Law. I dwelt on the prospects of great events, immense developments, splendid adventures ahead, on lines that would alter the whole status of the Empire.

I got encouragement. I felt sure that he would join us before long.

So there were prospects that the New Year, 1923, would be our year, the Empire year. That was the hope held up before those who had faith and confidence, who have never faltered in adversity or defeat. In the late autumn of the year there would be an Imperial Conference. From that Conference we shall gain a foundation for a structure on which to build the Economic Empire.

Radiant and full of promise, the year 1923 opens before us!

Bonar Law came back from Paris. I met him. I am in a position to say to him: We have every reason to hope for increased newspaper support. I tell him that it looks as if Lord Rothermere and I can make a united front in support of him with a vigorous newspaper campaign.

By this time the Empire policy is uppermost in Bonar Law's mind. He is turning with increasing frequency to the conception of an Empire Customs Union, a limited partnership of necessity in the case of the Dominions, a full partnership in the case of the Crown Colonies.

He tells me that he is considering methods. The plans will involve several decisions of the highest moment: an Imperial Conference in the autumn, followed perhaps next year by an election with the hated Food Taxes in the forefront of the programme. Conservatives believed that these taxes had wrecked them in the past.

It would be necessary to lead the Party with patience to an acceptance of the risks of an appeal to the country on a policy which had three times suffered defeat at the hands of the electorate—the policy of taxes on foreign foodstuffs, formerly rejected, and that almost unanimously, by a tired, weary, beaten Party in 1913. It was rejected at a General Election in 1906, again in January 1910, and once more in December 1910. Then in the month of January 1913 the Conservative Members of the House of Commons rose in revolt against the foreign Food Taxes. They were driven to it by Lord Northcliffe and the campaign in his newspapers, supported by Lord Derby who was, in fact, at that time a Conservative Free Trader.

When the storm began to beat on us, I invited Bonar Law to Ashton-under-Lyne which I represented in the House of Commons. At a meeting where there was a crowded audience and an immense array of press reporters Bonar Law hoisted the foreign Food Tax flag to the top of the mast. That was what precipitated the rebellion of the Conservative Members. I had hoped that Bonar Law's speech would forestall the mutiny but instead it brought the mutiny to a head. When Bonar Law found that his followers would go no further, he proposed to resign. A memorial was presented to him signed by all the Conservative M.P.s, and he agreed to resume the Leadership. I said "all Conservative M.P.s", but four names did not appear on the memorial. Mine was one of them. It had to be. I could not sign. That is, of course, all forgotten at this moment.

It was in mid-January, 1923, that Reginald McKenna, Keynes and I joined Bonar Law at Downing Street for dinner. The discussion turned on the claim of the Americans for settlement of British war debts to them irrespective of debt settlement to Britain by France, Italy or Russia.[1]

Britain, according to U.S.A. claims, must pay back money sent to Britain and spent by the Treasury, in part, for the specific purpose of supporting these allies France,

[1] Mr. Baldwin, the Chancellor of the Exchequer, was in Washington, and asking authority from Bonar Law to settle the debt on U.S.A. terms.

Italy and Russia. Bonar Law was convinced that the U.S. settlement without corresponding payment from Europe of their debts to Britain would result in disaster —as it did.

McKenna and Keynes supported him most vigorously. Of how Bonar Law was trapped and tricked into signing the outrageous debt settlement I hope to write in my next volume.

All our hopes and prospects were shattered by the illness of Bonar Law which claimed him for the remaining days of his life. The advantages of Bonar Law's Administration remained to benefit all mankind.

And the greatest benefit is the story of the threatened war with Turkey. Here was a crisis. The British Government was ready to take arms. An alternative leader arose. The public rallied to his support. They were determined to pursue the paths of peace. The results were swift and certain. Where we had been threatened with war, where the storm clouds had darkened the sky, we now followed paths of peace with the bright sunshine of tranquillity. And to Bonar Law we give credit for that blessed relief.

Lloyd George, when strife and hostilities resulting from the General Election had been softened by time and events, asked me for news of his former colleague and antagonist of 1922.

I knew that Bonar Law would welcome a meeting as he much regretted the breaking up of a close friendship formed during the war in the five years when they worked together. Bonar Law never doubted that Lloyd George in the hour of peril in 1916-1918 had triumphed over national doubt, discord and defeatism.[1] A lunch was arranged at The Vineyard, my house in Fulham.

[1] See Lloyd George in War and Peace in Appendix 63.

It was for me an emotional moment. Though my
loyalty was given entirely to Bonar Law, I did indeed
like my Lloyd George. It was on September 13th that
he wrote to Bonar Law.

Bron-y-de,
Churt,
Surrey
Sept. 13th, 1923

My dear Bonar,

I was very amused when Max told me last night that on your
return to the House of Commons you meant to spend the rest
of your years supporting the Government of the day in all its
difficulties. I told him that I had exactly the same design for
my own future but that when I imparted it to you my patriotic
professions were invariably received with incredulity. You were
right. I find it most difficult to be a tolerant judge of the defects
of my successors! Impartiality is a virtue that wears badly.
Mine is already in tatters. I have just written a preface to a book
in which I slang everybody with perfect impartiality. I was
delighted to see you once more & to see you looking ever so
much better than I did when I passed through a similar
experience.

We must have another meal at Max's. He was in a condition
of ribald high spirits last night.

Ever sincerely

D. Ll. G.

Here were two men who had served in the highest
office of state and each had come to an end. Bonar Law
had come to the end of his life and the shadows of death
were already gathering round him. Lloyd George had
many years to live but the shadows of decline were
gathering round him. There were to be flashes of revived
activity, moments of brilliance and an occasional false
hope of further greatness still to be achieved. But these
manifestations meant nothing. The path led inexorably

downwards. The heights were behind and the valley was ever deepening before. Lloyd George was never again to hold any public office.

Those two men of the shadows were as different as any two men could well be. Bonar Law was modest and self-effacing. He and Lloyd George had first come together in 1916. Then it was that Bonar Law, called upon to form a Government, relinquished the honour to Lloyd George. Bonar Law was content that all the public glory and the triumph should go to his colleague, whom he served with unswerving loyalty. He had never sought the first place for himself. When confronted with necessity he accepted it with reluctance and laid it down with relief. Ambition was a word in a dictionary he had never opened.

By contrast, Lloyd George was alive with ambition. He had always sought the heights—and when he grasped the last glittering prize he could not bear to let it go. In the end it was violently snatched from him. He was brilliant where Bonar Law was quiet. He was circuitous where Bonar Law was simple and direct. Gratitude meant little more to him than ambition meant to Bonar Law.

Yet here were these two different men, plainly attached to each other, talking intimately together over long-forgotten incidents and events, mostly unimportant; quarrels and disputes of 1922, altogether forgotten. They were men who had done the country the greatest service, each in his own way. In spite of their contrasting characters they respected each other and with affectionate phrases they addressed each other. They had tasted the fruits of power and felt its penalties. Now they had come to the last meeting in the eventide of understanding. They parted in an atmosphere of companionship. They were two friends destined never to meet

again. Lloyd George would recite in Welsh a favourite
quotation. His translation was:

> *News of death I get from yonder*
> *News of death brings sorrow here,*
> *In the lexicon of Heaven*
> *E'en its name will not appear.*

On a cold and cheerless morning in November 1923
Bonar Law's ashes were buried in Westminster Abbey.

ACKNOWLEDGMENTS

I acknowledge the gracious permission of Her Majesty the Queen to make use of material from the Royal Archives, Windsor Castle.

I wish also to thank Earl Baldwin of Bewdley; Margaret, Countess of Birkenhead; Viscount Brentford; The Rt. Hon. Sir Winston Churchill, K.G., O.M., C.H.; The Earl of Crawford and Balcarres, K.T., G.B.E.; The Rt. Hon. Viscount Davidson, G.C.V.O., C.H., C.B.; The Earl of Derby; The late Viscount Fitzalan of Derwent; Mrs. Gathorne Young; The Kedleston Trustees; Major John Maxse; Mrs. Terence Maxwell; Mr. R. J. Minney; Miss Judy Montagu; Mr. John Morris; Mrs. Barrie Nicoll; The Public Trustee; The Rt. Hon. the Marquis of Salisbury, K.G.; Viscountess Templewood; the late The Rt. Hon. Earl Winterton; and Viscount Younger of Leckie, for permission to publish correspondence. My thanks are also due to Frances, Countess Lloyd-George, who read the narrative, and to Margery, Viscountess Greenwood, D.B.E., Mr. A. R. M. Geddes, O.B.E., and Mr. Colm Brogan, who supplied me with helpful information, and Mr. Bill Martin for drawings of The Vineyard.

I acknowledge with thanks permission for the use of copyright material from:

Sir David Low, for permission to use his cartoon.

Mr. Randolph Churchill, M.B.E., for consent to publish extracts from his book, *Lord Derby, King of Lancashire*.

Hutchinson & Co. (Publishers) Ltd., for extracts from *My Political Life, Vol. II*, by L. S. Amery, and from *Reminiscences* by Marchioness Curzon of Kedleston, G.B.E.

Hodder & Stoughton, and Raymond Savage, for extracts from *Salvidge of Liverpool* by Stanley Salvidge.

Odhams Press for permission to quote letters from *The World Crisis, Vol. V: The Aftermath*, by Winston S. Churchill.

Charles Scribner's Sons, for permission to quote letters from *The World Crisis, Vol. V: The Aftermath*, by Winston S. Churchill (Copyright 1929 Charles Scribner's Sons; renewal copyright © 1957 Winston S. Churchill).

Miss Jean Riley and Miss Rosemary Brooks have been devoted helpers, reading and correcting errors and mistakes, and confirming quotations. And Mrs. Elton willingly undertook the tedious duty of preparing the Index.

Appendices
Index

APPENDICES

1. EDWIN MONTAGU TO LORD READING

May 12th, 1921

To anybody who understands political economy, or pretends to, nothing is so disgusting as the Anti-Dumping Bill now going through the House of Commons . . . I have got to grin and bear it, but it does disgust one with political life to know that we Liberals in the Government have got to defend this Bill and that even the Conservative leaders realise that it is ridiculous but have got to play up to their man. Asquith made the best speech yesterday that he has made since his return to the House—vigorous, humorous, incisive, splendid. I felt myself in cordial agreement with everything he said, and went dismally into the Division Lobby against him.

2. SIR GEORGE YOUNGER TO BONAR LAW

Private & Confidential

Leckie,
Gargunnock,
Stirlingshire, N.B.
2nd Jany 1921

My dear Bonar,

You spoke to me before I left about the dis-proportion of Peers in the two Party Lists of Honours, but when one comes to look through the published list it becomes a much more serious affair & there should be a proper understanding for the future on this subject.

Peers. Excluding Seaforth whose restoration is probably the work of Lady Midleton (& whose wife is rich) you have three on the P.M.'s list & only one on ours. I know nothing of the politics of Brooks Marshall, but Beardmore is & always has been a Unionist. (Incidentally I may tell you that his financial position just now isn't too sound, & no one can get money out of him. The underwriters were left with 95% of his recent issue of Notes.)

To elevate Vaughan-Davies is to put you & us in a hole, as our expectant M.P.s were all told that no Bye Election must be brought about from this cause.

Flannery,[1] for example, has been a perfect nuisance to me for weeks past, & I have always put him off with that answer.

If you set the Baron's P.C. against a Peer they have still one to the good, & with probably an interest in Seaforth as well.

Baronets. This is surely an absurdly long list, and no wonder, if he knew of it, that Stamfordham knocked our modest one severely. Excluding the two Admirals, there are 19 left, of which we got five with the greatest difficulty. I see Macmaster's name now; so if we count him, that is six.

Baden Powell, Hewitt, and Oppenheimer, are not I think Party at all but the remaining 10 are, so here you have 10 against 6.

In this 10 is Mills, chairman of Ebbw Vale, who is one of my pet candidates, & for whom I have been trying to find a seat for the last month or two, whom I mean to run on the first suitable opportunity.

This is poaching on our preserves with a vengeance, & it is by no means the first time this has happened.

There was a similar case last time & an even more glaring one in the list before that, & I have written Guest about it.

I said nothing on the previous occasions, but this kind of thing makes one's position with our own people impossible, and there must be a stopper put upon it once & for all.

He has a fellow . . .[2] on his list. This man & his friends have

---

[1] Sir James Fortescue-Flannery was a distinguished member of Parliament and had been a powerful supporter of Joseph Chamberlain. He sat in Parliament altogether for 28 years. He held a safe seat, the Maldon Division of Essex. There was no danger of a Government defeat at a by-election. He was certainly entitled to a peerage, but as a result of Coalition exigencies he died a Baronet at the age of 92.

[2] In 1918 Churchill had refused to support . . .'s claim to an honour:

Private   *Ministry of Munitions of War*
                                        *Whitehall Place, S.W.*1
                                               Dec. 9, '18
Dear Davies,

Mr. Churchill thinks he ought to let you know that he was approached on Saturday, to his great surprise, by an acquaintance who shd have known better, with a suggestion that he should procure a baronetcy for a certain . . ., and receive £5000 on delivery of the goods. Naturally the intermediary received short shrift—& Mr. Churchill thinks you may wish to make a note, to be borne in mind if the idea of any honour for Mr. . . . is mooted again.

                              Yours
                              E. M. [Eddie Marsh]

tried me hard to recommend him & have made offers so brutally frank that I made up my mind to have nothing to do with him, & showed him the cold shoulder. I suppose he has gone to Freddie & captured him.

Well, he is welcome to that acquisition, but I have written to our Chairman, Sir Alex Leith, to make it clear that we have no responsibility for this Honour. After I turned him down I was at . . . , & found that this fellow at the most critical stage of the War was discovered to be hoarding huge quantities of food, & they had him up & fined him nearly £1000.

You can understand how he has been ostracised there ever since, & I think he has left the place.

Quite a scandalous thing to honour such a man, & you will not be surprised that I have repudiated liability, as of course he is a Unionist. I should not have said a word if he had been C.L. It would have been no business of mine.

I should think that such a man as Cox is also sure to be a Unionist, but I don't really know.

Knights. Excluding the Colonial lot, there are 42, & of those I should say 9 were Non Party.

That leaves 19 on the P.M.'s List & 14 on ours so again they score heavily.

I should never have grumbled if we had had half of the list, but considering how Talbot had to work to secure his modest lot, considering the men we had to take down to let in fellows like . . . , there is little wonder that I am protesting.

Not only should we have half, but it wouldn't be unreasonable if we expected rather more than that, & I hope you'll insist on at least half for the future & also suggest a much smaller list.

There must also be a stop to Freddie poaching our men. I haven't a doubt that if I had got Mills a seat, & got him into the House he would have proved a generous annual subscriber, & it was for us & not for Freddie to give him something more later on. Freddie has written in reply to my letter about the £2500 & stating its purpose.

I think it safer not to reply till I have seen you in the end of the week. I hope to be in London on Friday.

Yours tr.

Geo. Younger

P.S. I'm awfully sorry to bother you with this screed, but I must get it off my chest & I want you to be thinking over the solution before we meet. I'm fed up with these people. Pray don't answer this.

3. STANLEY BALDWIN TO BONAR LAW

Board of Trade,
Great George Street, s.w.1
2 April 1921

My dear Bonar,

I cannot tell you what pleasure your letter gave me: my whole heart was in my work with you, and I don't mind confessing to you that I nearly took advantage of the shuffle to go back to private life and to business.

But it came over me that were I to do that I should have fallen far from the standard that you have set for so long and I should have felt later as ashamed of myself as you would have been of me.

I owe you a great deal and I still marvel at your patience with me on the Bench at the beginning of 1917 when I was all at sea.

Our friendship indeed remains, for it was welded and tested in stern years.

Take great care of yourself and don't try and do too much.

You must now be realising how tired you were.

But we shall be very glad to see you back.

My love to Isabel.

Ever yours
Stanley Baldwin

4. WINSTON CHURCHILL TO DAVID LLOYD GEORGE[1]

June 11, 1921

I have had a talk this morning with Venizelos. I explained to him the conclusions of our conference at Chequers, and he was in agreement with them. I agree with you that we should say to Constantine—"Here are the terms which we think should be offered to Kemal now. If you accept them we will put them before Kemal, if possible in conjunction with France. We should tell Kemal that if he refuses them, we shall help the Greeks in every possible way, and that if the Greeks gain a success the terms will have to be altered proportionately to Kemal's disadvantage." We should further tell Constantine that he should delay his offensive until he has reorganized his army by the reinstatement of competent Venizelist Generals. If he agrees with all that we ask of him, both in the matter of the terms to the Turks and in the matter of reorganizing the army, and if Kemal continues obdurate so that the arrangements with Constantine actually come into effect, we should not hesitate to recognise him. If unhappily we are forced to work with this man and with the Greeks, there is no sense in not doing everything possible to secure success. Half-measures and half-hearted support have been the bane of all the policy we have pursued, whether towards Russia or Turkey, since the Armistice, and they have conducted us to our present disastrous position.

As to the terms, I think they must include the evacuation of Smyrna by the Greek Army. I do not think anything less than that gives a fair chance of winning French co-operation or of procuring Kemalist agreement. The question of the guarantees to be taken either by a local force or by an international force for the protection of the lives of the Christians need not be finally decided at this stage, but I agree with you that effective guarantees must be obtained to prevent massacre.

I do not think there is any time to lose. If the Greeks go off on another half-cock offensive, the last card will have been played and lost and we shall neither have a Turkish peace nor a Greek army.

In taking the line I am now doing on the Greco-Turkish problem, I am sure you will understand that my view as to the objective at which we are aiming has never altered. It has always been and it is

From *The Aftermath*, pp. 395-6.

still, the making of a peace with Turkey which shall be a real peace
and one achieved at the earliest possible moment. I entirely disagree,
as you know and as I have repeatedly placed on record, with the whole
policy of the Treaty of Sèvres, and the results which have arisen from
it have been those which I have again and again ventured to predict.
But in the difficult situation in which we now stand I am doing my
utmost to find a way out of our embarrassments which will not leave
us absolutely defenceless before an exultant and unreasonable
antagonist.

5. MISS STEVENSON'S DIARY

April 2nd, 1926

He [Reading] came down to Lympne one afternoon with Hewart,
& L.G. told them both of the intended changes—Reading for India
and Hewart for the L.C.J. They stayed the night. After dinner we
had a sing-song—I played the piano—all sorts of tunes, & Reading
sang some sea shanties & Hewart a comical song of the circuit—very
effectively. Everyone in great high spirits & very pleased with themselves.

Everyone now acknowledges that Reading's appointment has been
an unqualified success—though many were against him at the time,
on account of his being a Jew.

6. DAVID LLOYD GEORGE TO LORD BIRKENHEAD

10 *Downing Street,*
Feb 11, 1921

My dear Lord Chancellor,
I fail to see the point of your lengthy typewritten document with
its quotation from the Judicature Act. I never suggested to you the
subjects of your elaborate protest. My only proposal to you was that
I should appoint a distinguished lawyer on the express understanding
that he should retire at 80. If it is contrary to the Judicature Act to
stipulate that high legal functionaries should not cling to their posts
into years of decrepitude, then it is high time these Acts were amended.

To take the Attorney General from his present position under existing conditions would be a national disservice. He very nobly responded to the appeal made to him by B.L. [Bonar Law][1] & myself in the interests of the nation to forego his claim. He is much too honourable and loyal a man to allow anyone to persuade him to break faith.

As to Finlay's capacity Carson whom you will admit is the most eminent advocate of the day, told me the profession would regard his appointment with great satisfaction.

Ever sincerely,
D. Lloyd George

7. LORD BIRKENHEAD TO DAVID LLOYD GEORGE

House of Lords
Feb 11th 1921

My dear Prime Minister,

1. The question has never arisen whether a judge cd properly be put under a condition to retire at the age of 80 because so far as I know no-one has ever been made a judge at an age which suggested such a stipulation. Campbell was 70 when he became L.C.J. but his vitality was amazing: he was, I think, a record. Carson has not practised before Finlay since the latter became Ld Chancellor. I have sat with him continuously. I by no means say that he is unfit for judicial work but he is not the man he was and I do not think that he cd undertake the office of L.C.J. The appointment is yours and if you appoint him I shall loyally co-operate with him but *I most earnestly hope that if you do you will make him L.C.J. without any condition*, relying upon his age to terminate his tenure of office within a reasonable time. If any condition is imposed I am sure that we shall find ourselves exposed to the risks and difficulties suggested in my letter the suggestion of which was the object of that letter.

2. I have no conceivable object in the matter except to help the Government. I have no conceivable personal motive in desiring to see the A.G. [Attorney-General] become L.C.J. at this moment. What does it matter to me? So far from advising the A.G. to do anything which is not honourable I have most carefully limited the opinion

[1] Bonar Law, on the contrary, favoured Hewart's appointment.

I gave him to the point already indicated to yourself that a judge cannot be appointed sub condicione be that condition written or verbal. Nor did I volunteer this opinion. He came to see me and invited it on the night of my return.

3. The appointment is of course yours but as Mr. Gladstone pointed out in the Collier crisis: "In such cases the public will suppose and will rightly and necessarily suppose that the Lord Chancellor is privy & assentient to the policy adopted, and my noble & learned friend was so privy and assentient."

It is surely better that possible objections should be stated by me who in effect must share the responsibility than from less friendly lips.

Yours sincerely,

Birkenhead

8. SIR GEORGE YOUNGER TO BONAR LAW

1, *Sanctuary Buildings,*
Gt. Smith Street, s.w.1
April 13th, 1921

My dear Bonar,

In sending you the enclosed letter and Resolution, I shall take the opportunity of writing you a few lines to say how very glad I am to know that your progress is satisfactory, and to think what a mercy it is that you are out of this peck of troubles under which the Government and the Country are again placed by the present crisis. I really begin to think it almost lucky that you had such a hard time in Glasgow, and that it brought on the breakdown which finally settled the question of your resignation. If you had gone on till now, and had become immersed in all these troubles, with the grave responsibilities attaching to the Government in the matter, results might have been much more serious, and it is really with a feeling of thankfulness that you are out of it all, that I am writing to-day. I have refrained from doing so any sooner, as there has really been nothing of any great importance to tell you and nothing that I am sure you do not already know from Davidson.

I had a very satisfactory interview with Austen about my own position here after the Carlton Club Meeting, and told him that you had asked me to, at all events, see him over the stile before I thought of retiring. I said that I proposed to do so but that the present Session must be the extreme limit of my work, and as there was to be no Autumn Session, arrangements must be made in time to allow my work to be carried on during the Recess. It is lucky in a way that this is likely to be the situation, as it will give the new man, whoever he is, a chance of settling down before the troublesome work of the next Session begins. It is impossible to expect any fellow of the age and Parliamentary experience which I have had, to undertake the terrible drudgery and constant worries of this post. Nobody would be quite such a fool as to do so, particularly as no-one of that age would be likely to have any ambition to serve by occupying the post. It will therefore have to be filled by a younger man, and I still have a strong feeling that Davidson would do the work well. I have not made any definite proposal yet to Austen on the subject, because really there is no opportunity for him just now to consider questions of that kind, but I propose to do so the moment the situation becomes easier.

The one trouble about putting a youngish man in my place is that ludicrous arrangement by which he immediately becomes Chairman of the Executive Committee of the National Union. You know how almost intolerable my position was, on more than one occasion, when the Executive, which is a most meddlesome body, was at daggers drawn with yourself, and I often wonder yet how one managed to sail through the difficulties by which we were confronted.

We have divorced the Central Office Organisation from that of the National Union at this Office under the new arrangements Fraser and I have made, so that the two departments are absolutely distinct in personnel, with the single exception of myself. The selection of a Chairman here would be rendered much easier if the rules of the National Union were changed, and the President for the year, who is always a man of Parliamentary position and experience, were also, as he ought to be, Chairman of the Executive Committee. The present arrangement was made by Maitland, with the sole object of keeping the power in his own hands, and that folly has very nearly proved to be our undoing at some of the occasions I have already alluded to. The Chairman of the Organisation should be ex-officio perhaps a member of the Committee, but he should attend in a detached capacity, with no responsibility whatever for any decision at which the Committee may arrive, and with complete freedom to represent the views of his Chief and to remain unaffected by any decision the Committee might arrive at, in case of a difference of opinion between the two.

This change would make Davidson quite a good man to fill the post of Chairman, more particularly as, apart from his common sense and ability, he has been working in close connection with the P.M. during a good many years, and will be able, I think, to pull with him and his Whips better than anyone I can think of at the present moment.

The new appointments, on the whole, have given reasonable satisfaction, but many of our old hands are terribly annoyed by the ineptitude of No. 10, in announcing the selection of James Hope as Chairman of Committee. I never knew such people to make blunders, and it is thought by very many in the House, who are willing to accept Whitley, as showing a complete disregard of the independence of the House of Commons in such matters and their acceptance as a foregone conclusion of anything the Government may propose. Nothing could have been more foolish or inept, and I should think expression will be given to it when Whitley's election is proposed.

The appointment of Lawrence as L.C.J. has already been scoffed at. It is such an obvious expedient to keep Hewart out of his natural promotion and to fulfil the condition on which it is quite well known he was asked to subordinate his claims.

I am very sorry for Peter Sanders in his appointment. He has taken it admirably and made no complaint of any kind, but I can see that he has felt it. Edmund tells me, however, that the P.M. was very keen he should not be made Whip and that Leslie Wilson was his suggestion. He is a very charming fellow, and so far as the Members of the House are concerned, will be I think very popular, but his difficulties are great, he knows nothing really about the procedure, and less about the necessary time tables, and it will take him all his time to get through his first Session without some mistakes. Sanders and Talbot between them have hitherto been responsible for that rather difficult part of the job, and with both of them out of office, it will not be very easy for Wilson.

I have rambled on at much too great a length, and must release you. Do not think it at all necessary to write me, and as for the Resolution I am sending you, the next Meeting of the Executive will not be held until the second Tuesday in May, and there is lots of time about acknowledging that. The less you do just now in the way of writing the better.

My best wishes for your continued progress,

Yours ever,

Geo. Younger

9. CURZON TO LADY CURZON

Extract from letter   *April 22nd,* 1921

I am also in trouble about the extraordinary tactics of the P.M. over Lympne. He has been trying by every manner of means to keep me from going—on the ground that it ought to be a conference between Briand and himself alone. When however it transpired that the former insisted on bringing Berthelot as there were other F.O. questions to be discussed—I sent Vansittart over to enquire whether I should be expected to go as well.

He returned no answer but telephoned this morning to Vansittart my private sec—without even consulting me—ordering him to go to Lympne tomorrow in my stead. Being quite ignorant whether this is merely one of his inconsiderate slapdash movements or whether it masks as it appears to do a deliberate affront I asked A.J.B. to come round & see me which he did before lunch. He was very much perturbed and thought the action deplorable. He promised to go after lunch (with Maud C[unard]) and find out from Hankey exactly what it all meant and let me know what he advised.

Girlie I am getting very tired of working or trying to work with that man. He wants his Forn. Sec. to be a valet almost a drudge and he has no regard for the convenances or civilities of official life.

10. CURZON TO LADY CURZON

Extract from letter   *April 23rd* 1921

Soon after I had closed my letter to you for F.O. bag, A.J.B. came in to say that he had seen both Hankey and P.M. Apparently the suggestion that Vansittart should go down had emanated from Hankey who thought that if I was absent from illness I should like to be represented by my P.S. Both he and P.M. apologised profusely for having asked—or rather instructed him—without even telling me. A.J.B. protests most earnestly to me that it would be a calamity if I were to resign. But I think I can see from his manner that he realizes how impossible the position is and that I may sooner or later be driven to it. To me he discourses about the peculiarities of the temperament & character of L.G. which he regards with stupefaction. I wonder what he says to him about me!

11. WINSTON CHURCHILL TO DAVID LLOYD GEORGE

Colonial Office,
Downing Street, s.w.1
June 9

My *dear Prime Minister,*

I am vy much taken with the suggestion wh. you made today, amid what I thought to be general agreement, that we shd. meet the U.S. objection to our Palestine & Mesopotamia mandates & the covetousness of Standard Oil by stating that while we are perfectly ready to discharge the duties we have assumed, & believe that ultimately these countries will be a benefit to the Mandatory Power, nevertheless we are willing to hand over to the charge of the U.S. either or both of the Middle Eastern mandates we now hold, if they shd. desire to assume them. I shd. like to be able to announce this myself on Tuesday. If you approve & Curzon agrees, may I arrange to have the matter submitted to the Cabinet on Monday morning?

Yours vy sincerely
Winston S. Churchill

12. WINSTON CHURCHILL TO LORD CURZON

Colonial Office,
Downing Street, s.w.1
June 9, 1921

My *dear George,*

I have sent the enclosed letter to the Prime Minister as the result of our talk at luncheon today. I will not of course bring it before the

Cabinet unless you agree from the point of view of Anglo American relations; but I see great advantages in it.

                                        Yours vy sincerely

                                                Winston S. Churchill

13. LORD CURZON TO DAVID LLOYD GEORGE

Private   *Foreign Office*, s.w.1

                                                June 10 1921

My dear Prime Minister,

Winston has sent me a copy of his letter to you about the suggestion for offering the Mandates to America, in which he asks if the idea be approved that he may be allowed to announce it on Tuesday.

This is of course out of the question.

All the consequences of so notable an act will require to be thought out in advance—they will be very far reaching. It is a question which clearly touches our allies as well as ourselves. The League of Nations is also involved.

For the Colonial Secy. to announce such a decision (even if arrived at) in the course of a speech explaining his policy or defending his Department in the House of Commons is not to be thought of.

I shall be in a position to discuss all these considerations if and when we take the case in Cabinet. But I should like to guard against the impression that a hasty decision can either be arrived at or announced.

I rather regret Hardinge's unauthorised conversation with Millerand, for the latter has pinned himself to an attitude about Lerond which makes it more difficult for us to persevere.

I am wrestling with the draft of Hardinge's about Greece and hope to get it off to you tonight.

                                        Yours sincerely,

                                                Curzon

14. DAVID LLOYD GEORGE TO WINSTON CHURCHILL

11th June 1921

My dear Colonial Secretary,

I have carefully thought over your suggestion regarding the Mandates for Mesopotamia and Palestine, and on reflection am not in favour of any public announcement being made at this stage.

Whatever may be the merits of offering either Mandate or both to the U.S.A., I am certain that a statement in the House of Commons, without previous reference to the American Government, is not the manner in which the subject should be broached. It could only suggest that we regarded these Mandates as useless burdens, to be unloaded without consideration on any other Power which would take them from us. To convey such an impression would, I think, be most unfortunate in its effects both on this country and on the United States. If the U.S. refused, as they undoubtedly would, a formidable agitation might arise here to abandon such burdensome possessions. The American Government might also very reasonably resent our making a proposal of such importance without consultation through the public Press. If we really want them to take either Mandate or both, that is not the way to set about it.

I feel, moreover, that the subject is one in which we should unquestionably consult the Dominion Prime Ministers and the representative of India. The Dominions and India contributed largely to these conquests and showed considerable concern in their disposal during the Paris Conference. They are here primarily to discuss Imperial and foreign policy, and the obligations which they entail; and they would justly complain at our taking such action as you propose without reference to them, when they are actually on the spot. This is the more important as they are all deeply interested and concerned in any course of action affecting our relations with the United States.

I am quite willing, however, that the Cabinet should discuss the question at an early date with a view to raising it, if that were agreed, in the Imperial Conference.

Ever sincerely,

D. *Lloyd George*

15. LORD CURZON TO WINSTON CHURCHILL

Private & Personal   *13th June* 1921

My dear Winston,

I hope you will pardon my saying that I am rendered a little anxious by your references in public speeches to foreign affairs. If you were only to develop on these occasions positions or arguments to which Cabinet affirmation had recently or definitely been given there would be less objection, although even so I think that public pronouncements on such matters should emanate from the Prime Minister or the Foreign Secretary rather than from their Colleagues, however important.

But on two recent occasions you have made public references to the Egyptian question (which does not lie in your Department) which were without Cabinet authority, which in each case have evoked an immediate protest from Egypt, and which have rendered the already difficult task of the Foreign Secretary there more difficult.

The first was your reference to Egypt in a speech some time ago, treating Egypt by implication as though it were an incorporated part of the British Empire—a remark which caused great annoyance to the Nationalists.

The second was your remark last week, which (vide Allenby's telegram No. 402 of June 11th) had an equally disturbing effect on the Egyptian Prime Minister.

In the same speech you developed propositions about the necessity of co-operation between Great Britain, France and Germany in the stabilisation of Europe, which were at once assumed by the Press to be invested with special Cabinet authority, and which, although I do not dissent from them in principle or even in form, would have been the better if the Foreign Secretary had been consulted before they were delivered.

I am aware that it is difficult to draw a precise line between what a Cabinet Minister of your experience and authority may say or should not say, and that much has to be left to the tact and discretion of the Minister. But experience shows that incursions into Foreign Affairs by Ministers other than those directly responsible (witness J. Chamberlain and the "long spoon") are seldom attended with much advantage, and not infrequently with some peril; and the twofold case of Egypt, where my task is one of almost inconceivable difficulty, is, I think, a pertinent illustration.

I should not dream of making a speech about the Middle East (Palestine or Mesopotamia) now that you have taken them over, without prior reference to you; although I may say that the connection between them and the Foreign Office, and perhaps myself in particular, is far closer than any that can be predicated between Egypt and the Colonial Office; and I only ask from you the same consideration which I should myself extend.

I am sending a copy of this letter to the Prime Minister since I think he ought to be made aware of my views; and I beg of you in conclusion to rest assured that my protest does not involve the slightest derogation from the great authority and power of your public speeches. Rather it is a tribute to them, since the Foreign Office finds itself involved and committed thereby, in circumstances where it has not been consulted, and may even disagree.

I am

Yours sincerely,

Curzon

16. WINSTON CHURCHILL TO LORD CURZON

Colonial Office,
Downing Street, s.w.1
June 13, 1921

My dear George,

I always speak with very great care on these matters, & I have many years experience to guide me as to what is due to the special position of the Foreign Secretary in external affairs or the Chancellor of Exchequer on finance. But certain broad aspects of these central problems must be treated of by Ministers in public speech from time to time if any contact is to be maintained between the Cabinet as a whole & the constituencies. I am sure in my remarks about the European problem I was well within the limits of past precedents, & I am vy glad to know that you did not disagree in general with what I said. So far as Egypt is concerned, I claim a greater liberty. The

Milner Report was made public in August last, I understand with your acquiescence, without the Cabinet being consulted in any way; & I am not at all prepared to sit still & mute & watch the people of this country being slowly committed to the loss of this great & splendid monument of British administrative skill & energy. Here again, however, the line wh. I took was in strict accord with the line which the Cabinet took up when it first had an opportunity of being consulted; tho' I can quite understand that those in Egypt who wish to see our troops relegated to "drinking condensed water on the banks of the Suez Canal" will not appreciate the reference.

However, I can assure you that it is my earnest desire not to hamper you but to help you, & that if my remarks at Manchester had not been of such a very general & even obvious character, I shd. certainly have talked them over with you beforehand.

Yours vy sincerely,

Winston S. Churchill

17. DAVID LLOYD GEORGE TO AUSTEN CHAMBERLAIN

Criccieth,
14th June, 1921

My dear Chamberlain,

You seem to have done very well over the "guillotine" resolutions. The gain in every respect is worth all the temporary defection. It is not a Bill[1] to loiter over and it lends itself to endless obstruction of the most mischievous kind. It might very well upset our arrangements for an August adjournment. That I regard as fundamental to the strategic position.

Economy. Geddes and Younger are quite right and I agree it would be well to have Geddes at our first conference on this question.

Newspapers. I am afraid you must take action. My reluctance was entirely due to the fact that we undoubtedly used these newspapers during the General Election campaign and we were therefore liable to exactly the same prosecution that we propose instituting now. That is why I would rather the prosecution should be instituted by some private person, say for instance Herbert Jessel, rather than that it

---

[1] Safeguarding of Industries Bill.

should be taken in hand by the Attorney General. However, whatever action you take I stand in and I leave it entirely to you to decide after consulting the Attorney General and Poole. My organisation will certainly take exactly the same responsibility as yours in the matter.

Addison. I have written McCurdy to tell him to co-operate with Leslie Wilson in ascertaining the actual position.

Curzon is going for Winston over his unauthorised pronouncement on questions of foreign policy. He has written him a strong letter on the subject. Curzon is undoubtedly right, but I hope there will be no flare up until I arrive. Winston has always been in the habit of making these pronouncements on his own. He did it under the Asquith administration constantly whenever there was a chance of a real limelight effect!

I shall be returning to Chequers on Friday night, and I trust to London on Monday.

Ever sincerely,

D. Lloyd George

18. DAVID LLOYD GEORGE TO LORD CURZON

10, *Downing Street,*
Whitehall, s.w.1.
Criccieth. 14*th June,* 1921

My dear Foreign Secretary,

I agree with you that it is most improper and dangerous for any Minister to make a pronouncement upon questions of foreign policy, not only without having had previous consultation with the Foreign Secretary, but without actually a specific request from him to do so. Declarations about domestic politics land us in trouble at home, but that is capable of being smoothed over with a jest. But when you come to foreign affairs you are in a much more perilous realm.

It just happens that I wrote Derby yesterday on exactly the same subject. He had sent me a letter which was evidently intended for publication on the subject of an alliance with France and he invited me to reply with a view to sending the correspondence to the newspapers. I wrote back immediately to say that it was a subject upon which not merely the Foreign Secretary but the Cabinet as a whole ought to be consulted before any pronouncement was made and that therefore I could not give him an answer until I had discussed it with you and until we had both put it before the Cabinet. An alliance with France, and certainly an alliance between France, Germany and ourselves is so momentous a project that it ought not to be left to any individual Minister to declare a policy upon it. It must be discussed at an early Cabinet but until then there must be [no] pronouncements. Before the Cabinet comes to any decision on the subject we ought to know how the project would be viewed (1) at home (2) in France & if [we] decide to make the plunge it ought to be in return for some definite assurances on the part of France as to her attitude on questions which concern us.

Ever sincerely,

D. Lloyd George

19. WINSTON CHURCHILL TO LORD CURZON

Private

Colonial Office,

Downing Street, s.w.1.

15.6.21

My dear George

The enclosed telegram, if in any way well-founded, seems to me to be of the utmost importance. As you know, I am prepared to support hostile measures against Turkey as the sole means of procuring a reasonable attitude on their part. It looks as if they had already been alarmed by the offended attitude of England & France. *It seems*[1] I beg you not to lose this opportunity of action. It seems to me vital to use every effort to postpone the Greek offensive & to address Constantine in the sense of our Chequers conversation. Also to send a really authoritative embassage, armed with the Greek compliance, if possible from France & Britain—at any rate from Britain—to clinch matters with Kemal. If Kemal really agrees to terms like these, we ought not to hesitate to put all forms of pressure upon Greece, including if necessary naval action off Smyrna or the Piraeus, to compel them to close with them.

[1] The words in italic are crossed out in the original.

I do trust & beg you will seize this chance of leading us out of the horrible muddle in wh. we are now wallowing.

Yours vy sincerely

Winston S. Churchill

20. LORD BEAVERBROOK TO BONAR LAW
(*Undated. April* 1921)

My dear Bonar,

Come home now. The public is satisfied & you might as well be comfortable. I offer you my little house until you find your new home. Please do accept it. Send a telegram to say when you arrive. Everything will be ready.

In politics we wait upon the coal strike. Austin is making a success. The P.M. is active & his interest in his own situation never falters. Evidently he never gets bored with power. Winston is very-very-very-very-angry. F.E. [Birkenhead] is as bitter as Winston is angry. The Co.Libs. [Coalition Liberals] won't have the exchange clauses of the anti-dumping bill. George Terrell & his friends won't be happy until they get them. This is the next jump for Austin. He got over the Speakership hurdle with ease.

Derby is going strong & foolishly. He intended to combat L.G.'s Labour speech at a Saturday meeting of the Unionist Assn. L.G. saw him on Friday & asked him to go to Ireland in disguise. Hence Derby's speech.

Londonderry[1] is in the dumps. He doesn't approve of Freddie Guest[2] as a Chief. Sutherland[3] is in open revolt breathing fury. L.G. told him that the Under Whips resolved in a body not to work under him or with him. Sutherland doesn't believe.

Northcliffe is coming—& on Sunday he entertains 5000 at lunch at White City.

L.G. told Heddle of the Hulton Press that he hoped the anti-dumping clauses relating to exchange would be killed by criticism. He continues to lead Govt. & Opposition.[4] Asquith is his deputy

[1] Under Secretary at the Air Ministry.
[2] Guest was appointed Secretary of State for Air in succession to Churchill.
[3] Lloyd George's personal press intermediary.
[4] Leading the Protectionists in the Government and the Free Traders in the Opposition.

leader—of the Govt. The old boy gets weaker & worse. He cannot fight but his speeches about Courtney Ilbert & Lowther are unrivalled. . . .

Yours ever,

Max

21. BONAR LAW TO LORD BEAVERBROOK

Hotel Lotti,

7 et 9 Rue de Castiglione,

Paris

30 *April* 1921

My dear Max

Thank you very much for your letter which gives me more news than any I have had.

I shall not go back to England for a while for I should not know what to do in London with the House sitting.

Indeed when I go back it will be difficult to get started in a normal life but if I go at all this summer (before the end of the Session) I think I shall go during the Whitsuntide recess.

Austen must be doing well since you praise his success but I wonder how he and L.G. get on together.

Though I know that I shall be terribly bored before long for want of occupation I am still very glad that I am out of it for I really was not fit for the job and it had become a night-mare to me.

I think I shall be able to stay here for a week or two anyway as I expect to get bridge as well as chess and so far I rather like doing nothing.

Thank you so much for offering your house but I am sure it would be a mistake to go back so soon.

Write me again soon. I want Isabel to go back now with her husband but it is not yet decided whether she will go or not.

Love to you all,

Yours ever,

A. Bonar Law

22. LORD BEAVERBROOK TO BONAR LAW

Vineyard,
Hurlingham Road,
Fulham, s.w.6
13.5.21

My dear Bonar,

I am disappointed. But do come at the end of May. Why not? You needn't go to the House. You can stay at this little house—& you needn't see anybody. You are out of it and entitled to take any course you choose. The advantage in your return for a time is very great. Besides, if you want something to do, you can join boards in the City. McKenna tells me that he has asked you to join his board. Why not?

About politics. George has decided to do away with an intermediary in the leadership of the Tories. He gets on well with Austin who continues to make much of the need for loyalty. But George fears for the permanency of Austin's leadership. The latter gets tired at ten P.M. and cannot lead with efficiency. He is like Asquith after dinner—but for another reason. But George is content.

Derby gives breakfasts on Thursdays & George is meeting the whole Tory Party in relays. Yesterday he rejected proposals for Irish truce & spoke of "long tradition & unbroken loyalty of Tory party" as the instrument with which he would crush out insurrection in Ireland. And when he spoke of Mr. Balfour's policy at the Irish Office in terms of warmest admiration & approval the enthusiasm of the Liverpool members was unbounded.

At the Cabinet yesterday the decision was taken to reject all overtures for a truce during elections—except on condition of surrender of arms. The division of opinion was sharp, all Co-Liberals to the left except Sir A. Mond with Curzon on the Cross Benches. All Unionist opinion with the P.M. including Horne who had taken up an attitude of compromise on the previous day. Horne explained his change of view with disarming frankness—he had enjoyed in the meantime the advantage of a talk with the P.M.

Mond is the new recruit to the Tory ranks & a very popular aristocrat he has become. He promises the end of Addison reforms.

He led the pro-French party in the German Reparations Committee. He is the spokesman of the Tariff Reform Party. The only weakness is a certain leaning towards the Miners pool.

That brings me to Horne again. The miners say he intends to marry Lady Markham (widow of the late Sir Arthur). Hence his firmness over the wages dispute. My own opinion is that he will choose youth & beauty as well as wealth. But you never can tell about these Scotchmen.

This ends this——

Yours ever

Max

23. LORD BEAVERBROOK TO SIR ROBERT BORDEN

Private

2, Garden Court,
Temple, E.C.4
12th May 1921

My dear Borden,

I have received your letter, and I am so glad to hear from you again. I had hoped you would come over here during the summer. Perhaps it is still a possibility although Kemp seems to think it is unlikely. If I had known you were in Ottawa, I would have written you about the Bonar Law development here.

The Government is passing through difficult times on account of internal differences. The strike wards off the political crisis. Churchill is the bitter enemy of George. He has just grounds for his hostility. The Prime Minister will make enormous efforts to placate him in the near future. So far he has left Churchill to himself ever since the "return from Egypt".

F. E. Smith means to challenge Chamberlain's leadership of the Tory party. He may not defeat him but he will diminish Chamberlain's authority. Curzon too has pretensions. I am told that Lady Curzon means to give us a son, so that good government is assured for another generation.

I am going to see Kemp this afternoon. From what I hear, I am afraid that he is not very well.

Chamberlain is doing very well; but he displays a very small percentage of Bonar Law's efficiency in the Leadership of the House. He

does not control his temper and after 10 p.m. he shows failing powers.
With kindest regards,

Yours sincerely,

Max

24. DAVID LLOYD GEORGE TO BONAR LAW

Chequers
June 7th, 1921

My dear Bonar,

I have been in daily expectation since you quitted this world of
trouble of hearing from you how you were getting on in the realms
of bliss. As you will have perceived from the papers—if you have
either time or inclination to glance at them—whilst you are engaged
in steadily bringing your blood pressure down events are conspiring
to work mine up. One perplexity after another. Crises chasing each
other like the shadows of clouds across the landscape. Miners, Unemployment, Reparation, Silesia, and as always Ireland. Come back as
soon as you can and we might then negotiate a swap. You could go
on with the swimming of the rapids whilst I do the resting on the
banks!

I have had a temporary breakdown—at least Dawson assures me—
much to my disappointment it is only temporary—and I am here
recruiting. He counselled a fortnight, but I can hardly give that time.

It is a whirling world and you are well out of it. I often envy you.
But I am sincerely glad to hear accounts of the improvement in your
health. I miss your counsel more than I can tell you, although nothing
could be finer than the way Chamberlain is bearing his share in the
partnership. He is loyal, straight and sensible.

When are you returning? Let me know. I want to see you.

Ever sincerely yours

D. Lloyd George

25. BONAR LAW TO DAVID LLOYD GEORGE

Hotel Lotti,
7 et 9 Rue de Castiglione,
Paris
8 June 1921

My dear L.G.

I thank you for your letter which I am very glad to receive though I did not suppose that you had forgotten that I was still alive.

First as to myself. I am so far as feelings are concerned in better health than I have been in for four years & my sister who was over here last week says that the lines have all gone out of my face & that I look 20 years younger.

I am leading a life which if I were young would be perfectly disgraceful. I get up late, play bridge in a club from half past four for three hours & after dinner go to a second rate café & play chess till bedtime. So far I am not bored but this will not amuse me indefinitely. I have seen a French Doctor here (he is Clemenceau's Doctor & a very intimate friend of his) & he tells me that I will be all right with care but—he advises me not to play either tennis or golf or to return to politics. I do not intend to obey him as regards golf & I am sure Horder will not agree with him.

To drop out of everything is quite possible to me but I often think that if you had been driven to follow my example you would long before this have been utterly miserable. I have of course been following everything in England very closely & have quite understood that you have been passing through & are still passing through a worse time than any I had.

So far as I can judge you have done the best that was possible but even the best is not very good.

Do you remember one time when walking from the House at night I said to you that terribly bad trade, unemployment & all the rest of it was as certain in a year or two as that we were alive & your reply was "Well we must get out of it before that happens." This St. George's election is a surprise to me but any Govt in existing conditions must be unpopular & indeed it is a mystery to me that your Govt. should have retained so much strength for so long a time.

I am sure that if it were possible you would like to let some one else have a try at it for a while but I do not see the possibility. You are like Macbeth isn't it "For me there is nor moving hence nor tarrying here—I 'gin to be a weary neath the Sun". I don't guarantee the accuracy of the quotation but it is something like it.

I am going to London for a short time in ten days or so & I shall at once let you know when I get there as I should like so much to have a talk with you.

Yours sincerely,

A. Bonar Law

26. LORD BIRKENHEAD TO BONAR LAW

House of Lords, s.w.1
June 9, 1921

My dear Bonar,

Thanks very much for your letter which I should have answered before. I am simply delighted to hear such good accounts of your health from Max. It is very wonderful and a source of rejoicing to your friends.

But with the restoration of health new problems will arise. I remember telling you when you spoke to me of resigning that I doubted whether one who had handled so many immense problems could ever be content, unless health completely failed, with the obscurity of private life, or the substitution of less important employment.

You cannot allow yourself to be permanently exiled in Paris a place which I should think you would soon come to dislike acutely. You may prolong your stay but you cannot make it indefinite. And as you have to come home I should come whenever you want. Surely it is a misplaced delicacy to think you cannot return without causing embarrassment. You can only avoid this

    (I) By a permanent exile
    (II) By dying

As on the whole I suspect that you would think either price too high you will have to come and might as well come now or soon. You need not decide upon any course or policy but be guided by developments and you can remain silent as long as you find it desirable or tolerable. In fact there can be no doubt that it is to the public interest that a man of your experience and ability should be there to give advice, looking at the problems of the day detachedly though with fairly friendly eyes.

I am glad you have taken up golf again. I have developed a tennis elbow after playing with impunity for 40 years and can only play once a fortnight at present. So I have taken up golf for exercise in the interval. I am very bad; but we can have some games when you return.

I heard from Max that you had most kindly interested yourself in my promotion. I did not mention it to a living soul. I was too proud to go to L.G. and not prepared to recognise that Austin as leader in the H.C. had anything whatever to do with the matter. It was like you to remember it and kind as you have always been to me.

We think the coal strike over now; but of crises uno avolso non deficit alter. All your premonitions about the (corn?) subsidy have been borne out and at the moment of writing I am listening to that ass Carrington now Lincolnshire denouncing the withdrawal of the subsidy as a gross breach of Government faith. The consequences will be very bad in agricultural constituencies. The step seems to be necessary but what a commentary on the arguments the P.M. and others rammed down our throats in the autumn. I remember feeling great doubts about the Bill at the time—doubts which were not diminished by your apprehensions and as you will gather from Max's press there is a devil of a fuss going on or brewing up about the Graeco-Turk situation. Winston seems to have become almost pro-Greek having always hated them. I suspect the explanation is that the Kemalists are being helped by the Bolshevists & W. will support anyone who attacks them.

I must stop this long rigmarole. Come back soon.

F. E.

27. SIR GEORGE YOUNGER TO AUSTEN CHAMBERLAIN

1, Sanctuary Buildings,
Great Smith Street, s.w.1
June 10th, 1921

My dear Austen,

I think it not undesirable that you should see the enclosed special supplement made to the Daily Press Summary which we prepare each morning at this Office. It deals with the newspaper comments on the St. George's By-Election.

The two elements, indeed probably the three elements which contributed to the unfortunate result in that Division were first a good deal of personal dislike of Jessel, who, though a fairly able fellow, has an extremely unfortunate manner, has been working for a long time to secure the reversion of that seat and was not regarded as the type of man who ought to have followed such a man as our friend Walter Long. They have been used in that constituency to being represented by rather prominent men, and Jessel was not placed by anybody in that category.

The second reason is the strong anti-semitic feeling which is very prominent at the present time. Far too many Jews have been placed in prominent positions by the present Government. Unluckily a Jew named Gluckstein is the present Mayor of Westminster, and there was a very strong feeling against adding to their prominence and against another Jew as Member for the Division. The Palestine stunt was very cleverly utilised by Rothermere and his friends; indeed very unfairly used against Jessel, but it had its influence, and such as it was wholly adverse to him.

The last, and perhaps the most serious difficulty for him, was the anti-waste propaganda against the Government, and it cannot be denied that that can be made most effective use of in present circumstances. After the Birmingham Conference last year, the Prime Minister asked Bonar what my general impressions were about the Party attitude generally towards the Government, and I then wrote a memorandum in which I said that the most vivid impression left upon me, not only by the proceedings at the Conference, but by the conversations I had had with large numbers of prominent and consistent supporters whom I met at Birmingham, was that the one difficulty the Government had to face was the fact that it had failed to tackle and to deal with the grave extravagances, which were obvious to everyone, in connection with the administration of many of the Departments, and I was satisfied that if some drastic action was not at once taken by them to reduce public expenditure, there would be a revolt which would, in a short time prove to be their undoing. In St. George's, which largely consists of voters who are struggling with a huge Income Tax and Super Tax, and finding the greatest difficulty in making two ends meet, there was a most fertile stage for the effective use of Anti-waste propaganda. No doubt it was exaggerated. No doubt people forget that there is a definite obligation amounting to nearly 500 millions a year which must be met by any Government, unless Great Britain is to default. Of course that is always conveniently omitted by those gentlemen who are making the attack, and it gets snowed under by examples of extravagances, known and seen, not important in themselves so far as their cost is concerned, but providing most effective ammunition for creating the atmosphere which resulted in the return of the Anti-waste candidate.

Now all this is most important in the consideration of our attitude towards the action of such newspapers as the *Daily Mirror* in overriding and ignoring, what I believe to be and the Attorney General agrees with me are the clear provisions of the Act of Parliament, and if the Ministers desire to protect themselves, apart from the protection of their supporters, against a continuance of these practices, they must either at once consent to raising the question in the Courts in connection with the recent election, or they must bring in a Bill to make it perfectly clear that the exhibition of posters, the free distribution of newspapers etc are a breach of the Law, and the one or other course must be taken immediately, or we shall be at the mercy of any newspaper proprietor, or any rich candidate who is in a position to subsidise a campaign of this kind. I must, therefore, press for an immediate consideration and statement of the course we are to take. Poole has seen the Attorney General, who is quite decided in his opinion that a gross breach of the Act has been committed at Hereford, at Dover, at Dudley and now at St. George's. Rothermere has announced already, and I have private information also to the same effect, that they mean to fight any election anywhere near the Metropolis on the same lines as they did at St. George's, and by the same means, and there is no time to be lost in acting.

If the Prime Minister does not consent to join us in such an action, I think we ought to go on without him. I am not disposed to wait any longer and I am not disposed to submit to a continuation of these practices, and I wish therefore to press upon you to authorise me to proceed, if there is any further delay on the part of the Prime Minister in coming to a decision.

Yours sincerely,

Geo. Younger

28. AUSTEN CHAMBERLAIN TO DAVID LLOYD GEORGE

11, *Downing Street,*
Whitehall, s.w.
13th June 1921

My dear Prime Minister,

Your letter of the 10th reached me on my return to town late yesterday afternoon. I scarcely liked to try the long-distance telephone for the matters about which I have to write to you.

First, as regards Addison. I can easily defer the debate till Thursday week, and possibly later. But the more I answer questions on the subject—and it is raised every time that I deal with the course of business—the more we get committed, and the more difficult it becomes for Addison to withdraw. At the same time I think it is necessary that you should see him, and that you have a better chance of preserving his friendship if you speak to him yourself, than if your message comes in writing or through a third party. I left Addison under no doubt as to the feelings of my Party—and, indeed, I told him that nothing but your personal influence could possibly carry the vote, and that, even if you were successful, it would only be because this House of Commons would not finally refuse anything of which you made a personal point. If I were now to tell him that he must resign, I think he would receive such a message very ill from me. He regards himself as your man, and his appointment as your appointment, and I do not think he would accept his *congé* from anyone but yourself.

(2). St. George's Election. I agree with all you say. I send you a copy of a letter of Younger's—not written for your eye, but one which I think it is important that you should see. The use of the Press as an election agency, and for the purpose of evading the law in respect of the limitation of expenses, is most serious. If we do not check it at once, we shall be confronted with the same kind of attack in every constituency in the Metropolis and the Home Counties, and I think it will be fatal to us. I would therefore urge most strongly that we should jointly take action against both Rothermere and Beaverbrook on the elections in which they have been concerned. I hope that you will consent to our two Central Offices acting in common in this matter. If you feel that you must have a conference with the lawyers before giving your assent, I beg that we may have a meeting at the earliest possible moment.

(3). Economy. I entirely agree with what you say, and I have before me a letter from Eric Geddes, of which I also send you a copy, giving his first impressions as Chairman of the Committee to settle which Government departments were to be moved out to Acton. I will ask the Chancellor to have a talk with Mond, and as soon as you are able to attend a conference I should say that the five of us, i.e. yourself, Horne, Geddes, Mond and myself, had better meet.

Lastly, as to the Corn Subsidy. I think Boscawen's difficulty was that he is still negotiating with the farmers, and he was afraid to go into any details lest they should injuriously affect his prospects of success.

We can manage without you this week; but by next week I think it will be time for you to come and pick us up and dress our wounds! I hope by that time you will be feeling like a giant refreshed. No constitution but yours would have stood so successfully the immense strain to which you have subjected it.

Yrs sincerely,

Austen Chamberlain

P.S. Leslie Wilson & McCurdy will have a joint report on the Addison question by Wednesday. McC. is getting more pessimistic again & Wilson says it is hopeless!

29. DAVID LLOYD GEORGE TO DR. ADDISON

War Office,
Whitehall, s.w.
31.3.1921

My dear Addison,

When Worthington Evans was appointed Minister without portfolio, as you know I strongly urged you to take it. I was anxious for many reasons that you should be free to assist me in my general political work. However you could not then see your way to accept.

The resignation of Bonar Law forces me to make very considerable changes in the Ministry, and I propose that there should be a change in the Ministry of Health. But as I am anxious to secure your help I should like you still to remain in the Cabinet & to occupy the post of

Minister without portfolio. In this post you will be able to afford me the kind of assistance which I really stand very much in need of, in coordinating the political effort of the Government and adjusting it to the needs and sympathies of the new electorate.

Please let me know at once whether you accept, as the announcements must be made at the latter end of this week.

Trusting you have had a good holiday.

Ever sincerely,

D. Lloyd George

30. AUSTEN CHAMBERLAIN TO DAVID LLOYD GEORGE

Personal & Secret   11, *Downing Street,*
                                                 Whitehall, s.w.
                                                 9th June 1921

My dear Prime Minister,

I am glad to hear that you are making good progress and that Sassoon found you in good spirits. I gave your message to Kellaway, who took it very nicely and recognised that it warned him against a fault to which he is prone to succumb.

There is one matter about which I think I ought to write to you at once, for it is causing me considerable anxiety. There is no concealing the fact that for the moment the authority of the Government is somewhat shaken by our action in regard to Members' remuneration and by the inconvenient result of the Westminster election. We shall, I expect, have a difficult situation this afternoon in connection with the Post Office charges. But ahead of us there lies a more serious trouble. I am being pressed to name a day for the discussion of Addison's salary, and I think I must appoint to-day fortnight for the purpose. But I am really concerned as to the result.

Let me begin by saying that I recognise your difficulties and that I will stand by you in whatever decision you take. That being clearly understood, I must tell you that my Whips give me a worse report of the feeling of our Party in respect of this matter than on anything else. Even men who have never voted against us before declare that they will not vote with us on this occasion. If they do not vote against us, the most that they will contemplate is abstention, and an undoubted majority of Unionists is likely to go into the lobby against us. We can, of course expect no help from the Independent Liberals or the Labour Party. McCurdy is making some enquiry as to the feeling amongst Coalition Liberals and will report to me to-morrow. But from what he has said it would seem that there is as much disinclination to support the vote among your followers as among mine, and that we must expect a large abstention of Coalition Liberals.

The grounds of opposition are, first, that a Minister without portfolio is unnecessary: that we had suppressed the office when Worthington Evans became Secretary of State for War, and only revived it in order to provide a billet for a Minister who had failed in his previous post.

Secondly, that even if it were proved that there is work for a Minister without portfolio, Addison is not the man for such a position.

You know exactly how much there is of truth in both these contentions. I have endeavoured privately by myself and by the Whips to represent to Members the other considerations which a Prime Minister is bound to take into account, even though it may be difficult or impossible to state them publicly. But we have met with no success, and I am obliged to tell you—as, indeed, I am frankly told by the Whips—that my influence with the Party will not be sufficient to carry the vote, and that the only chance of averting defeat is that you should yourself undertake its defence and exert all your influence and authority. Even so, our members will vote most reluctantly, and I cannot at present say definitely what the result would be except that I think your influence in the present House of Commons is sufficient to carry anything if it is personally exerted!

There is the story I have to tell, and a very disagreeable one it is. I have no solution to offer, and can only say in conclusion, as I said at my opening, that I will back you whatever you decide.

Yrs sincerely,

Austen Chamberlain

31. AUSTEN CHAMBERLAIN TO DAVID LLOYD GEORGE

Personal & Secret   11 *Downing Street,*
                                                         Whitehall, s.w.
                                                          10.6.21

My dear Prime Minister,

You will laugh over the P.O. vote & the collapse of the Opposition. They bungled their affairs as usual & Kellaway did very well; otherwise we should have had a much worse time.

Addison has just been in to say that he thought that you, & not I, ought to defend his appointment. I told him quite frankly that I had already written to you that the feeling among my people was so strong that nothing but your personal influence could carry the vote. A. did not know this but took the view that since you made the appointment he was entitled to claim your advocacy. He was afraid of hurting my feelings by suggesting that I should give way to you in the matter. How little he knows me!

MacCurdy reports the state of feeling among the Coalition Liberals as better than he had expected—abstentions likely but not hostile votes *unless* the Press works up an agitation. Of course they will do so & are indeed already beginning.

My congratulations & best wishes to your son on his marriage.

Yrs. sincerely

Austen Chamberlain

P.S. I forgot to say that Addison told me that a dinner is being organised in his honour & that Carson will take the Chair at it. A. is led to expect a large gathering—not of course confined to M.P.s.

32.   AUSTEN CHAMBERLAIN TO DAVID LLOYD GEORGE

Secret   11, *Downing Street,*
                                                        Whitehall, s.w.
                                                        15*th June* 1921

My dear Prime Minister,

Many thanks for your letter of the 14th, all of which is satisfactory.

We had a meeting of the Cabinet Committee on Irish affairs this morning at which Macready and John Anderson were present. Hankey will send you a full report of it but the proceedings are of so secret a character that no other copy of the notes will be taken and we have returned our copies of the document which we were considering.

Next week will be a very busy one for you and I should like to have an hour's quiet talk with you before you return to town. I was going to spend Saturday and Sunday at the Buxtons for a gardeners' party, but if it were perfectly convenient to you I should like to motor down to Chequers on Sunday afternoon and discuss some of the matters which have come to a head in your absence, especially the Irish situation. If you will let me know whether it would be convenient to you to see me at Chequers at 5 o'clock on Sunday, or in London at any time that afternoon or evening, I would make my arrangements to keep the appointment. I do not at present know where Buxton's place is but I do not think it is very far from London and I believe that I could easily motor up on the Sunday morning and get down to Chequers in the course of the afternoon. In any case if it suits you to see me, that is more important than looking at Lady Buxton's garden and I would arrange to meet your convenience.

Since dictating this I have looked at your letter again & I see that you expect to reach Chequers on Friday night. May I come down to see you on Saturday morning? This would suit me best of all.

Henderson has told Leslie Wilson that he cannot expect Labour support on Addison's salary. The *D. Mail* announced A's resignation this morning. A. has denied it. He is not I think in a pleasant mood. He said to Oliver "It was the P.M.'s appointment & it is for him to see it through."

Is it worth your while to consider a suggestion made to me by

Younger—viz. that A. should take no salary from public funds but that you should make it up to him from your party fund? I doubt it, but pass it on for what it is worth.

You will have seen in the papers the memorial signed by 150 Coalition Unionists and 7 Coalition Liberals. It was brought to me by Godfrey Locker Lampson & I fairly let myself go and gave him a sample of my temper. Of his 156 signatories 87 absented themselves & 14 voted against the Govt. on Henderson's motion to add 15 millions to our pensions expenditure! What right have they to hector & threaten?

Yrs sincerely
Austen Chamberlain

33. DAVID LLOYD GEORGE TO C. A. MCCURDY

Criccieth,
14th June, 1921

My dear McCurdy,

I congratulate you on the success of your meetings. They seem to be going exceptionally well and ought to make a very great difference in the ultimate political situation. The country needs educating and I am clear that there must be a systematic and well organised campaign throughout the country during the late autumn and winter. It will rally our forces: it will instruct the electorate and it will incidentally have a real effect upon the course of the next session. We ought to be ready for all contingencies. However, I will talk to you about this later on.

What I am specially concerned about now is this agitation about Addison. I felt it coming for a very long time, long before Addison could be persuaded to leave the Ministry of Health. I did my best to get him to take the Ministry without Portfolio a year or two ago. Whether he was succeeding or not, he was creating the impression of failure. However, he refused to take my advice upon that occasion and I am very much afraid that it is now too late to save him. According to all I hear, the majority of the Unionists will either vote against him or abstain. The Wee Frees and probably Labour will vote against if they know that by that means they have a chance of inflicting a serious defeat upon the Government. The Liberal Coalitionists alone can be depended upon and I am not quite clear how many of them will vote. As at present informed it seems to me that we are in for a bad defeat unless Addison realises the position in time. That is the report which comes to me from many quarters. I am anxious that you and Leslie Wilson should make enquiries and that you should present a report to Chamberlain and myself. It would be folly for Addison himself to risk a personal defeat. It does not help him personally to bring down the Government over his own unpopularity. If there had been a question of principle involved and Addison had been a real success in his Department and was being sacrificed purely because he had done his duty too well, I should take the challenge, but I have not been in the least satisfied with the way in which he handled the housing question, & he has behaved sulkily and stupidly since his transference. However, you will let me know what the position is by the time I return. If possible, I should like to hear from you and Leslie Wilson by Saturday. If you will hand the report to J. T. Davies he will forward it to me.

D. Lloyd George

34. AUSTEN CHAMBERLAIN TO DAVID LLOYD GEORGE

House of Commons
15/6/21, 10 p.m.

Secret
My dear Prime Minister,

Since I wrote to you this afternoon I have seen an interview given by Addison to the *Eveg. Standard*.

Addison has put in the fire what little fat still remained out of it. From my point of view he could have done nothing worse. It was expressly explained to me that the Members memorial of which I wrote did not refer to Addison. He fits the cap to his own head. He singles out Banbury by name & by implication suggests that he (Addison) is of more importance than the Fleet. Finally he attempts to turn what was in part a genuine movement for economy & in part an attack on his own administration into a revolt of Unionists against Coalition Liberals.

Under these circumstances I cannot promise you a sufficient number of Unionist votes to secure victory even tho' you were to exert your personal influence to support him & most of the votes which you would secure would be reluctantly given.

I think I know your intentions. To make your path easier if I can, I am sending Addison a letter which concludes: "I told you that I was ready to support the Prime Minister throughout this question. I must now tell you that this attack upon Unionists generally makes it impossible for me to give any such help. I felt the greatest sympathy with you & desired to show all the loyalty that you had a right to expect from a colleague. But you have destroyed by your own act any possibility of usefulness on my part."

I enclose the interview.

Yrs. sincerely,
Austen Chamberlain

35. C. A. MCCURDY TO DAVID LLOYD GEORGE

Memorandum   17*th June*, 1921

From careful inquiries it would appear that on a simple Vote for Five Thousand a year for the Minister without Portfolio it would be difficult for the Government to avoid a defeat.

The Labour and Wee Free vote would probably be almost solid against us. The balance of Conservative votes in favour of the Government would be very small, and I do not think we could rely on more than fifty Coalition Liberal votes. Three or four Coalition Liberal votes would probably be cast against the Government.

The general feeling in the House is first a genuine doubt as to whether Dr. Addison is fulfilling any necessary functions in his present post, and as to whether this is a post which ought to be continued any longer.

This doubt is quickened by alarm at the anti-waste propaganda in the country, and a fear of being placarded as one who voted for an unnecessary Five Thousand Pounds a year.

On the other hand, there is some re-action, owing to resentment at newspaper propaganda of this kind.

Dr. Addison's interview with the *Evening Standard* has made matters worse for him, as he has chosen deliberately to accuse the Conservative Coalitionists of being animated by disloyalty to their Liberal colleagues, and by a desire to break up the Coalition. I do not believe there is any substantial ground for this suggestion.

It is obviously undesirable that anyone should be able to say, however untruly, that a Liberal Minister has been dropped either in deference to anti-waste propaganda, or in consequence of a Conservative plot, as Dr. Addison himself suggests.

Dr. Addison's immediate resignation would not, therefore, afford a smooth and satisfactory solution of the difficulty.

I venture to suggest as the line for the Prime Minister to take:—

(1) An appreciation of Dr. Addison's services, both as Minister of Health, and in his present position.

(2) An explanation that the need for winding up business before the Autumn Recess, complicated by a Coal strike which takes Ministers away from their own Departments every day of the week to serve on Emergency Committees, have rendered the assistance of a Minister without Portfolio quite essential during this Session.

(3) That there has never been any intention of making the post permanent, and that the post will come to an end in August when the House rises.

Leslie Wilson agrees with me that on such a statement Conservative support would be freely forthcoming.

This does not drop Dr. Addison, nor does it commit the Prime Minister as to his future.

C. A. M.

36. LORD BIRKENHEAD TO DAVID LLOYD GEORGE

Secret   *House of Lords*, s.w.1
June 23rd, 1921

My dear P.M.

Winston has just shown me an article in today's *Manchester Guardian*. It is a tissue of lies from beginning to end. You gave me the Woolsack. You made it possible for me to win distinction on it. You have delighted myself & my wife by recommending me for a Viscountcy.

There is absolutely no office in the state which at this moment or at any moment which I can forsee I would exchange for mine. When you can find time for a quiet evening I should like a talk with you and

I will candidly tell you the only ambition I have left in public life. It is one of which you would not and could not disapprove.

Yours ever

F. E.

I am making a public contradiction.

37. SIR JOHN T. DAVIES TO LLOYD GEORGE

Thames House

Dec 9th (1936)

My dear Chief,

I received your letter today. I am glad to know that you are going to see the new Trustees and explain to them your reasons for increasing the Committee. I do not think it quite right to say the Chairman objects to anyone—that is too strong a word. He doesn't know Addison except by name and he fears that if & when he again becomes a Minister in a Labour Cabinet and say a bye-election takes place at a time when you might not approve of their policy the Committee might be asked to vote funds to put up a candidate in opposition to Labour. It was such a contingency as this he had in mind. He cordially approves of Miss Lloyd George's nomination. He also agrees to put another £1000 into the special fund, in fact he goes further & would like to see that fund augmented by £25,000 or even £30,000 before the change takes place so as to ensure that cash is available over which the new enlarged committee will have no control. Personally, I agree with him . . .

I paid a visit to Avalon and found the young lady just on her return from the morning session at school & in a hurry to get back in the afternoon: she was very excited about two youngsters of her own age who had been chasing her round the playground and she said "she *let* one of them catch her." Isn't she growing up to be a fine child with health and beauty in her whole being. She follows the party on a map and showed me exactly where they were at the moment and where they had been . . .

Yrs. ever. With love to all

from everyone

J. T.

38. SIR SAMUEL HOARE TO LORD BEAVERBROOK

House of Commons
18 *Cadogan Gardens*, s.w.3
June 8th 1921

Dear Beaverbrook,

Many thanks for your letter of the 7th.[1] I am afraid that I cannot get down until 11.30. I hope this will not inconvenience you. If this is too late, will you have a telephone message sent to me at Kensington 4162. If I hear nothing from you I will turn up about 11.30.

I have had a long talk to Guinness with reference to our conversation particularly about Ireland. Could you meet him and me sometime and have a short further talk on the subject with a view to our taking action in the House. If so, perhaps you could let me know to-morrow when it would suit you to see us.

Yours sincerely,
Samuel Hoare

39. SIR SAMUEL HOARE TO LORD BEAVERBROOK

Pte & Personal   18 *Cadogan Gardens*, s.w.3
June 13th 1921

Dear Beaverbrook,

Guinness and I have been thinking over our conversation with you, and as a result it occurs to me that you ought to be fully informed as to what we have done up to the present.

Accordingly I send you two enclosures, not so much to trouble you to read them as to bring them to the attention of those of your people who are dealing with the question of fiscal autonomy.

(1) A copy of an article I wrote with the approval of my friends in the House for the *Nineteenth Century* of last October. The article excited a good deal of attention at the time and there was a leading article on it in *The Times*. It was upon the policy set out in it that we

[1] Invitation was to play tennis.

moved innumerable fiscal autonomy amendments during the autumn to the Home Rule Bill. All our amendments without exception, met with contemptuous indifference from the Government, particularly from Worthington Evans and Fisher who were in charge of the Bill.

(2) A copy of a memorandum that we presented to the Prime Minister at the end of March. The Prime Minister, Austen Chamberlain, Greenwood and Edmund Talbot discussed the subject with us for most of an afternoon. Having run our Secret Service in Russia and Italy for four years, I knew enough of intelligence methods to convince the Prime Minister that his show in Ireland was rotten from top to bottom. Greenwood tried to bluff, but the case against our Intelligence in Ireland is overwhelming. I could write books about it. No one has seen this memorandum as far as we know except the Ministers to whom we handed it and ourselves. I would therefore ask you to treat it as confidential except for yourself and your man who is dealing with Irish questions. It ought not on any account to be quoted, but there would be no objection, if it is worth while and you desire to accumulate a case against the present regime, to say that the Prime Minister and the Government were given full warning on the subject before Easter. I might add that Lloyd George showed great momentary interest in my views, but nothing seems to have happened except that the rotten regime has become more rotten.

I think that if there were a campaign, we could get rather more than the ten Members of whom I spoke to you, and that as soon as it was evident that the wind was blowing our way, most of the Coalition would come over.

As to Greece, Venezelos paid me a long visit on Friday afternoon and convinced me that, whilst his views have not changed on the subject of Greek aspirations, he himself is not the centre of any Greek intrigue that there may be. He is quite frankly bored with politics and not in the least anxious to meddle with Greek affairs.

Yours sincerely,
Samuel Hoare

40. SIR JAMES CRAIG

Sir James Craig, created Viscount Craigavon in 1927, was fifty years of age in 1921. He was married and had two sons and one daughter. He was tall and broad-shouldered. He might have come straight from the farmyard though he had been a stockbroker. He had a broken nose and looked like a hard-drinking (which he was not) farmer fresh from the chase. In debate in the Commons he could talk on any subject for time without end but never holding the attention of the Members. He was often called upon by the Whips to keep the House going through dinner hour. He was friendly with Tim Healy though at the same time claiming that my own intimacy with Healy might lead to public misunderstanding of the opposition of Bonar Law to Irish Home Rule. Craig disliked Churchill. But I met him in London on a Sunday morning in 1940 and took him to Churchill's home at Chartwell where the two Prime Ministers appeared to be on most friendly terms. Craig died in November 1940.

41. MISS STEVENSON'S DIARY
July 22nd, 1921

Went to the Royal Garden Party yesterday and was introduced to Mrs. Asquith, above all people. She was very nice and I was agreeably surprised in her. She does not repel: on the contrary she rather attracts. She is a sort of kind Nancy Astor, whereas Nancy A [stor] is a good looking Mrs. A[squith]. She mentioned Megan and I said the P.M. always said how kind Mrs. A[squith] was to her. "Not so kind as my husband was to him," was her retort.

42. DAVID LLOYD GEORGE TO LORD DAWSON

10 *Downing Street*
24th *October*, 1921

My dear Dawson,

You are a brave man to have defied Mrs. Grundy in her best parlour. But the outcry has already frizzled away.[1] . . .

I have many a time sat down to write to thank you for the great kindness you showed me in Scotland. I know the sacrifices you made to come to that rain-sodden glen to rescue me from what might have been a serious illness. You alone did that. And I also feel that I owe

---

[1] Lord Dawson had made a speech in the House of Lords in favour of Birth Control and had been severely criticised.

a debt of gratitude to Lady Dawson for the sacrifice she made in letting you go. I am ever so much better for my Gairloch experiences. In spite of my dental mishap I came back really rested and invigorated.

Ever sincerely,

D. Lloyd George

43. DAVID LLOYD GEORGE TO AUSTEN CHAMBERLAIN

Flowerdale House,
Gairloch,
Ross-shire
September 21st, 1921

My dear Chamberlain,

I am sending down to-night by bag a short précis of an informal discussion which I have had here with such Ministers as were close at hand, in addition to the Unemployment Committee of the Cabinet who had already arranged to come up and see me this week. I also enclose a copy of the draft reply on which we have agreed provisionally. I am in no hurry to despatch it and we shall consider it again tomorrow morning when Horne arrives. It needs very careful consideration—more than any previous one—and there is more to be gained than lost by keeping them on tenterhooks in Dublin for a time.

Everyone is agreed that we have to weigh two chief considerations very carefully:—

(1) In the first place, we have to make quite certain that we have in no way compromised our position as regards allegiance to the Crown and the integrity of the Empire in the endeavour to secure a conference. There was some division of opinion amongst us here to-day as to how far we should insist again literally upon this consideration or by making it implicit help de Valera out of his difficulty. The general view was that without yielding anything to the extremists in Dublin we should not make de Valera's position more difficult in dealing with them, and if possible, indicate a way by which he can come into the conference. There was considerable discussion, as you will see in the précis, regarding the form which would best carry out this idea, but so far we are pretty generally agreed upon the draft which I enclose.

(2) The other consideration chiefly in our minds was the great importance of carrying the opinion of the Empire, and of this country in particular, with us. It was generally felt that the country expects a conference to take place, and will not be quite satisfied that everything has been done to prevent rupture unless a conference is held. Opinions vary as to the weight which should be attached to this consideration. It is to some extent a question of presentation of the issue, but there is no doubt that the more conciliatory tone of de Valera's two latest communications has, to some extent, taken the edge off British feeling against him, which was running very high.

I shall be glad to hear from you by telegram on Friday, when you have had time to consider the draft, whether you approve the principle or not, and I will of course wait until I have had a letter from you before despatching it. I will not send the reply, in any case, until next week.

I am sending instructions to the Cabinet office to say that if Ministers approve a telegram to that effect will be sufficient, but that if they have alterations to suggest they should send them by post.

I am much better to-day, but Dawson tells me that I should not leave here at the earliest until the end of next week. I hope you have had a reasonably good holiday.

D. *Lloyd George*

44. LADY LLOYD-GEORGE'S AUTOBIOGRAPHY

Sometimes L.G., "F.E." and Churchill would gather together over a friend's table,[1] and I had the privilege of being present. I need hardly say that the conversation was a first-class entertainment. From time to time, however, it appeared to me to develop into a triple monologue, as the three of them developed their views, not one of them listening to the other, each taking a delight in his own exposition, rather than in that of his companions.

[1] The Vineyard.

45. BONAR LAW TO LORD ROTHERMERE

Private   16 *November* 1921

My dear Rothermere,

I was very glad to get your telegram but not surprised for I remember very well the tremendously energetic and effective fight which you put up for Ulster before the war.

I had a long talk with your son and he promised to write to you fully about it. I still hope that L.G. will find that to proceed on the lines which he contemplated would mean the irretrievable smashing of the Coalition and I believe a very nasty position for himself personally. I hope, therefore, that he will find some other way of dealing with the situation than to expect the Ulster Party to go back on all its pledges.

I arranged with your son that if any new developments came of which I was aware I would see him again and he will make an appointment with me at any time he thinks it useful.

Yours sincerely

A. Bonar Law

46. LORD DERBY TO DAVID LLOYD GEORGE
(*With covering letter to J. T. Davies*)

Knowsley,
Prescot,
Lancashire
22 *December* 1921

My dear Davies

The enclosed is a personal letter to the Prime Minister giving him certain information he asked for. It is rather urgent and I should be much obliged if you would see that he gets it at the earliest possible moment. All good wishes for Xmas and New year.

Yours v sincerely

Derby

Confidential

My dear P.M.

I have received the answer from Sir Percy Woodhouse and I enclose it for you. As you will see his opinion is very much against an immediate Election and he gives his reasons.

The one which I think particularly strong is his idea that trade will improve. I see Sir Edwin Stockton who is President of the Manchester Chamber of Commerce, made a speech very much in the same direction a few days ago.

About the Reform of the House of Lords of course, there is no doubt whatever, if you went to the Country now, before introducing such a Bill, you would be accused of breach of faith. At the same time I feel that any Bill that you bring in will have the tendency to still further divide our Party rather than bring it together, as I am quite certain a Bill that would be acceptable to the House of Lords would not be acceptable to the House of Commons, and vice versa. If you have a Bill for the Reform of the House of Lords ready on the stocks, I am not sure that I would not show it now to the people who are most active in the direction of the Reform of that Chamber, namely Selborne and Salisbury. If it was a Bill that they would accept with minor alterations, then probably it would be better to introduce the Bill, but if they condemn it root and branch it would only mean they would offer violent opposition to it in the House of Lords and it would mean a fight between the two Houses which would be fatal just before an Election.

There is another factor that I think is against an immediate election and that is the delay by Dail Eireann in ratifying the Treaty. There is no doubt it has strengthened the case of the Die-Hards. It is making a lot of waverers incline more to their side because if what is a great gift on the part of England is not to be received in the spirit in which it is given, it does not look as if there would be any real peace in Ireland. I gather that the Delegates are doing their best to get it accepted but it certainly is a case of looking a gift horse in the mouth.

I should be much obliged if you would let me know what your idea is because, as I told you, I ought to telegraph for my eldest son to come back. As I see that you have apparently come to no arrangement with the French and are going to the south of France on the 8th of January I rather conclude that you have made up your mind not to have an election in January. I wish you were going to Cannes a week later. I shall be there then as I am going out myself on the 17th and I might unofficially have been of a little use to you.

To go back to the question of an Election would you like me to make any further enquiries from other parts of Lancashire? I could easily do so if you wished.

All good wishes to you & yours for Xmas & the New year.

Yours v sincerely

Derby

47. LORD DERBY TO DAVID LLOYD GEORGE

Confidential

Knowsley,
Prescot,
Lancashire
24th December 1921

Dear P.M.

Here is yet another letter, from Sir Edwin Stockton, in which you see he differs from Woodhouse. He is a very good opinion but when it comes to electioneering I am not quite certain that Woodhouse is not the most reliable. At the same time I send you on the letter as Stockton gives very clearly his reasons advocating an immediate election. Unless I hear from you to the contrary I shall not send for my boy to come home. I can catch him any time up to about the 10th of January. After that he will be away shooting and I cannot get him till the middle of March.

All good wishes for Xmas & New Year.

Yours sincerely

Derby

48. SIR GEORGE YOUNGER TO DAVID LLOYD GEORGE

Unionist Central Office,
Palace Chambers,
Bridge Street,
Westminster, s.w.1
January 4th, 1922

Dear Prime Minister,

At Austen's request I send you copies of a Memorandum from this Office, prepared by Sir Malcolm Fraser, with which I fully agree, and of a letter from myself on the subject of the suggested early Election.

I only came here yesterday for a couple of days, but I have seen many of our Members, and one and all are opposed to any Election in the near future, generally for the reasons given in my letter, and all declare that if an Election be forced upon them, they will not stand as Coalitionists, but as Independent Unionists. They tell me that so far as they have been able to ascertain, this intention is generally held, and I am not at all surprised that it should be so, as, during the last few months, the most difficult of my tasks has been to prevent the spread of a revolt of this kind, and to keep our people together in support of the present state of things.

I hold most strongly the views expressed in my letter to Austen. I should regard it as a disaster to the best interests of the country if an Election were held in the present circumstances. I see no justification for it, and no sufficient reason could be advanced in support of it, and I believe it would be a most risky operation, and that it would do infinite harm to the National interests. Holding those views so strongly as I do, and believing that an Election now would rightly be regarded as an unfair advantage taken by the Party in power, it would be my duty to use what influence I have to oppose it. This is no time to think of personal or Party interests, and although the breaking up of our combination would be a serious matter, and a very great regret to myself, I would rather see that happen than be in any way involved in what I regard as an indefensible act.

You will understand that having seen the Memoranda submitted to you by McCurdy and Sutherland, my letter and Fraser's Memorandum express our considered view.

Yours very sincerely,

Geo. Younger

49. DAVID LLOYD GEORGE TO AUSTEN CHAMBERLAIN

(Cannes)

January 10, 1922

My dear Chamberlain,

As to the Election, although I have had several talks with Horne, Worthington, and Winston, the greater pre-occupations of golf(!) and the conference have left me no time for really thinking out the problem. When I return you and I can survey the whole situation and then take our decision.

As I told you before leaving, my view would depend largely upon the result of investigations made as to the trade and electoral prospects throughout the country. On the moral issue I have never had any doubt that we were fully entitled to ask the King for a dissolution. Our opponents would have been demanding it on that ground had it not been that they felt very doubtful about the result. I observe that Malcolm Fraser favours an Election in the early summer months. We can consider all the alternatives when we meet. Meanwhile, I am opposed to any declarations being made by responsible Ministers. In fact, it would be an offence to the Sovereign and contrary to all traditions to do so. Moreover, even if we decide that the time is not opportune, there is a good deal to be said for leaving the minds of friend and foe alike in suspense for two reasons. (1) It will help to get through the Irish settlement. (2) It will force our organisations to set their house in order. Up to the present most of the organising has been left to the Labour and Wee Free Parties. We have trusted too much to our overwhelming strength.

Younger has, in my judgment, behaved disgracefully. He was consulted confidentially on a most confidential subject. He was shown a document prepared by the Chief Coalition Liberal Whip. When you informed me that you meant to send a copy to him I certainly relied that, as a man of honour, he would not reveal it. He has rushed to the Press; carried on an active campaign; disclosed the most intimate and secret information which would never have been imparted to him unless we had depended upon his being gentleman enough to keep counsel. His action has caused serious damage which it will be difficult to repair. His suggestion that the General Election is a Coalition Liberal stunt is absolutely untrue. The suggestion came, in the first instance, as you are aware, from Unionist quarters. Prominent Unionists were the first to urge it upon us, and McCurdy only came in when I consulted him upon the idea which had been pressed upon me notably by F. E. As for myself, I definitely declared that, although on moral grounds I felt we had a right to declare an Election and that on other grounds there was a good deal to be said for it, still, I would come to no conclusion in my own mind until I had heard from you what the views of the Conservative organisers were, as well as those of my own—after full investigation made by both. I also urged that trade would have a very great influence on my mind, and I proposed that an inquiry should be made on that subject. However, we will discuss all these things on my return.

The Conference is now going well. As usual there have been unpleasant incidents with the French which you have always to work through before you begin business with them. The International Conference [at Genoa] has been agreed to, and I think we are on the way to the solution of the reparation problem. The French were very opposed at first to bringing the Germans here, but the Italians and the Belgians supported our view that the agreement was much more likely to be carried out if arrived at after a discussion with the representatives of the German Government. I am hoping the Conference will be over by Saturday, in which case I shall be back probably on Monday.

You seem to be having rather bad weather in England.

Ever sincerely,

D. Lloyd George

50. CHURCHILL AND RUSSIA

Churchill was always hostile to Lloyd George's Russian plans. He wished to maintain support given to the Russian Imperial Forces then threatening Petrograd. Lloyd George insisted upon abandoning the project.

Churchill objected to receiving a Russian Trade Delegation under

Krassin, and he persisted in his warnings about the Bolshevik threat to peace.

Krassin was received at Downing Street. Churchill, enquiring about his reception, said: "Did you shake hands with the hairy baboon?"

Then the American Ambassador warned Lloyd George that his Government would not shake hands with the Russians. Lloyd George replied: "I'll tell you what to do. If you don't want to shake hands with the Bolsheviks, you let us do it, and then you shake hands with us."

Lady Lloyd-George wrote in her Autobiography about these events:

"L.G. [Lloyd George] and Churchill remained diametrically and obstinately opposed to each other on Russian policy, and on the question of the recognition of the new Russian Government. L.G. continued to work, with many setbacks, for an understanding with Russia, realising the vital importance of not quarrelling with this vast country, and the folly of trying to stem the flood which had been let loose by Lenin. But he was hindered and opposed at every turn by his own colleagues and by his Allies, the French. And when, in 1922, L.G. announced his intention of attempting to treat with the Russians at Genoa in the hope of furthering the peace of Europe, Churchill did his best to wreck the plans for the forthcoming Conference, and Poincaré succeeded in torpedoing the Conference itself."

"Now, in 1922, the divergence in outlook between himself and his Conservative colleagues was widening, especially in relation to the British attitude towards Russia. Churchill headed a group which strongly opposed any recognition of Russia. He made considerable trouble for L.G. before the Genoa Conference, refusing to support L.G.'s programme, while L.G. again threatened to resign if Cabinet support were withdrawn. He got his way. Through weeks of arduous negotiation he persisted in his attempts for a plan for Europe—many times he was faced with the break-up of the Conference and the failure of his endeavours."

51. DAVID LLOYD GEORGE TO SIR ROBERT HORNE

Brynawelon,
Criccieth
March 22nd, 1922

My dear Horne,

I told you I thought Winston would be a real wrecker. The enclosed correspondence will show you my apprehensions were justified. To go to Genoa under the conditions that would satisfy Winston would be futile and humiliating in the extreme. Unless Genoa leads to a real European peace it is no use going there. It is an essential part of the Genoa programme that there should be a European pact of peace which will involve an undertaking by Russia not to attack her neighbours, and by Poland and Roumania not to attack Russia. I cannot see how that is possible without recognizing Russia. You might as well have asked Germany to recognize a treaty without recognizing the Government which signed it.

I wish you would see Chamberlain and tell him that as far as Curzon and you and I are concerned we are pledged up to the eyes by the Cannes proposals & could not recede. I certainly could not go to Genoa on Winston's terms. That means I must go altogether if they are insisted upon. You cannot put the Cannes conditions to the Russian delegates and then if they accept them still refuse recognition. They are put forward in the Cannes project as conditions of recognition. We must act straightforwardly even with Revolutionaries.

I trust you are none the worse for your flying visit to Wales.

Ever sincerely,

D. Lloyd George

52. J. T. DAVIES TO MISS STEVENSON

Criccieth
Tuesday [21 March 1922]

Dear Frances:

The P.M. is ever so much better and after setting the course he is going to take before Genoa he is much happier. If the House will not give him an overwhelming vote then he cannot go on, but if it does, it will strengthen his hands at Genoa. It appears as if the reaction was setting in. That's what I gather from the post—letter after letter sympathizing with him and telling him to go on! The greater question of course is that of health—I was very worried last week but am much easier in my mind now, though your letter about Tom Phillips is very disquieting. If there is anything in what Phillips says then Dawson ought to get him thoroughly overhauled; and that before it is too late! Whether for good or ill I can see that he means to stick to Coalition with the Tories. Personally I regret this and I should regret it still more if he were a younger man, for after all leading a great progressive party of liberals and moderate labour requires new stunts, new programmes, new policies, new campaigns, and I doubt whether the P.M. is fit enough for that now even with six months rest. I do not mean to say he is getting too old but his great work of the last few years must have told upon him more than he and we realise; I can quite see therefore that a continuance of the present Coalition is what he desires if he can go on with it without suffering loss of prestige or dignity.

53. LADY LLOYD-GEORGE'S AUTOBIOGRAPHY

He [Lloyd George] was very depressed, and what cheered him most, even at this critical time, was to have a "wild west" story read to him. I used to chaff him, saying after we had read the first page, that I would tell him the rest of the story, for they were all the same—the lone rider, the lovely girl, the villain, the misunderstanding, the vindication of the hero and the happy ending. But he never ceased to enjoy them and they never ceased to distract him.

54. DAVID LLOYD GEORGE TO LORD STAMFORDHAM

10 *Downing Street,*
Whitehall, s.w.1

Dear Stamfordham,
    Campbell Stuart—the Managing Director of *The Times*—has been here to see me about a project he has elaborated for securing *The Times*

for a really national trust that will run the paper on independent
national & patriotic lines free from the pernicious influences that have
done so much harm to the Country during recent years. He has the
money behind him subscribed by men of the highest character.

Before launching his scheme he is very anxious to have an
opportunity of placing it before the King. He rightly regards *The
Times* as a great national institution. He does not want to use His
Majesty's name but he would like to know as a loyal subject & a
devoted believer in the throne & the Empire that he has the King's
approval.

If he came up to Balmoral could he be given the honour of a few
minutes audience? Kindly let me know.

Ever sincerely,

D. Lloyd George

55. EDWIN MONTAGU TO LORD BEAVERBROOK

Private and confidential

4, *Gordon Place*,
Bloomsbury
13*th March*, 1922

My dear Max,

This is what I should say if I were you. But I say "if I were you"
because I do not in the least agree with you. The views which Lord
Reading has expressed now have been expressed over and over again
before. This telegram, and everything connected with it, is just a
subterfuge of the Prime Minister's. I believe it would be a calamity
if Lord Reading were to resign. I have not the slightest doubt that
he thinks so too, and my prayer to you would be to leave him alone.

Yrs.

Ed. Montagu

Curzon wants a copy of his letter. Shall I send it to him you have the
only one.

56. DAVID LLOYD GEORGE TO LORD CURZON

10 *Downing Street*
Sept. 15*th* 1922

My dear Foreign Secretary,

I have heard nothing of Venizelos' projected visit to England except from the Press.

As you know I have been careful not to see anyone representing either Greece or Turkey as I have been most anxious not to interfere with the very difficult hand you had to play. I saw Gounaris at Cannes at your request but you were present at the interview & directed its course. Apart from that I have steadfastly refused to see anyone representing or professing to represent the belligerent parties. At Genoa at your urgent suggestion I declined to see the Greeks. In the Cabinet I have confined my intervention to steadily supporting your policy.

From the moment Greece threw over Venizelos & placed its destinies in the hands of Constantine I realized that a pro-Greek policy in Anatolia was doomed & I have agreed with you that the best we could hope to achieve in that quarter was to secure some protection for the Xtian minorities. That hope is now slender.

I also strongly support your views as to European Turkey. But I feel that we might do more to organize Balkan support for that policy. Our Ministers at Bucharest and Belgrade have been unaccountably impotent. If we secure the active support of Roumania & Jugo Slavia—& their interests are identical with ours—then French & Italian intrigues will be neutralized.

However we can discuss these questions at the Cabinet this afternoon. The country would be behind us in any steps we took to keep the Turk out of Europe. The Slavs & Roumanians would gladly supply troops.

Ever sincerely,

D. Lloyd George

57. DAVID LLOYD GEORGE TO KING GEORGE V

10 *Downing Street,*
Whitehall, s.w.1
16*th October,* 1922

The Prime Minister with his humble duty to Your Majesty

Last night's meeting of Ministers revealed the fact that there existed a strong feeling in the Conservative Party that a party meeting should be summoned to consider the situation before a final decision is taken as to the advice to be tendered to Your Majesty on the subject of an immediate dissolution.

The Conservative leaders have therefore called a meeting of the members of the party in the House of Commons for Thursday next. Upon the decision taken at that important gathering will depend the continued existence of the Coalition. If the decision is adverse I should have no alternative but to ask Your Majesty to accept my resignation of the high office to which Your Majesty graciously called me six years ago. My colleagues will follow my example in that respect.

As soon as the party meeting is over I will inform Your Majesty of the result and effect.

I remain,
Ever Your Majesty's obedient servant,

D. Lloyd George

58. KING GEORGE V TO DAVID LLOYD GEORGE

York Cottage,
Sandringham,
Norfolk
Oct: 16*th,* 1922

My dear Prime Minister

I write to thank you for your letter which I have just received. I shall anxiously await your report of Thursday's meeting. It is my hope that the result will not cause the break up of my Government for many reasons, especially when questions like Ireland & the Near East are still unsettled.

I trust you will be able to remain my Prime Minister.

Believe me

very sincerely yours

George R.I.

59. SIR GEORGE YOUNGER TO BONAR LAW

January 15th, 1923

I am not in a position to state definitely that he [Farquhar] did collect money for the Election expenses and handed that money to the Lloyd George Executive, but I have every reason to believe that he did so, and hope to be able to prove this one of these days.

The salient points of the position are:

(1) That he was Treasurer of our Party and had no right to collect funds for any other than our own Central Fund so long as he retained that position.

(2) That there has never been any fusion of funds during the existence of the Coalition, and that collections made by Farquhar either for elections or ordinary expenditure were paid into our own Central Fund, just as Lloyd George's Fund was used by his Treasurer and Executive.

(3) When any joint financial responsibilities were undertaken the costs were halved and each Party paid by cheque on its own Fund.

(4) In any case the Coalition had come to an end before the General Election and Farquhar's reported statement that he had collected money for the Coalition does not hold water.

60. BONAR LAW TO LORD FITZALAN

24th January, 1923

Dear Edmund,

You have noticed the trouble there was with poor old Farquhar. I have seen him twice and there is now no question of his hesitating to sign the cheques for the actual party funds but I have still a strong suspicion that he has handed sums, and perhaps large sums, to L.G.

for his party while he was acting as our Treasurer. He is so "gaga" that one does not know what to make of him but among the many statements he made to me was one which he repeated several times—that he had given no money to L.G. funds which was not ear-marked for that purpose. Hicks, the accountant, has been seeing him and he has become sane enough to realise that that was not a wise thing to say so that he has said to Hicks that he has given no money at all to L.G. except £80,000 from Astor. He spoke to me also about this and said that at the same time he handed over £80,000 to you. This he did, so he tells me, on the ground that Astor had left him a perfectly free hand to deal with it as he liked. I said that in that case provided you, as representing our Party, knew what was being done I had not a word to say against it, but the poor old boy is so helpless that I would like to know whether even this story is literally accurate. I should be much obliged, therefore, if you would send me a telegram with the simple word "Yes" if he did give you the £80,000 and "No" if he did not . . .

61. LORD FITZALAN TO BONAR LAW

Hotel Beau Séjour
Cannes
Jan: 26. 1923

Dear Bonar,

In the interests of truth and at the same time in all due charity to poor old Horace a straight "Yes" or "No" as asked for in reply to your letter is impossible.

My recollection is this.

Horace told me, I think about a year before the late [Lord] Astor's death, that the latter had given him £200,000 (I think that was the sum named) to do exactly what he liked with.

That of this sum he had given to the King for some War Charity H.M. was particularly interested in, I think he said £50,000 and the balance he had divided between our party funds and Lloyd George.

I don't remember his mentioning any specific sum as going to L.G.

If I am wrong in the £50,000 going to the King and it was perhaps

£40,000 and the balance was equally divided, then L.G. would have had £80,000.

But no money was "handed" to me as stated in your letter. I was not consulted as to what should be done with the money. The thing was a fait accompli when I heard of it. He simply happened to tell me what had been given and what had been done with it.

You will therefore see I could not reply "Yes" to your letter as no £80,000 or anything else was ever "handed" to me, nor would I like to say "No" as apparently L.G. did get £80,000 or something like it, though not with my knowledge till after he had got it.

I have therefore wired to you "Not literally accurate writing Edmund".

At the time of the election I heard Horace talking in the wild way he was doing. I tried to speak to him seriously, but he would not listen and was quite hopeless and I don't think he is responsible. He certainly cannot be relied on.

62. LORD DERBY

According to *Lord Derby* by Randolph Churchill, his Lordship recorded his answer in his diary entry of the same date: "Bonar Law then said something which disquieted me, because he said there may be a point of difference between him and me on the question of tariffs. This looks as if he was still thinking of putting on a tariff. I told him perfectly frankly that if he did he and I should part company."

Again on the next day Lord Derby's diary, which I quote from the same source (Randolph Churchill's biography), described a meeting of those who were designated for office in the new administration: "Then there was rather a disturbing incident. He gave it to be understood his views on Tariff Reform were unchanged and of course if he is going to bring that up he is going to split the Party again at the beginning."

63. LLOYD GEORGE IN WAR AND PEACE

Bonar Law had firmly believed that Britain was drifting into a peace of surrender or even defeat. Lloyd George would provide the drive and also command the public confidence which would turn defeat into victory. Bonar Law was convinced that Britain had found its leader in the dark hour when disaster was staring her in the face. And his hopes were realized.

Lloyd George led the nation to victory though confronted by desperate perils. He faced a terrible task when full command of the nation came to him. He had special difficulties. There were no road signs on the journey he had to undertake. As Britain had not been engaged in a major war since the Crimea, there were no precedents and there was no experience he could rely on. He had to improvise everything and at the time when one major mistake could have been fatal. Also he had no personal knowledge of war on any scale.

He had the further terrible disability that he was pestered by the King. George V intrigued with the Generals against him, right up to the post-War election. Lloyd George did not have full Conservative support. There were too many rankling memories of his pre-War speeches for that. Nor did he have full Liberal support. The Lloyd George Liberals were much too weak a part of the divided Party, and Asquith Liberals regarded him as something worse than a traitor.

Liberal enmity was actively promoted by McKenna and deeply resented by Lloyd George. An incident was the cause of bitter complaint by both of them.

Readers of my book *Men and Power* will recall the exciting incident of the "Lost Box" containing a revised document, which if disclosed to Parliament might have altered the trend of events. Lloyd George was the beneficiary of the "Lost Box". Another Red Dispatch Box gave him much trouble and tried him to the utmost in devising explanations.

According to his critics he was at that time leading the opposition to Asquith's Administration, though holding second place in that Government. A meeting of several discontented Conservative Coalition Ministers was held. F. E. Smith, as secretary, prepared a minute of the proceedings for Lloyd George's information and forwarded the document in a Red Box addressed to the "Chancellor of the Exchequer" (and of course these Red Box communications go direct to the Minister who holds the key). But Lloyd George had just left the Exchequer for higher and better War employment. Reginald McKenna, who had succeeded him as Chancellor, opened the Box, read the memo., showed it to his political associates. Gross treachery, double dealing and political assassination was McKenna's description of the document. After two days' delay McKenna sent the Box on to Lloyd George. A "rocket", as they say in military circles, was the only possible way out for Lloyd George. He wrote McKenna: "Next time a letter comes into your hands by mistake, put it back into the same Box and send it to the right person at once—*after reading it.*"

Lloyd George and McKenna were never reconciled. McKenna persisted in his charge of "Traitor" and Lloyd George cried "He stole my letter."

He got nothing but hatred from the Generals who in that war fiercely opposed any civilian attempt to interfere with their strategy. Though Lloyd George had a deep and well-founded distrust of the Generals, his political instinct warned him that it would not be safe to go against popular idols such as Haig and Robertson. Consequently he could and would conspire against Haig and seek to undermine him, but he would not assert his authority and insist that campaigns of senseless slaughter must cease. He was and had to be the politician, the man who tried to gauge the current and not to go against it. Failure to heed that same current would have driven him from power.

It is right to say that Lloyd George always had an eye on the newspapers which were mostly under the spell of the Generals. Perhaps to some extent it was for that reason that he made so few changes in the High Command when he knew that he ought to have made many. He had always one eye on victory but he never failed to keep the other eye on the movement of public opinion. He was only too conscious of the glamour of the highly publicised Generals. He feared Haig and he mistrusted Robertson. These two held the support of King and Commons in their keeping and acting in unison could and would have brought Lloyd George down if he had given them the chance.

Nor did Lloyd George have full public support. He was not spared the horror of huge and ever mounting casualty lists which were setting up an unconscious war resistance among the people when he came to power. That war resistance was expressed in the famous Lansdowne Peace Letter and also in much industrial trouble. The people of

Britain had no notion of what total war was like. They were quite unaccustomed to doing with too little food, and they were angered by the countless regulations which interfered with their daily lives. The Defence of the Realm Act was intensely unpopular.

There was the further heavy disability that the people could not see a possible defeat in terms of catastrophe. They imagined that defeat would mean the loss of gold from the Bank of England by way of indemnity. They thought they would suffer no more than France had suffered in 1871.

After the 1918 election the Press regarded Lloyd George with increasing hostility. This, strange as it may seem, was the hour when George V at last decided that Lloyd George was indispensable. He gave full support to his Prime Minister at the very time when Lloyd George's fate was sealed.

It was a magnanimous decision. For the King had been annoyed by a certain indifference to Royal favour and indeed a somewhat insolent attitude by Lloyd George on occasion. When offered an audience on a Saturday morning, Lloyd George exclaimed: "Damn the King! Saturday is the only day I have to play golf." He sent a reply: "I was going away for the week-end, but of course if the King wishes an audience of me, I will put it off." The King graciously replied that Monday would do as well. "God bless His Majesty!" said Lloyd George.

As a gesture of good will and confidence George V asked Lloyd George to carry the state sword before the King at the opening of Parliament. Lloyd George dodged the invitation. To his intimates he said: "I won't be a flunkey."[1]

The Lords had supported him in the days of danger but when the sky was clear they were bitterly hostile to him. Their condemnation of Lloyd George was a constant source of debate and discussion in the Gilded Chamber.

Struggling against these obstacles, Lloyd George once threatened to resign. It was in the garden at 10 Downing Street that he said to me, "I am a C3 character," referring to the lowest medical category for the forces. "I want a C3 job." He of course had no intention of resigning but Churchill would never have made the suggestion.

I shall not call him George, he hated it. He considered this form of address almost as an insult. Bonar Law was not aware of Lloyd

[1] See Appendix 64, Lloyd George on the Dearth of Kings from Miss Stevenson's diary, February 18th, 1934.

George's attitude and when speaking of him invariably called him George. However when he addressed the Prime Minister he called him at first Lloyd George, and afterwards L.G. When Lloyd George took to himself a title in 1945 he adopted a hyphen and became in fact Earl Lloyd-George of Dwyfor.

He was of course devious. He was inclined to secure his ends by methods of which Bonar Law did not always approve. Lloyd George was not above misrepresenting the character and motives of those who stood in his way. He could be bitter in his public and private attacks on his opponents.

But he took a lenient and charitable view of human frailties. This compassionate nature found practical expression when attempts were made to exclude unmarried mothers from benefits under Government projects. Lloyd George, pointing to a member of a hostile deputation of ladies, said: "Who is she to talk of immorality? Why, her husband lived on immorality! He was President of the Divorce Court."

He did not have many intimate friends. The late Lord Reading was attached to him and also Lord Riddell, but in time he lost both. Riddell was his chosen companion and the relationship was exceedingly close for thirteen years. Several volumes of an interesting and absorbing diary are devoted almost entirely to the sayings and doings of Lloyd George. A column in *News of the World*, Riddell's own paper, was the best informed gossip page and particularly on political subjects. Riddell himself was often the writer.

As an orator Lloyd George was superb. I remember him speaking of a Nonconformist village high up on the hillside when a neighbour rode in the night time to bring the Nonconformist Minister to a dying man, passing the house where the Anglican parson would have been only too willing to go to the death-bed. When he spoke of the hoof beats clattering on the roadside, you could positively hear the passing horse.

He had a marvellous command of imagery and powers of repartee. Before his downfall he dominated the House of Commons. There was none to equal him. And he had a pleasant voice, a very pleasant voice. With sympathetic look and gesture, with a welcoming smile, and with seductive and vibrant voice he could win any man's interest —or woman.

Lloyd George's conversation was entertaining and indeed invariably exciting too. He spoke about the personal idiosyncrasies of those who came in contact with him and with extraordinary insight and understanding. Certainly he was not above discussing the social weaknesses of those who served under him.

It cannot be denied that Lloyd George lived for the day and the hour. He had no thought of history. He often indulged in reminiscence but seldom about the great events with which he was so intimately connected.

There was however a story going back to the First War and of Germany's invasion of Belgium which has always held my interest. The Belgian Government, he said, were on the point of giving way, and allowing the Germans to pass through their territory, when M. Vandervelde, the Socialist leader, came to the Ministry, and taking a letter out of his pocket, said: "Jaurès has been murdered: this is a letter from the French Socialists asking me to go to Paris and lead them. Unless you can tell me that Belgium will resist violation, I will shake the dust of Belgium from my feet, and take my stand among the French—and France shall know the reason why." This came to the ears of the Belgian King, who sent for Vandervelde, and together they turned the tide and Belgium declared war on Germany.

Lloyd George was fond of talking about the great days of Liberal ascendancy before the First World War. He talked frequently about his triumphs in the little community in Wales where he practised law as a solicitor. The memory of his battles in Welsh courtrooms against the pretensions of the Established Church and the aristocracy aroused him, and he of course aroused the simple people of Wales.

I have told of an occasion when, after many days working intimately with Lloyd George, the end was attained: the fall of Asquith. Lloyd George was called upon to form a Government. All day long I sat in my room at the Hyde Park Hotel waiting for the telephone call from him which would have been a confirmation of the pledge he had given me under the trees at Cherkley that I would be his President of the Board of Trade. Silence reigned. The telephone did not ring. I worried over the profound silence. How I longed for the sound of that voice that I knew so well and that I had heard so often during the days when the political upheaval was in the making.

After the election of 1935 Lloyd George returned from his own campaign in high spirits and good humour after having suffered a very severe defeat, and after having held only four seats, including his own.

In the following week-end there was not a single telephone message for Lloyd George from any source, political or otherwise.

The telephone was silent. When I heard of this experience I was reminded of my own lonely vigil and for Lloyd George I had deep sympathy.

He had a passion for churches, preachers, hymns and psalms. His devotion did not appear to be religious fervour, but just a deep response of the emotions.

Lloyd George himself of course loved to sing Welsh hymns. On occasional Sundays he and his entire family and Miss Stevenson would go to the service at Castle Street Chapel and on their return would sing together what Lloyd George called "the glorious Welsh hymns". He would discuss Welsh preachers, assessing their preaching, describing their personal appearance and occasionally finding some idiosyncrasy to describe with high good humour.

He was familiar with the New Testament. Saint James was his favourite and he often read aloud with much feeling the chapter denouncing the rich, though by this time he was himself "passing rich": "Go to now, ye rich men, weep and howl for your miseries that shall come upon you."

David Davies, M.P. and one-time Lloyd George's Parliamentary Private Secretary, held his job for long by amusing Lloyd George with stories about Welsh preachers. One of them was about a sermon on the parable of the ten virgins which the preacher concluded with a flourish, "Oh my Brethren! where would you rather be—with the five wise virgins in the light? Or with the five foolish virgins in the dark?"

Lloyd George was of course deeply interested in agriculture. He had a real liking for the farm and devotion to the farming community. He had no talent for managing his own farming property. He did not even have any real understanding of husbandry. However he pretended that his farm paid. He made such a statement on one occasion to Churchill who was also engaging in agriculture. Churchill said, "I am going to make my farm pay, whatever it costs."

I also had a farm. At that time it was a chicken farm. Lloyd George asked me how many chickens I had. I replied that I had about 25,000. "And how many pigs have you got?" I asked. "Perhaps 500," he said. As he drove away from Cherkley where these conversations took place, Lloyd George laughingly enquired of his companion, "How many pigs did I say I had?" On being told "500", he said, "Of course I have not got anywhere near as many at that. But he hasn't got 25,000 chickens either." He was right about his own exaggeration but not about my affairs. I did have 25,000 chickens, and when I disposed of them I made a loss of £8,353.

Lloyd George frequently referred to himself in the words of Robert Louis Stevenson as "a bonnie fighter". Another passage in Stevenson described even more accurately his character and attitude to events. " 'Is it only me they're after, or the pair of us? . . . How many would ye think there would be of them?' I [David Balfour] asked.

" 'That depends,' said Alan [Breck]. 'If it was only you, they would like send two-three lively, brisk young birkies, and if they thought that I was to appear in the employ, I dare say ten or twelve,' said he."

64. MISS STEVENSON'S DIARY

February 18th, 1934

The Dearth of Kings:

"We talked of Kings, L.G. [Lloyd George] saying that now there was no King of outstanding strength in Europe, with the possible exception of the King of Serbia. I suggested our own, but L.G. said: 'Quite frankly, he is not a man of strength. He is admirable and reliable, but has never interfered in any emergency, and would not be capable of doing so should any emergency arise. If he had someone strong behind him to act, he would carry out orders, faithfully and with courage. But nothing more. I look upon this event,' [death of Albert, King of the Belgians] said L.G. 'as an ominous one for Europe. It may have serious results in the present unsettled state of the Continent.' There were just two or three pillars one regarded as being bulwarks against trouble—Mussolini, and the King of the Belgians amongst them ('and incidentally he is not a Belgian,' said L.G.). L.G. regards Hitler as a very great man."

INDEX

Abdulla, King of Transjordan, 33
Addison, Christopher, Vt Addison, 31, 41 n.1, 61–4, 67, 70–1, 75–80, 133, 141, 258, 262, 270–9, 280
  Letters from, 78 n.1
  Letters to, 271
Aga Khan, 149–50
Aitken, W. M., see Beaverbrook
Albert, King of the Belgians, 305, 307
Alexander, King of Greece, 153, 205
Alexander, King of Yugoslavia, 307
Allenby, Sir Edmund, Vt Allenby, 255
Amery, L. S., 210, 212, 222
Anderson, Sir John, Vt Waverley, 275
Anti-waste campaign, 27, 269, 278
Asquith, H. H., Earl of Oxford & Asquith, 9, 27, 52, 58, 114, 209–10, 213, 241, 260, 262, 283, 301, 305
Asquith, Margot, Countess of Oxford & Asquith, 283
Astor, J. J., 147
Astor, Nancy, Viscountess Astor, 76 n.2, 283
Astor, W. W., Vt Astor, 203, 299
Australia, 109, 161

Baden-Powell, Sir Robert, Lord Baden-Powell, 242
Baldwin, Stanley, Earl Baldwin of Bewdley : considers resignation, 28, 244; proposed for Exchequer, 33 n.1, and for India Office, 155; and Chanak,

165–6; and Carlton Club meeting, 190, 193, 201, 223; appointed Chancellor of Exchequer, 210; and general election, 1922, 217–18; and Beaverbrook, 224; and U.S. debt, 231 n.1; mentioned as P.M., 103, 197
  Letter from, 244
Balfour, A. J., Earl of Balfour, 44; opposes coalition, 1910, 177; Curzon consults on Lympne conference, 39–40, 251–2; tennis at The Vineyard, 65 n.2; and Irish negotiations, 85, 89, 262; on Poincaré, 144 n.1; pro-Greek, 152–3, 164–5; urges Derby to take India Office, 155; supports Ll. G., 174, 177, 184, 188, 213 n.1; and Carlton Club meeting, 202; and party funds, 204
Balsan, Mme, 129
Banbury, Sir F. G., 277
Barnes, George N., 100
Barton, Robert, 96
Beardmore, Sir William, Lord Invernairn, 241
Beaverbrook, Lord (Sir W. M. Aitken)—
  for tariff campaigns by, see Tariff Reform policy
  Ormsby-Gore and, 40 n.3, Sassoon and, 49; owns The Vineyard, 65 n.2, 285
  attempts to bring Law back to politics, 51–2, 64–7, 71–5, 80, 90, 260–4, 266–7
  breach of election law by,